W9-AYO-901

The World Book Encyclopedia of

People and Places

ma Solomon Islands Ecuador Somalia Martiniq
ina Brunei Costa Rica Angola Uzbekistan Cuba
udi Arabia Dominica Samoa Dominican Republ
Zimbabwe Russia Equatorial Guinea Bulgaria
Antigua and Barbuda Federated States of Mic
hamas Gabon Faeroe Islands Kazakhstan Gamb
outh Africa Germany Barbados Benin Great Bri
adeiras Bermuda Greater Antilles Greece Cam
wanda Mali Bahrain Grenada Puerto Rico Gua
ncent and the Grenadines Guatemala Belgium
rra Guyana Haiti Bermuda Honduras Senegal Co
Marino Papua New Guinea Indonesia Iraq Italy
anistan Kiribati Jordan Kenya North Korea Ku
Brazil Latvia Mali Lebanon Belize Vanuatu Ma
ia Malawi Bangladesh Malaysia Benin Marshal
itania Cape Verde Mexico Guadeloupe Mongolia
oldova Morocco Albania Namibia Bermuda Aust
therlands Niger Fiji Nigeria Finland Tuvalu Rus
mbourg Oman Botswana Pacific Islands Pakis
inea Paraguay Peru Portugal Qatar Gibraltar R
Maldives Saint Christopher and Nevis Hong K
aint Vincent and the Grenadines Jordan São To
Seychelles Sierra Leone Singapore Burundi Sr
n Lesotho Suriname Swaziland New Caledonia
witzerland Congo Monaco Syria Tahiti Guinea
Thailand Madagascar Nauru Israel Togo Denn
Zealand Nicaragua Trinidad and Tobago Tunisi
Republic of Ireland Liechtenstein Tuvalu Uga
rates Peru United States Australia Lesser Anti
olivia Antarctica Venezuela Vietnam Bulgaria
tern Sahara Western Samoa Yemen Morocco Tu
Cook Islands Zambia Iceland Papua New Guine
land Taiwan Afghanistan Jamaica Italy Jordan
ibati North Korea Lebanon Argentina South K
Latvia Lithuania Macao Belize El Salvador Ma
adesh Malaysia Benin Marshall Islands Liberia
e Guadeloupe Mexico Libya Mongolia Central A
nia Luxembourg Chile Mozambique Morocco Bo
Benin Ghana Norway Netherlands Finland Rwa
n Oman Pakistan Niger Malta Nepal Romania
New Guinea Paraguay Peru Portugal Cuba Mada
ltar Maldives San Marino Rwanda Seychelles
Christopher and Nevis Brazil Saint Lucia Saint
dines Burundi São Tomé and Príncipe Iran Sier
non Islands Ecuador Somalia Martinique Hunga
n China Brunei Costa Rica Cuba Jamaica Ethiopi

The World Book Encyclopedia of

People and Places

VOLUME 6/U-Z

Index

World Book, Inc.
a Scott Fetzer company
Chicago London Sydney Toronto

Staff

1995 revised printing

Created by Mitchell Beazley International and Bertelsmann Lexikon Verlag

This edition published by
World Book, Inc.
525 W. Monroe Street
Chicago, IL 60661

ISBN 0-7166-3794-4
Library of Congress Catalog Card No. 94-61377
Printed in the United States of America

7 8 9 10 11 12 99 98 97 96 95

Burma Solomon Islands Ecuador
Somalia Martinique Bhutan Spai
hina Costa Rica Brunei Benin Cu
ngola Mali Marshall Islands Sin
American Samoa Dominica Saudi
Dominican Republic Poland Easte
Zimbabwe Equatorial Guinea Djib
Ethiopia Faeroe Islands Burkina
Antigua and Barbuda Canada Fed
States of Micronesia France Baha
Gabon Philippines Russia Palau
Africa Germany Barbados Benin
Britain Azores and Madeiras Grea
Antilles Bermuda Greece Cameroo
Greenland Bahrain Grenada Puert
Guam Mali Egypt Congo Guatema
Belgium Panama Guinea Andorra
Bermuda Haiti Honduras Colombi
Senegal Papua New Guinea Ukrai
Indonesia Jamaica Italy Taiwan Ir
Martinique Afghanistan Kiribati
Kenya North Korea Kuwait Laos
Korea Brazil Latvia Lebanon Beli
Vanuatu Macao El Salvador Mala
Bangladesh Malaysia Marshall Isl
Mauritania Bermuda Cape Verde
Guadeloupe Mongolia Central Afr
Republic Albania Morocco Namib
Austria Nepal South Africa Ghana
Netherlands Niger Fiji Finland Ni
Cyprus Norway Japan Oman Luxe
Pacific Islands Ukraine Pakistan
Botswana Papua New Guinea Para
Peru Reunion Qatar Portugal Rom
Gibraltar Rwanda Maldives Saint
Christopher and Nevis Hong Kong
Saint Lucia Saint Vincent and the
Grenadines San Marino Iran São
and Príncipe Seychelles Sri Lanka
Burundi Singapore Cambodia Tog
Lesotho Sudan Suriname Swazilan
Caledonia Algeria Sweden Switze
Congo Monaco Tonga Tahiti Guine
Bissau Tanzania Comoros Madaga
Thailand Israel Nauru Sierra Leon
Benin Denmark New Zealand Solo

Front cover acknowledgments:
large photo, A. Boccacrio, The Image Bank
left inset, Bernard Gerard, Gamma/Frank Spooner
center inset, Mark & Evelyne Bernheim, Susan Griggs
right inset, Dave Brinicombe, Hutchison Library

Back cover acknowledgment:
Peter Miller, The Image Bank

ma Solomon Islands Ecuador Somalia Martiniqu
ina Brunei Costa Rica Angola Uzbekistan Cuba
udi Arabia Dominica Samoa Dominican Republi
Zimbabwe Russia Equatorial Guinea Bulgaria E
Antigua and Barbuda Federated States of Mic
hamas Gabon Faeroe Islands Kazakhstan Gamb
outh Africa Germany Barbados Benin Great Bri
adeiras Bermuda Greater Antilles Greece Cam
wanda Mali Bahrain Grenada Puerto Rico Gua
ncent and the Grenadines Guatemala Belgium
ra Guyana Haiti Bermuda Honduras Senegal Co
Marino Papua New Guinea Indonesia Iraq Italy
anistan Kiribati Jordan Kenya North Korea Ku
Brazil Latvia Mali Lebanon Belize Vanuatu Ma
ia Malawi Bangladesh Malaysia Benin Marshall
tania Cape Verde Mexico Guadeloupe Mongolia
oldova Morocco Albania Namibia Bermuda Aust
therlands Niger Fiji Nigeria Finland Tuvalu Rus
mbourg Oman Botswana Pacific Islands Pakis
inea Paraguay Peru Portugal Qatar Gibraltar R
Maldives Saint Christopher and Nevis Hong K
aint Vincent and the Grenadines Jordan São To
Seychelles Sierra Leone Singapore Burundi Sr
n Lesotho Suriname Swaziland New Caledonia
witzerland Congo Monaco Syria Tahiti Guinea
Thailand Madagascar Nauru Israel Togo Denn
Zealand Nicaragua Trinidad and Tobago Tunisi
Republic of Ireland Liechtenstein Tuvalu Uga
rates Peru United States Australia Lesser Anti
olivia Antarctica Venezuela Vietnam Bulgaria
ern Sahara Western Samoa Yemen Morocco Tu
Cook Islands Zambia Iceland Papua New Guine
land Taiwan Afghanistan Jamaica Italy Jordan
ibati North Korea Lebanon Argentina South K
Latvia Lithuania Macao Belize El Salvador Ma
desh Malaysia Benin Marshall Islands Liberia
Guadeloupe Mexico Libya Mongolia Central A
nia Luxembourg Chile Mozambique Morocco B
Benin Ghana Norway Netherlands Finland Rwa
Oman Pakistan Niger Malta Nepal Romania
New Guinea Paraguay Peru Portugal Cuba Mada
tar Maldives San Marino Rwanda Seychelles
Christopher and Nevis Brazil Saint Lucia Saint
dines Burundi São Tomé and Príncipe Iran Sier
non Islands Ecuador Somalia Martinique Hunga
China Brunei Costa Rica Cuba Jamaica Ethiopi

Contents

ma Solomon Islands Ecuador Somalia Martiniqu
ina Brunei Costa Rica Angola Uzbekistan Cuba
udi Arabia Dominica Samoa Dominican Republi
Zimbabwe Russia Equatorial Guinea Bulgaria E
Antigua and Barbuda Federated States of Mic
hamas Gabon Faeroe Islands Kazakhstan Gamb
outh Africa Germany Barbados Benin Great Bri
adeiras Bermuda Greater Antilles Greece Came
wanda Mali Bahrain Grenada Puerto Rico Gua
ncent and the Grenadines Guatemala Belgium
ra Guyana Haiti Bermuda Honduras Senegal Co
Marino Papua New Guinea Indonesia Iraq Italy
anistan Kiribati Jordan Kenya North Korea Kuv
Brazil Latvia Mali Lebanon Belize Vanuatu Ma
ia Malawi Bangladesh Malaysia Benin Marshall
tania Cape Verde Mexico Guadeloupe Mongolia
ldova Morocco Albania Namibia Bermuda Aust
therlands Niger Fiji Nigeria Finland Tuvalu Rus
mbourg Oman Botswana Pacific Islands Pakis
inea Paraguay Peru Portugal Qatar Gibraltar R
Maldives Saint Christopher and Nevis Hong K
aint Vincent and the Grenadines Jordan São To
Seychelles Sierra Leone Singapore Burundi Sr
n Lesotho Suriname Swaziland New Caledonia
witzerland Congo Monaco Syria Tahiti Guinea
Thailand Madagascar Nauru Israel Togo Denn
Zealand Nicaragua Trinidad and Tobago Tunisi
Republic of Ireland Liechtenstein Tuvalu Ugar
rates Peru United States Australia Lesser Antil
olivia Antarctica Venezuela Vietnam Bulgaria
ern Sahara Western Samoa Yemen Morocco Tu
Cook Islands Zambia Iceland Papua New Guine
land Taiwan Afghanistan Jamaica Italy Jordan
ibati North Korea Lebanon Argentina South K
Latvia Lithuania Macao Belize El Salvador Ma
desh Malaysia Benin Marshall Islands Liberia
e Guadeloupe Mexico Libya Mongolia Central A
nia Luxembourg Chile Mozambique Morocco Be
Benin Ghana Norway Netherlands Finland Rwa
Oman Pakistan Niger Malta Nepal Romania
lew Guinea Paraguay Peru Portugal Cuba Mada
tar Maldives San Marino Rwanda Seychelles
Christopher and Nevis Brazil Saint Lucia Saint
dines Burundi São Tomé and Príncipe Iran Sier
non Islands Ecuador Somalia Martinique Hunga
China Brunei Costa Rica Cuba Jamaica Ethiopi

nutan Spain
in American
oland Easter
pia Burkina
esia Canada
alau Islands
Azores and
n Greenland
ussia Congo
ama Guinea
bia Hungary
wan Jamaica
Laos South
El Salvador
ands Liberia
tral African
Nepal Ghana
Japan Malta
Papua New
on Romania
Brazil Saint
nd Príncipe
nka Ukraine
eria Sweden
au Tanzania
Tonga New
tonia Ghana
United Arab
Vatican City
uritius Cuba
Yugoslavia
donesia Iran
uatu Kuwait
Laos Brazil
alawi Kenya
ritania Peru
an Republic
da Namibia
Cyprus Mali
wana Papua
car Reunion
Kong Saint
cent and the
eone Burma
Peru Finland
nin Djibouti

Uganda

Uganda is a densely populated country in east-central Africa. Since the early 1970's, Uganda has been troubled by war and political instability.

Government

The president of Uganda has great powers. He appoints a Cabinet of about 30 ministers to help carry out the operations of the government and names a National Resistance Council of about 25 members. The council serves as an unelected national legislature.

History

By the first hundred years after the birth of Christ, the people living in what is now Uganda were farmers and ironworkers. Later, they adopted a form of government headed by chiefs, and after 1300 several local kingdoms developed.

By about 1850, the Ganda people had formed the rich and powerful kingdom of Buganda, which had a large army and a highly developed government. During the 1860's, explorers and missionaries from Great Britain began arriving in the region. In 1894, Buganda was made a British protectorate that eventually included three other kingdoms.

Worshipers gather outside a Roman Catholic church, *right,* in Kampala, Uganda's capital. About 65 per cent of the people are Christian, a heritage that goes back to the 1800's, when British missionaries and explorers came to the region.

FACT BOX

THE COUNTRY
Official name: Republic of Uganda.
Capital: Kampala.
Land regions: Mainly high plateau covered by forests in south and savanna in north; highlands in east and west; Great Rift Valley in west.
Area: 93,065 sq. mi. (241,038 km^2).
Climate: Tropical, but modified by altitude. Daytime temperatures average 60° to 85° F. (16° to 29° C). More than 40 in. (100 cm) rain falls yearly.
Main rivers: Victoria Nile, Albert Nile (headwaters of White Nile).
Highest elevation: Margherita Peak, 16,762 ft. (5,109 m).
Lowest elevation: Lake Albert, 2,036 ft. (621 m).

THE GOVERNMENT
Form of government: Transitional.
Head of state: President.
Head of government: Prime minister.
Administrative areas: 4 regions, divided into 33 districts.
Legislature: National Resistance Council with 25 members appointed by president.
Court system: Court of Appeal, High Court, magistrates' courts.
Armed forces: About 70,000 troops.

THE PEOPLE
Estimated 1996 population: 19,278,000.
Official language: English.
Religions: Christianity (about 65%), traditional African religions (about 20%), Islam (16%).

THE ECONOMY
Currency: Shilling.
Gross national product (GNP) in 1992: $2.9 billion U.S.
Real annual growth rate (1985–92): 1.8%.
GNP per capita (1992): $170 U.S.
Balance of trade (1991): −$440 million U.S.

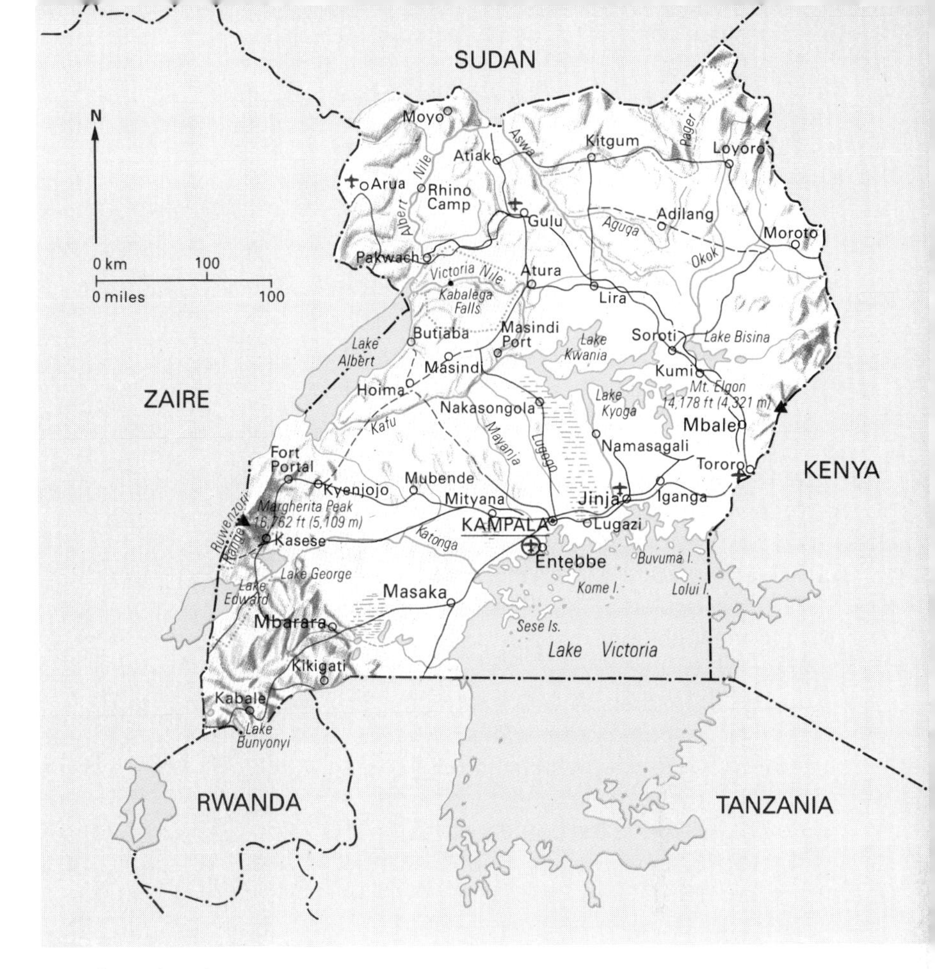

Uganda is a densely populated agricultural country in east-central Africa. Although the nation has rich mineral deposits, only copper is mined on a large scale. Many cargo ships operate on Uganda's large lakes.

An independence movement became strong among the Ganda people during the 1950's, and occasionally trouble erupted between the *kabaka* (king) of Buganda and the British. Uganda became an independent nation on Oct. 9, 1962, but each of the four kingdoms that had been united in the protectorate kept its own king until 1967.

Apollo Milton Obote, a member of a northern ethnic group, became prime minister of the new nation of Uganda in 1962, and in 1963, Sir Edward Mutesa II, the kabaka of Buganda, was elected president. When serious differences arose between the two, Obote dismissed Mutesa and took on the presidency himself. In 1967, a new Constitution made Uganda a republic and abolished the kingdoms.

Obote was overthrown in 1971 by the army, and Major General Idi Amin Dada, commander of the armed forces, headed the new military government. Amin was a cruel dictator. Many thousands of Ugandans were killed on Amin's orders or the orders of his supporters. In addition, he ordered some 50,000 Asian businessmen to leave Uganda and used their money to reward soldiers who were loyal to him. Political opposition was not allowed.

In 1978, Amin went to war with neighboring Tanzania over a border dispute, and the war resulted in his downfall. In 1979, Tanzanian troops, aided by Ugandans, defeated Uganda's army and overthrew Amin.

Ugandans who had opposed Amin took over the government, but they in turn were overthrown by the military in 1980, and in December of that year an election for a new civilian government was held. Obote returned from exile and won the presidency, but his opponents charged that the election was rigged and began a guerrilla war to oust him.

In July 1985, Obote was overthrown and General Tito Okello became president. Another group, called the National Resistance Movement (NRM), began fighting to overthrow Okello and captured the capital city of Kampala in January 1986. The NRM leader, Yoweri Museveni, then became president. By the end of 1986, Museveni had restored peace to most of Uganda. In March 1994, Ugandans elected a Constituent Assembly, which will draw up a new Constitution. Parliamentary elections were expected to take place in 1995.

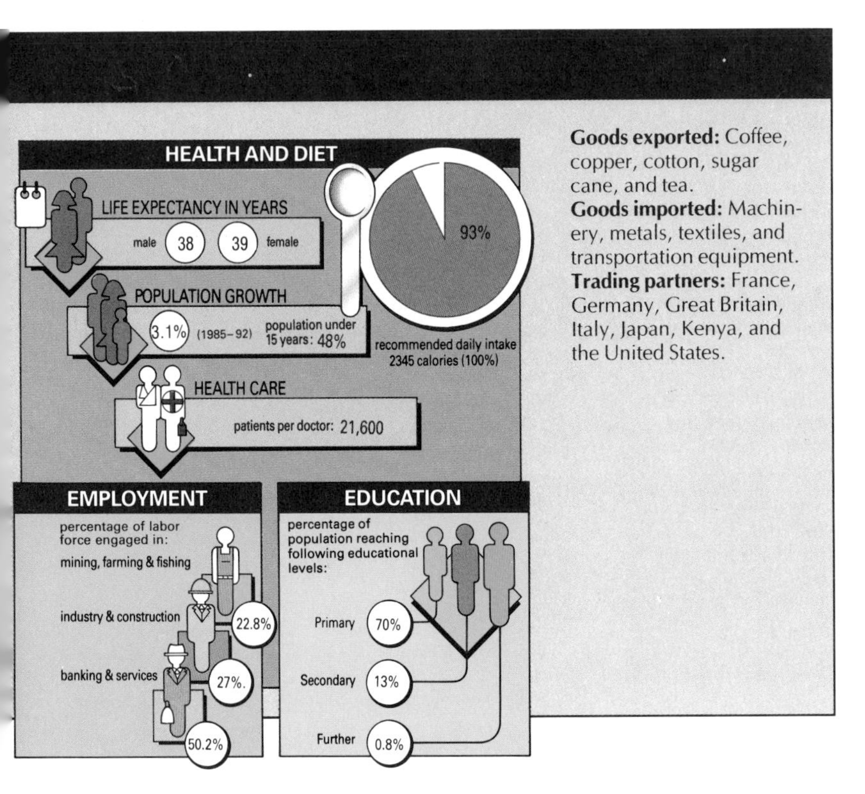

Environment and People

Uganda has a magnificent landscape, ranging from towering, snowcapped mountains to dense tropical forests. Large lakes cover more than a sixth of the nation. A great variety of wild animals roam vast national parks such as Kabalega Falls National Park in the northwest.

Most of the country consists of a plateau about 4,000 feet (1,200 meters) above sea level. In the south, thick rain forests grow, and in the north grassy savannas stretch across most of the land, though some northeastern areas are near-deserts.

In the highlands that run along the eastern and western borders, Mount Elgon towers more than 14,000 feet (4,000 meters) near the border with Kenya. The Ruwenzori Range, which includes the 16,762-foot (5,109-meter) Margherita Peak, rises along the border with Zaire. Just east of these western mountains lies the Great Rift Valley, a series of cracks in the earth's surface.

Within the Great Rift Valley lie Lakes Albert, Edward, and George. Part of Lake Victoria—the largest lake in Africa and the world's second largest freshwater lake after Lake Superior in North America—forms the southeastern corner of Uganda. The Victoria Nile and the Albert Nile and their branches, which form the headwaters of the White Nile (also called the Bahr al Jabal), drain most of Uganda.

Several of Uganda's lakes and rivers were named for members of the British royal family. Victoria was queen of England when the British explored and began to rule the Ugandan region, and Albert was her husband and prince. Edward, their eldest son, later became king of England.

Although Uganda has many rich mineral deposits, only copper is mined to any great degree. Uganda is mainly an agricultural country, and its people grow such crops as bananas, beans, cassava, corn, millet, and sweet potatoes for their own use. They grow coffee, cotton, sugar cane, and tea mostly for export.

Most Ugandans are black Africans, but they belong to more than 20 different ethnic groups. Almost every ethnic group has its own language, and no language is understood by everyone. English is the nation's official language.

A traditional hut makes a cozy sleeping place for Karamojong people of northeastern Uganda. The huts are made of clay, branches, and thatch.

Missionaries distribute food to children in northern Uganda, *right*. The people in this dry region face hardship when drought reduces the amount of pasture available to their cattle.

A Ugandan transports bananas to market on the back of a bicycle, *far right*. Bananas, one of the chief food crops of Ugandans, are grown mainly for the people themselves rather than for export.

Kabalega Falls plunges into the Victoria Nile River between Lake Victoria and Lake Albert. A beautiful national park surrounding the waterfall is home to a variety of wildlife, including elephants, hippopotamuses, and leopards.

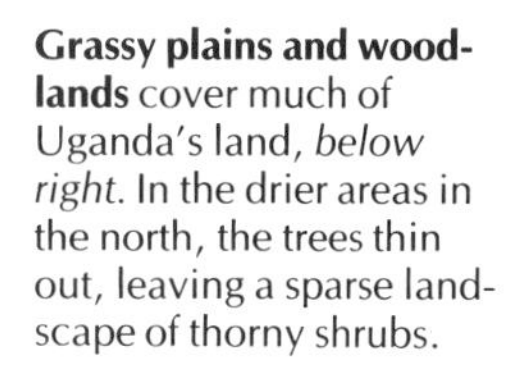

Grassy plains and woodlands cover much of Uganda's land, *below right.* In the drier areas in the north, the trees thin out, leaving a sparse landscape of thorny shrubs.

The Ganda, the largest and wealthiest ethnic group in the country, make up about 30 per cent of the population and live in central and southern Uganda. They speak a language called Luganda, which belongs to the Bantu language group.

Hundreds of years ago, ancestors of the Ganda developed the powerful kingdom of Buganda. Today, their political and social organization is one of the most highly developed in central Africa.

Most Ganda are farmers. Ganda women do much of the farm work. The people live in houses that have iron roofs and walls of cement, cinder block, or mud.

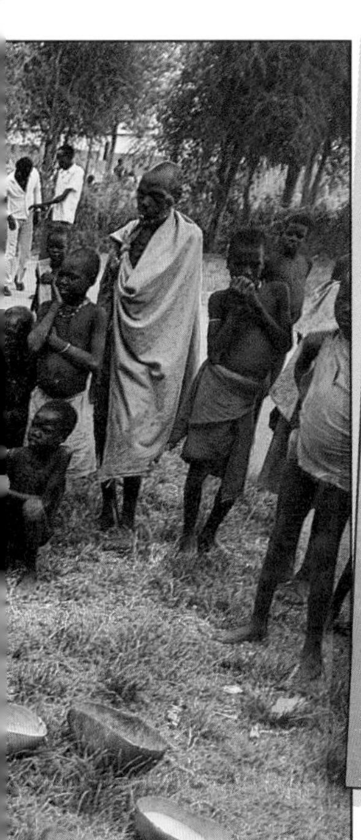

Most of Uganda's other ethnic groups are farmers as well. But the Karamojong in the northeast and several other groups in the drier sections of the country are herders who roam the land in search of pasture for their livestock.

About 65 per cent of Uganda's people are Christians, and many others practice traditional African religions. A small percentage are Muslims.

Unlike the people of many other African countries, more than 50 per cent of Ugandans can read and write. However, the country's educational system has declined sharply since the early 1970's due to war and political unrest.

Ukraine

Ukraine is a rich farming, industrial, and mining country in southeastern Europe. It consists mostly of fertile steppes. Ukraine is bordered by the Black Sea to the south and the Carpathian Mountains to the west.

Ukraine covers about 233,090 square miles (603,700 square kilometers) and has about 53,125,000 people. Kiev is the capital and largest city. Formerly a union republic of the U.S.S.R., Ukraine became an independent country and a charter member of the Commonwealth of Independent States (CIS), *above,* when the Soviet Union was dissolved in December 1991. (For a more detailed map of Ukraine, see the Commonwealth of Independent States article in volume 1 of this series.)

History

The long history of the Ukrainian people began with prehistoric agricultural tribes who inhabited the Dnepr and Dnestr river valleys. Later, Slavic peoples settled in the area. By the A.D. 800's, Vikings from Scandinavia called the *Varangian Russes* established a loose system of control over the land on both sides of the Dnepr River. In time, this region became the heart of the Kievan state, dominated by Kiev, the first powerful Russian city-state.

Following the reign of Yaroslav (1019-1054), which marked the height of Kiev's power, the Kievan state broke up into *principalities* (regions ruled by princes). In the mid-1300's, some of the principalities in Ukraine and Byelorussia (now Belarus) were taken over by the expanding Lithuanian and Polish states. Under their rule, the peasant farmers of Ukraine were bound to the land as serfs.

By 1795, Russia had gained control over most of Ukraine. In 1918, after the October Revolution, the Ukrainians established an independent non-Communist state. But by 1920, Communists brought most of Ukraine under their rule as a Soviet republic.

In 1929, hundreds of thousands of Ukrainians resisted the Soviet government's takeover of the small peasant farms. The Ukrainians' opposition to Soviet domination and its restrictions on their cultural freedom continued through the 1970's and 1980's.

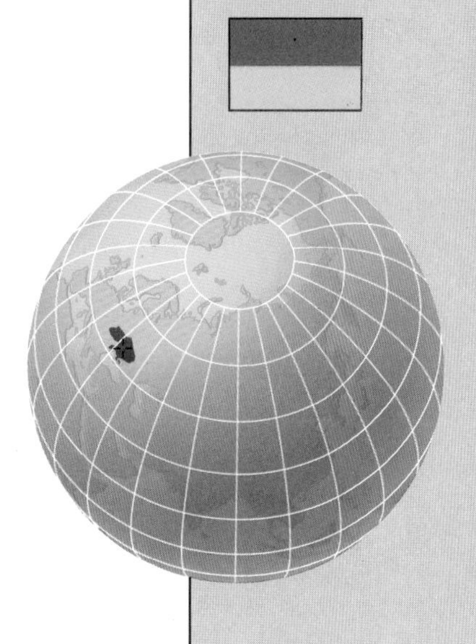

THE COUNTRY
Official name: Ukrayina (Ukraine).
Capital: Kiev.
Land regions: Dnepr-Pripyat Lowland, Northern Ukrainian Upland, Central Plateau, Eastern Carpathian Mountains, Coastal Plain, and Crimean Mountains.
Area: 233,090 sq. mi. (603,700 km^2).
Climate: Cold winters and warm summers.
Main rivers: Dnepr, Dnestr, and Donets.
Highest elevation: Mount Goverla, 6,762 ft. (2,061 m).
Lowest elevation: Sea level along the coast of the Black Sea.

THE GOVERNMENT
Form of government: Republic.
Head of state: President.
Head of government: President.
Administrative areas: 1 auton. republic, 24 *oblasts*.
Legislature: Supreme Council.
Court system: Supreme Court, lower courts.
Armed forces: 230,000 active troops.

THE PEOPLE
Estimated 1993 population: 53,125,000.
Official language: Ukrainian.
Religions: Ukrainian Orthodox, Ukrainian Catholic, Protestant, and Judaism.

THE ECONOMY
Currency: Ruble and karbovanet.
Gross national product (GNP) in 1991: $121.5 billion U.S.
Real annual growth rate (1991): 2.7%.
GNP per capita (1991): $2,340 U.S.
Balance of trade (1990): −$3.2 billion U.S.
Goods exported: Coal, construction equipment, manufactured goods, sugar beets, and wheat.
Goods imported: Consumer goods, natural gas, rubber, oil, and wood products.
Trading partners: Canada, Germany, Hungary, Iran, Poland, Russia, and Tajikistan.

Ukraine remained under the strict control of the Soviet central government until the late 1980's, when a new Ukrainian nationalist movement appeared. Many Ukrainians demanded greater control of the republic's government and economy. In 1990, the Ukrainian Parliament declared the republic's sovereignty, which meant that its laws took precedence over those of the Soviet Union. In 1991, in the midst of political upheaval in the Soviet Union following an attempted government coup in August, Ukraine declared itself independent.

In December 1991, Ukraine, along with Byelarus (now Belarus) and Russia, established a new association called the Commonwealth of Independent States (CIS). A week later, Soviet President Mikhail Gorbachev and Russian President Boris Yeltsin agreed to dissolve the Soviet Union by the end of the year and replace it with the CIS. Most of the remaining former Soviet republics joined the new commonwealth.

In early 1992, tension developed between Russia and Ukraine over control of the naval fleet in the Black Sea. Although Yeltsin claimed that the Black Sea fleet was now a part of the commonwealth, Ukraine's nationalist leaders maintained that most of the fleet was now their own.

Ukrainian farms produce sugar beets, meat and dairy products, and grain. Ukrainian farmers also raise barley, corn, rye, tobacco, and other crops.

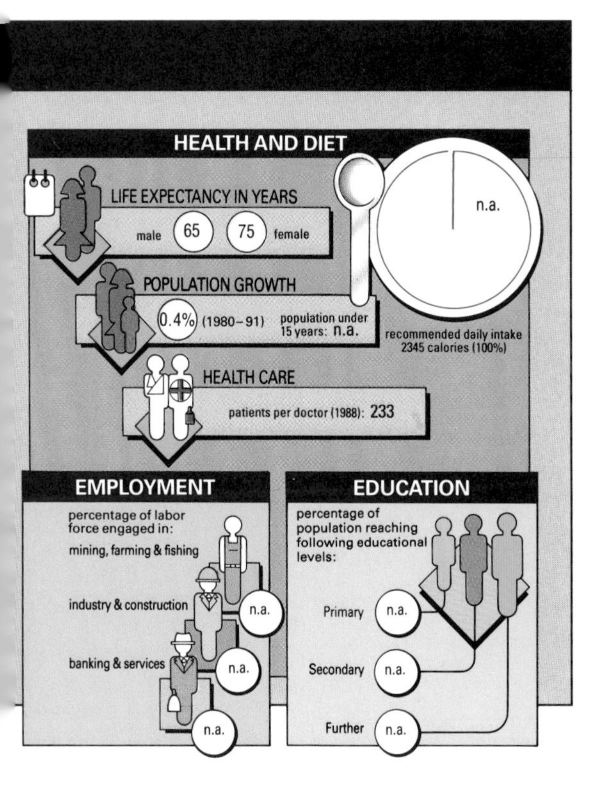

People

About 75 per cent of the people in Ukraine are Ukrainians, a Slavic nationality group that has its own customs and language. Most Ukrainians belong to the Eastern Orthodox, Ukrainian Catholic, and Baptist churches. Russians, a separate nationality group, make up about 20 per cent of the remaining population.

About 33 per cent of the Ukrainian people live in rural areas, where they maintain close ties to their families and farms. They are famous for *pysanky*, the unique folk art of decorating Easter eggs with elaborate designs. Ukrainians also enjoy dancing, and their music often features a stringed instrument called a *bandura*.

The United Arab Emirates

The United Arab Emirates (UAE) is a federation of seven independent Arab states at the southern end of the Persian Gulf. From west to east, the states are Abu Dhabi, Dubayy, Ash Shariqah, Ajman, Umm al Qaywayn, Ras al Khaymah, and Al Fujayrah. The capital city of each state has the same name as the state. Abu Dhabi also serves as the capital of the federation.

Each of the seven states of the UAE is an *emirate,* ruled by a prince called an *emir.* The emir controls his own state's political and economic affairs.

Together, the seven emirs form the Supreme Council of the UAE. The council names a president to serve as chief executive. It also appoints a prime minister to head a Council of Ministers, who supervise government departments. This federal government controls the UAE's foreign affairs and defense and plays a large role in economic and social development.

Most of the UAE's people are Arabs from rival tribes that have lived in the region for hundreds of years. Lack of agreement among the tribes has made it difficult to establish a unified nation.

The Arab states that now make up the UAE began to develop during the 1700's, when European nations had already established trading posts in the Persian Gulf area. Great Britain eventually became the strongest foreign power in the region.

Ras al Khaymah and Ash Shariqah became the first strong Arab states in the area. Their strength came from naval power as well as the wealth obtained from pearl diving and trading.

In the late 1700's and early 1800's, Ras al Khaymah and Ash Shariqah warred with other gulf states over control of the region's trade. Not only did the British aid the rivals of the two Arab states, but they destroyed the city of Ras al Khaymah.

In 1820, the British forced all the states to sign a truce forbidding warfare at sea. Other truces were later signed, and the region became known as the Trucial States. But rivalries over boundaries, pearl-diving rights, and other disputes led to wars among the states that continued into the mid-1900's.

By that time, Abu Dhabi and Dubayy had become the leading states in the area. Great Britain controlled all the states' foreign affairs, while guaranteeing them protection against invaders. Each emir continued to handle his own state's internal matters.

Then in the mid-1900's, foreign oil companies began to drill for oil in the Trucial States. In 1958, petroleum was discovered in

FACT BOX

THE COUNTRY
Official name: United Arab Emirates.
Capital: Abu Dhabi.
Land regions: Swamps and salt marshes on northern coast, desert inland, highlands in the east.
Area: 32,278 sq. mi. ($83,600 \text{ km}^2$).
Climate: Desert (hot and dry). Temperatures average above 90° F. (32° C) in summer, above 60° F. (16° C) in winter. Yearly rainfall averages less than 5 in. (13 cm). Mountains are cooler and wetter.
Highest elevation: Jabal Yibir, 5,010 ft. (1,527 m).
Lowest elevation: Salamiyah, a salt flat just below sea level.

THE GOVERNMENT
Form of government: Federation of emirates.
Head of state: President.
Head of government: Prime minister.
Administrative areas: 7 independent states.
Legislature: Federal National Council, with members appointed by emirs of the states.
Court system: Federal courts.
Armed forces: 43,000 troops.

THE PEOPLE
Estimated 1996 population: 1,820,000.
Official language: Arabic.
Religion: Islam (95%).

THE ECONOMY
Currency: Dirham.
Gross national product (GNP) in 1992: $37 billion U.S.
Real annual growth rate (1985–92): 0%.
GNP per capita (1992): $22,220 U.S.
Balance of trade (1991): +$7.3 billion U.S.
Goods exported: Dates, fish, natural gas, and petroleum.
Goods imported: Building supplies, clothing, food, household goods, and machinery.
Trading partners: Japan, the United States, and Western Europe.

Abu Dhabi, and in 1966 large oil deposits were found in Dubayy.

In 1971, the Trucial States gained full independence from Great Britain. Despite their long-time feuding, six of the states decided to form a union called the United Arab Emirates. The seventh—Ras al Khaymah—joined the federation in 1972.

Oil production began in Ash Shariqah in 1974, and oil profits enabled Abu Dhabi, Dubayy, and Ash Shariqah to develop into modern states. However, the oil industry brought people as well as wealth to the UAE. Thousands of workers came from neighboring Arab countries—as well as from India, Iran, and Pakistan—to work in the oil industry.

The United Arab Emirates, a federation of seven Arab states, extends along the eastern coast of the Arabian Peninsula. Abu Dhabi, the capital of one of the states, is also capital of the federation.

A modern shopping center forms an impressive part of the new *suk,* or market, in Ash Shariqah. The UAE's economy boomed in the 1970's, when oil production increased, but it suffered when oil prices fell in the 1980's.

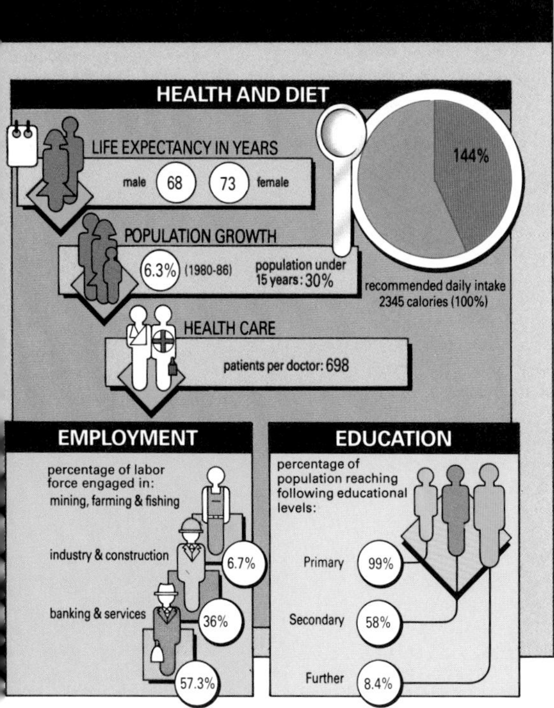

Most of the UAE's people are Arab Muslims. About 75 per cent of them live in urban areas, and most have modern houses or apartments. But in rural areas and on the outskirts of the cities, many people live in small thatched huts, as their ancestors did. Some of the people wear Western-style clothing, but most prefer traditional Arab robes.

Land and Economy

Before the mid-1900's, the region that is now the United Arab Emirates (UAE) was one of the most underdeveloped areas in the world.

The land itself has few natural resources, and the climate is hot with little rainfall. Humid swamps and salt marshes line much of the northern coast, while desert covers most of the inland area. Hills and mountains rise up in the eastern section.

Until the 1950's, most of the UAE's people earned a living by diving for pearls, fishing, herding camels, growing dates, or trading. The discovery of oil, beginning in the 1950's, brought sudden wealth into the region. New industries were created, and modern cities began to develop. Many of the people left their traditional ways of life and took jobs in the oil industry or other modern occupations.

Under the Provisional Constitution adopted in 1971, the emirs who rule the seven states of the UAE agreed to share their resources and work for the economic development of all the states. During the decade of the 1970's, the UAE's average income per person was among the highest in the world.

When thousands of people came from neighboring countries seeking jobs, the UAE was faced with housing shortages and other problems. But profits from the oil industry and other economic activities have helped the federal government build apartments, schools, hospitals, and roads to meet the needs of the growing population.

Most of the oil production of the UAE takes place in the states of Abu Dhabi, Dubayy, and Ash Shariqah. The rulers of these emirates earn huge profits selling oil to foreign countries. The exports are mainly crude oil, but the UAE also has refineries that process some of the oil into petroleum products.

The production of natural gas, which often is found near petroleum, also brings income into the UAE. In addition, the region has trading and banking facilities.

Other states of the UAE—Ajman, Umm al Qaywayn, Ras al Khaymah, and Al Fujayrah—have also begun producing some

Dubayy

Of all the United Arab Emirates, Dubayy has made the greatest effort to attract foreign businesses and investment, especially from Europe and North America. In the early 1970's, the state began an ambitious program to develop an international airport and harbor. Port Rashid is now a major shipping center, where goods are transferred from oceangoing vessels to *dhows* (Arabian sailing ships). Some of the dhows carry goods back and forth to the coast of Iran, less than 100 miles (160 kilometers) away. Persian carpets are just one of the many items traded in this duty-free zone.

oil. However, they continue to rely on agriculture and fishing as the basis of their economies.

Desert covers much of the region, so less than 1 per cent of the land of the UAE can be farmed. However, wells and oases dot the desert, and the hills and mountains in the eastern section generally receive more rainfall than the rest of the area. Farmers in the desert oases and the highlands grow dates, melons, tomatoes, and other crops, while desert nomads tend herds of camels, goats, and sheep.

People who live in the coastal areas earn their living by fishing. The UAE exports small amounts of fish and dates.

The craggy ruins of an ancient fortress in the hills of the United Arab Emirates are a reminder of the region's violent and warring past. These small eastern Arabian states often quarreled over control of the valuable trade that moved through the Persian Gulf.

Arab musicians, keeping traditions alive, hold the attention of a group of children. Oil income has enabled the United Arab Emirates to build many schools, and today most UAE children receive an education.

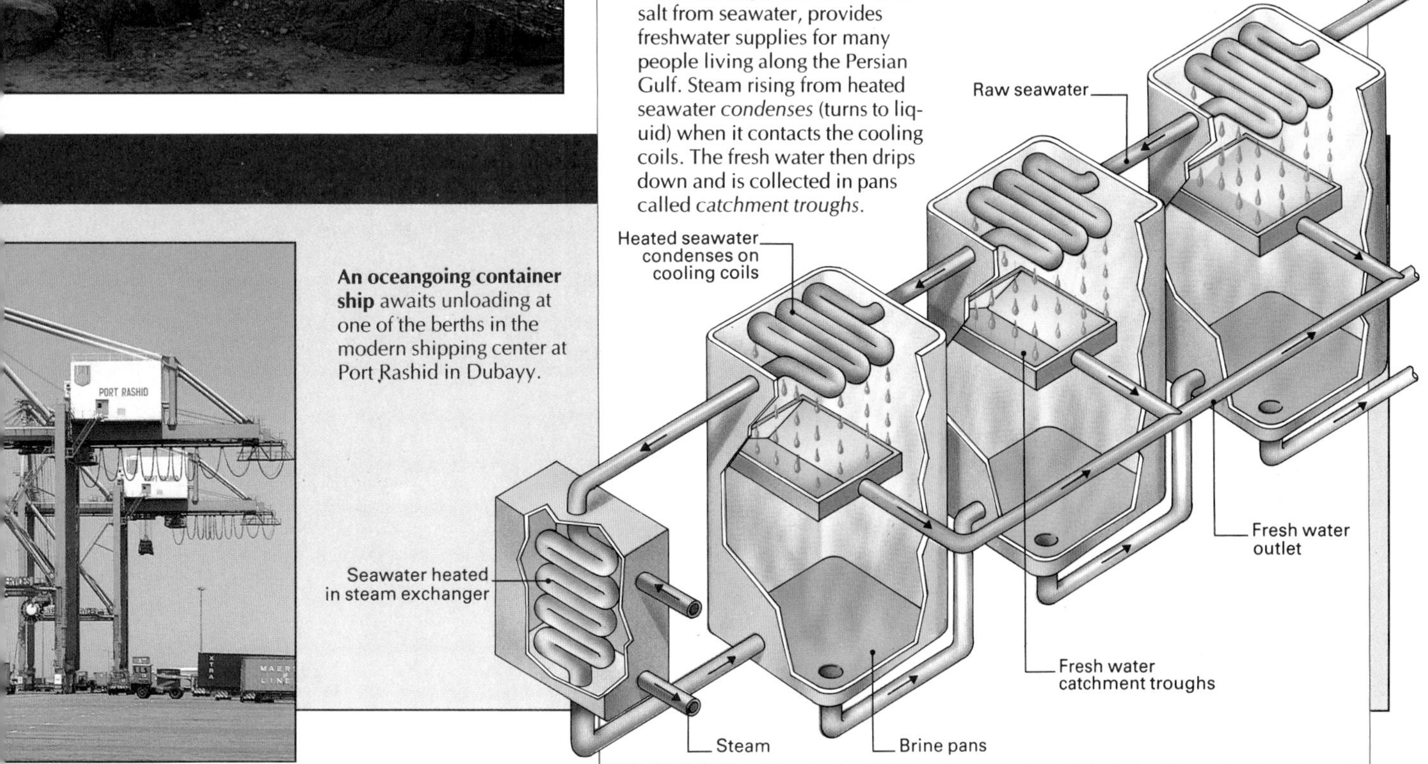

Desalination, or the removal of salt from seawater, provides freshwater supplies for many people living along the Persian Gulf. Steam rising from heated seawater *condenses* (turns to liquid) when it contacts the cooling coils. The fresh water then drips down and is collected in pans called *catchment troughs*.

An oceangoing container ship awaits unloading at one of the berths in the modern shipping center at Port Rashid in Dubayy.

The United States

The United States of America is the fourth largest country in the world. Only Russia, Canada, and China are larger. Only China and India have more people than the United States.

This mighty nation spans the middle of North America from the Atlantic Ocean to the Pacific Ocean. It also includes the huge state of Alaska in the northwest corner of North America and the island state of Hawaii, far out in the Pacific.

America's landscape is as varied as it is vast. It ranges from the warm, sunny beaches of California and Hawaii to the frozen northlands of Alaska, from the flat Midwestern plains to the towering Rocky Mountains, and from the swamps of Florida's Everglades to the desert of Nevada's Death Valley.

The United States also has rich and varied natural resources. Some of the most fertile soil on earth covers much of the Midwest. Vast forests flourish in the Northeast, Southeast, and Northwest. Under the ground lie huge deposits of valuable minerals. Excellent water transportation routes are provided by the five Great Lakes and by many rivers, including the Mississippi River system, which flows through the heart of the country.

These resources have helped make the United States one of the world's most highly developed and productive nations. The people of the United States enjoy the highest standard of living in the world.

Most Americans are descendants of European settlers who arrived in North America after the 1500's. Until then, the area that is now the United States was largely a wilderness. Small groups of Native Americans lived on the land between the Atlantic and the Pacific, Eskimos lived in what is now Alaska, and Polynesians lived in Hawaii.

For many Europeans, this New World offered an opportunity to build a new and better life. Spanish settlers came to Florida and the Southwest. English people and other Europeans settled along the east coast. In 1776, the Thirteen Colonies declared their independence from England. They founded a nation based on freedom and tolerance.

Through the years, immigrants from around the world have come to the United States. Since 1886, the Statue of Liberty in New York Harbor has welcomed many of these people to the New World.

Today the United States is sometimes called a "nation of immigrants." Some groups have suffered socially and economically, but through the laws passed by their elected representatives, the people of the United States continue to seek "liberty and justice for all."

The United States Today

The Constitution of the United States, written more than 200 years ago, established the United States as a federal republic. *Federal* means that power is shared between a national government and state governments, and in a *republic,* the people vote for leaders to represent them and guard their rights.

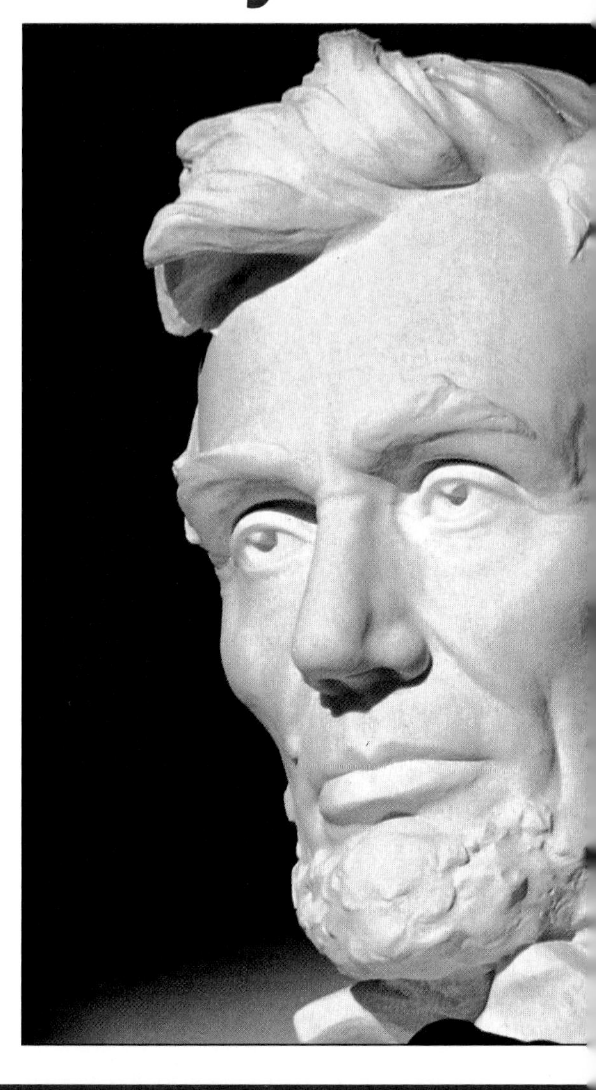

The federal government

The writers of the U.S. Constitution separated the federal government's power among three branches—the executive, the legislative, and the judicial.

The executive branch is headed by the President and includes executive departments and independent agencies. As chief executive, the President enforces federal laws, commands the armed forces, and conducts foreign affairs. The people elect the President to a four-year term through the electoral college, but no President can serve more than two terms.

The legislative branch is represented by the Congress, which is made up of two houses—the House of Representatives and the Senate. It also includes various agencies. The legislative branch makes the laws of the nation. Its powers include raising money through taxes, regulating trade between states, and declaring war.

FACT BOX

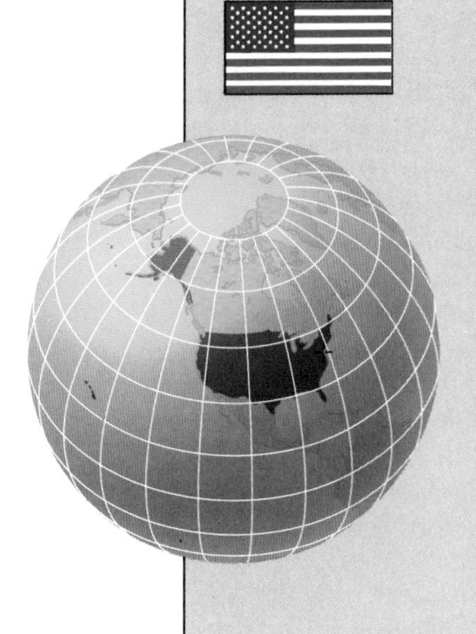

THE COUNTRY
Official name: United States of America.
Capital: Washington, D.C.
Area: 3,618,770 sq. mi. (9,372,571 km^2).
Land regions: Appalachian Highlands; Coastal Lowlands; Interior Plains; Ozark–Ouachita Highlands; Rocky Mountains; Western Plateaus, Basins, and Ranges; Pacific Ranges and Lowlands.
Climate: Northeast and north-central: warm summers and cold, snowy winters. South: hot summers and mild winters. West and Southwest: dry deserts and cool, wet mountains. Pacific Coast: mild.
Main rivers: Mississippi, Ohio, Missouri, Colorado.
Highest elevation: Mt. McKinley, 20,320 ft. (6,194 m).
Lowest elevation: Death Valley, 282 ft. (86 m) below sea level.

THE GOVERNMENT
Form of government: Republic.
Head of state: President.
Head of government: President, also chief executive.
Administrative areas: 50 states and the District of Columbia.
Legislature: A two-house Congress, including a Senate with 100 members, 2 from each state, elected to 6-year terms; and a House of Representatives with 435 members, state representation based on population, elected to 2-year terms.
Court system: Supreme Court, federal courts of appeal, and district courts.
Armed forces: About 771,800 troops.
Main outlying areas (dates acquired)
Commonwealths: Northern Mariana Islands (1947); Puerto Rico (1898).
Unincorporated territories: American Samoa (1900–1925);

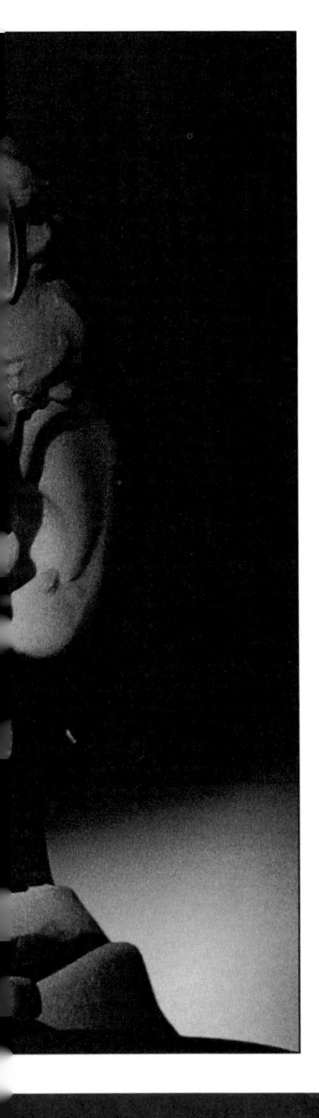

The number of representatives each state sends to the House of Representatives depends on the population of the state. However, regardless of its size or population, each state sends just two senators to Congress.

The judicial branch of the United States is a system of courts. The highest court in the land is the Supreme Court of the United States. The nine justices of the Supreme Court interpret the Constitution and hear cases that involve federal laws.

In addition to these specific powers, each branch of government has powers that check or balance the powers of the other two branches. For example, the President can veto bills from Congress and appoint the justices of the Supreme Court. Congress can override presidential vetoes and organize the federal courts. And the Supreme Court can declare executive orders and laws unconstitutional. This system of checks and balances prevents any branch from becoming too powerful.

A statue of Abraham Lincoln is part of the Lincoln Memorial in Washington, D.C. The beautiful white marble monument stands at the end of the National Mall and honors the democratic ideals of the 16th President of the United States. From a humble birth, Lincoln rose to the presidency, led the nation during the Civil War (1861–1865), and freed the slaves.

The state governments

Each of the 50 states can exercise powers given to the states—or not denied them—by the Constitution. Each state has its own constitution, with an executive branch (headed by a governor), a legislative branch (headed by a state legislature), and a judicial branch (headed by a state supreme court).

Some of the powers exercised by the states include the maintenance of law and order, administration of health and welfare services, and the regulation of business. The states also have the major responsibility for public education.

Government spending

Government plays a major role in the U.S. economy. Federal, state, and local governments employ about a fifth of all workers and buy a fifth of all the goods and services produced in the United States. The federal government spends part of its budget on social security benefits for American people, and both federal and state governments provide medical and welfare aid for the elderly and for the needy.

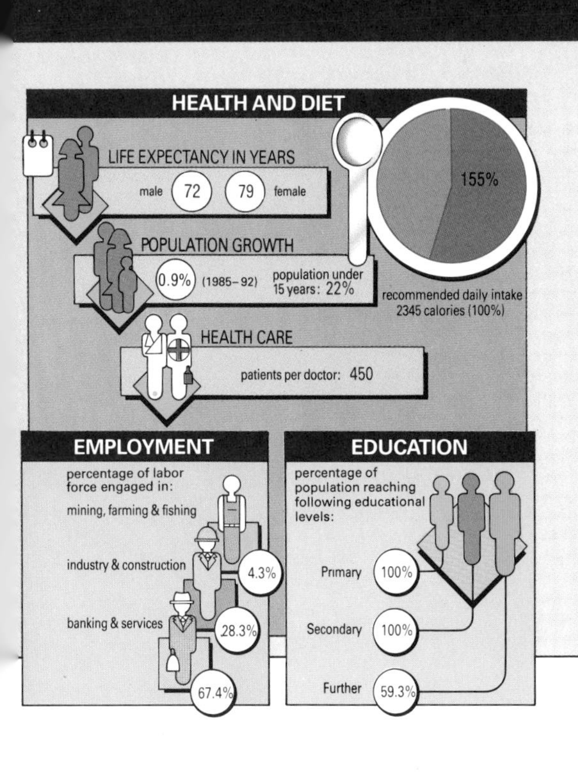

Baker Island and Jarvis Island (1856); Guam (1898); Johnston Island and Sand Island (1858); Kingman Reef (1922); Midway Island (1867); Virgin Islands (1917).
Unincorporated possessions: Howland Island (1856); Palmyra Island (1898); Wake Island (1898).
UN trust territory: Trust Territory of the Pacific Islands (1947).

THE PEOPLE
Estimated 1996 population: 264,015,000.
Official language: No official language. English most widely used. Spanish also spoken.
Religions: Protestant (31%), Roman Catholic (22%), Jewish (2%), Mormon (2%).

THE ECONOMY
Currency: Dollar.
Gross national product (GNP) in 1992: $5,904.8 billion U.S.
Real annual growth rate (1985–92): 1.1%.
GNP per capita (1992): $23,120 U.S.
Balance of trade (1992): −$101.8 billion U.S.
Goods exported: Agricultural products, chemicals, coal, machinery, and transportation equipment.
Goods imported: Food products, machinery, manufactured goods, minerals, and transportation equipment.
Trading partners: Canada, Germany, Great Britain, Japan, Mexico, and Taiwan.

The Fifty States

The 50 states that together form the United States cover an area of more than 3-1/2 million square miles (9 million square kilometers). The northernmost point is Point Barrow, Alaska, and the southernmost point is Ka Lae, Hawaii. The easternmost point lies at West Quoddy Head, Maine, and the westernmost point at Cape Wrangell on Attu Island in Alaska.

The 48 states that border one another between the Atlantic and Pacific oceans stretch across four time zones and 2,807 miles (4,517 kilometers) at the greatest distance. The states differ greatly in size, ranging from huge Alaska and Texas to tiny Rhode Island.

The 50 states are political divisions of the United States. Because the United States has a federal system of government, the states hold many of the powers assumed by national governments in most other countries. For example, states have a great deal of control over education, and they can pass many civil and criminal laws. Some states can be compared with many small countries in size, population, and economic output, as well as government.

In addition to the 50 states, the District of Columbia, the seat of the federal government, is an important part of the United States. The District of Columbia lies along the Potomac River between Virginia and Maryland. The 69-square-mile (179-square-kilometer) area was set aside by the government for the U.S. capital city of Washington. The United States also has island possessions and territories in the Caribbean Sea and Pacific Ocean.

The states of the United States are often divided into regions that share geography, climate, economy, traditions, and history with one another. Because America was largely settled from east to west, states on the East Coast and along the southern shores of the Great Lakes have long been centers of dense population. But in more recent times, people have been attracted by the mild climate and growing business opportunities in the Southern and Western Sun Belt states. Today, California has more residents than any other state.

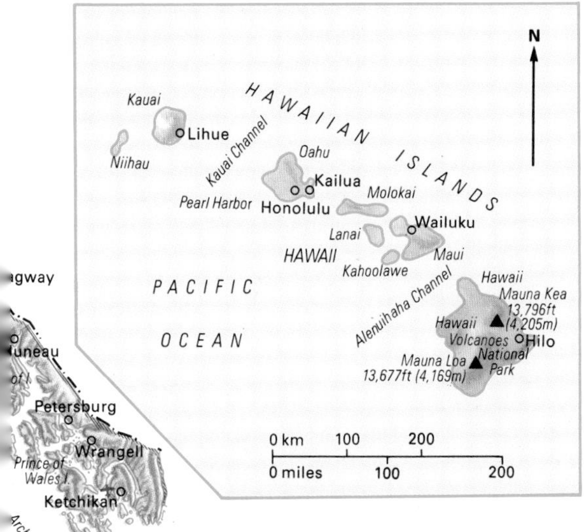

Fifty states make up the United States of America. The far Northeastern states, called New England, and the Middle Atlantic States were the first to be settled by Europeans. Today, great cities like Boston and New York are located there. West of the Appalachians, the states of the Midwest spread out over the plains of the Mississippi River system. This area is rich farm country, but it also became heavily industrialized, starting in the late 1800's. The warm South, once a region of slavery and farming, now has growing businesses and industries. Moving west, the Great Plains slope upward to the Rocky Mountains and the dry plateaus of the Southwest. This area offers some of the most spectacular scenery in the country. The Pacific Coast States have dense forests, rugged mountains, vast deserts, and wild ocean shores. The mild climate attracts tourists and new residents. Alaska and Hawaii, geographically separate from the other 48 states, are the newest states. Both became states in 1959.

East Coast States

The states that occupy what is now the northeast corner of the country were part of the original Thirteen Colonies. Along with the Southern Colonies, they declared their independence on July 4, 1776, and the United States was born.

These East Coast States are often considered two smaller regions: New England, consisting of Connecticut, Maine, Massachusetts, New Hampshire, Rhode Island, and Vermont; and the Middle Atlantic States, consisting of New Jersey, New York, and Pennsylvania.

Many New Englanders are descendants of the English Puritans who settled the Massachusetts Bay region in the 1600's. Dutch immigrants originally settled in what is now New York. Their city of New Amsterdam became the budding city of New York when England took control of the colony. William Penn, a Quaker, founded Pennsylvania as a place where people of every faith could enjoy religious freedom.

Varied land and a varied economy

The Appalachian Mountains stretch through the East Coast States as the White Mountains in New Hampshire, the Green Mountains in Vermont, the Catskill Mountains in New York, and the Allegheny Mountains in Pennsylvania. Lowlands hug the coast, and plains and a plateau lie west of the mountains. The Piedmont, an area of gently rolling hills west of the coastal lowlands, stretches from New York south to Alabama.

New England was the nation's first industrial center, and manufacturing is still its leading source of income. Much of New England is too hilly or rocky to grow crops on a large-scale, commercial basis, but the area produces dairy and poultry products and is famous for its maple syrup. New England's land and history contribute to the economy in still another way. Many tourists visit the region's historic sites, picturesque rural villages, fishing harbors, and fine ski resorts.

The deepwater harbors of the Middle Atlantic States and their large populations help make this area a major center of trade. Factories produce a variety of products, and coal is mined in Pennsylvania.

Farms dot the hillsides and plains in these states. Tourists are drawn to this area too, attracted by its forested mountains, scenic

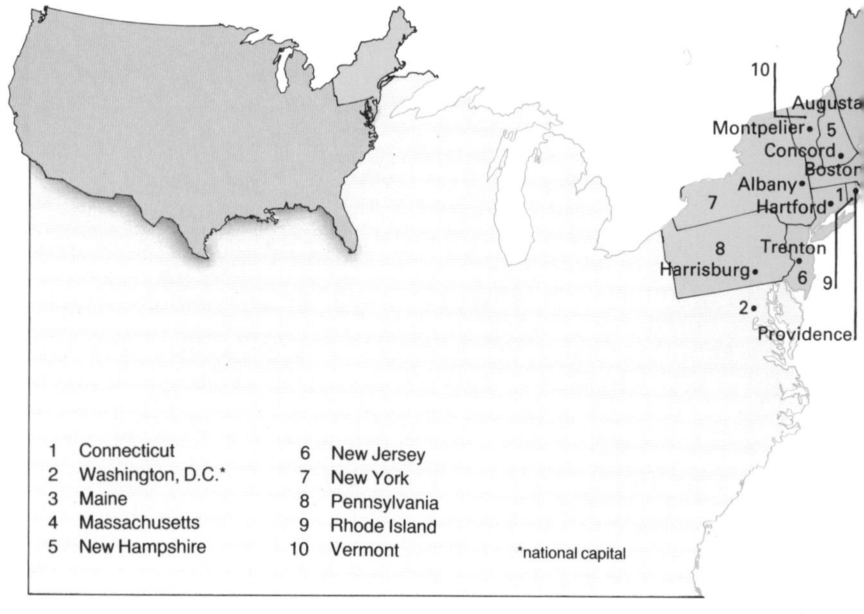

The Old State House, *far left,* is a historic landmark in Boston. Built in 1713, the State House was the seat of the colonial government. Today, the towers of Boston's downtown area rise around it.

Scarecrows watch over pumpkins for sale at a farm in Vermont. Famous for its maple syrup, its scenic autumn beauty, and its skiing, Vermont is the most rural and one of the least populated of the 50 states.

lakes and rivers, big cities, and historic sites such as Gettysburg, the Pennsylvania community that is famous as the site of the Civil War's Battle of Gettysburg. Another attraction for tourists, as well as nature-lovers, is the Appalachian National Scenic Trail, a hiking path almost 2,000 miles (3,200 kilometers) long. The trail begins in Maine and stretches through New England and the Middle Atlantic States into the Deep South.

The cities

The East Coast States have developed the largest *megalopolis* (great city) in the United States. A megalopolis is a region where two or more metropolitan areas have grown together. A huge megalopolis includes Boston, New York City, Philadelphia, Baltimore, and Washington, D.C.

Boston, with more than half a million people, is one of the oldest and most historic U.S. cities. It is New England's leading business center as well as a national center of learning.

New York City, with about 7 million people, is the largest U.S. city and the sixth largest in the world. As a center of international business and culture, New York affects much of what happens around the world.

Philadelphia, with more than 1-2/3 million people, was the birthplace of the United States. Philadelphians are now trying to renovate the run-down sections of the city. Development projects include stores, housing, and office buildings.

The U.S. Capitol provides the backdrop for a parade in Washington, D.C. The nation's capital is at the southern end of a huge megalopolis that includes Boston and New York City.

Busy New Yorkers throng Fifth Avenue in midtown Manhattan, *middle,* the oldest and most important borough in New York City. Rockefeller Center lies on Fifth Avenue, as do many fine stores.

Midwestern States

Twelve states lie in the heart, or center, of the United States and are sometimes even called "the heartland." The Midwestern States of Illinois, Indiana, Iowa, Kansas, Michigan, Minnesota, Missouri, Nebraska, North Dakota, Ohio, South Dakota, and Wisconsin cover a vast area of fairly flat and very fertile land. They produce food for the country and for the rest of the world.

The eastern states of this region—Illinois, Indiana, Michigan, Minnesota, Ohio, and Wisconsin—lie around four of the five Great Lakes. These lakes were the chief route taken by explorers and settlers traveling into what is now the Midwest. Thousands of other pioneers from the Eastern United States sailed down the Ohio River on large flatboats to Midwestern settlements.

The Great Plains—a vast grassland—stretches across the western part of the Midwest. The plains were opened to settlers when the U.S. government defeated Native Americans who lived there, forcing them to sign treaties that cleared the way for whites to live there.

Ranchers moved onto the land first, and soon the Great Plains was a vast cattle empire. Railroads expanded westward to provide transportation to eastern markets. Farmers known as *homesteaders* followed the ranchers onto the Great Plains. Such new inventions as barbed wire and improved windmills, along with free land, helped the homesteaders turn the plains into a productive agricultural region, where both cattle and crops could be raised.

The breadbasket

The Midwest is noted for its vast expanses of fertile soil. The Great Plains represents one of the world's chief wheat-growing areas. In addition to wheat, farms in the Midwest also produce enormous quantities of alfalfa, barley, corn, oats, and rye, as well as dairy products and livestock. Iowa and Illinois are the nation's leading soybean-producing states.

Many of the people who live in the rural areas of the Midwest today are the descendants of German, British, Swedish, and Norwegian settlers.

Industry, services, and cities

Although the Midwest is a major farming region, it also has large industrial cities and an important service economy. The Great Lakes were important in the industrial development of the United States and the Midwest, especially for the steel industry. These deep lakes provide a fast water route for ships carrying iron ore from ports in northern Michigan, Minnesota, and Wisconsin to steel mills in Indiana and Ohio. The Great Lakes are also the best way to ship the huge wheat crops from the Great Plains.

The U.S. automobile industry has been centered in Michigan since the early 1900's. Detroit, called the *Motor City,* was the birthplace of the first Ford car.

The railroads that helped settle the plains turned Chicago into a rail hub that now ranks as the nation's leading transportation center. Chicago is the only place where the Great Lakes connect with the huge Mississippi River system. This energetic city also has the world's tallest building and the world's busiest airport.

Other large industrial cities located along the Great Lakes include Milwaukee and Cleveland. In fact, the area from Milwaukee through Chicago and east to Pittsburgh is developing into a megalopolis. Many descendants of immigrants from northern, eastern, and southern Europe, as well as African Americans, live in the big cities of the Midwest.

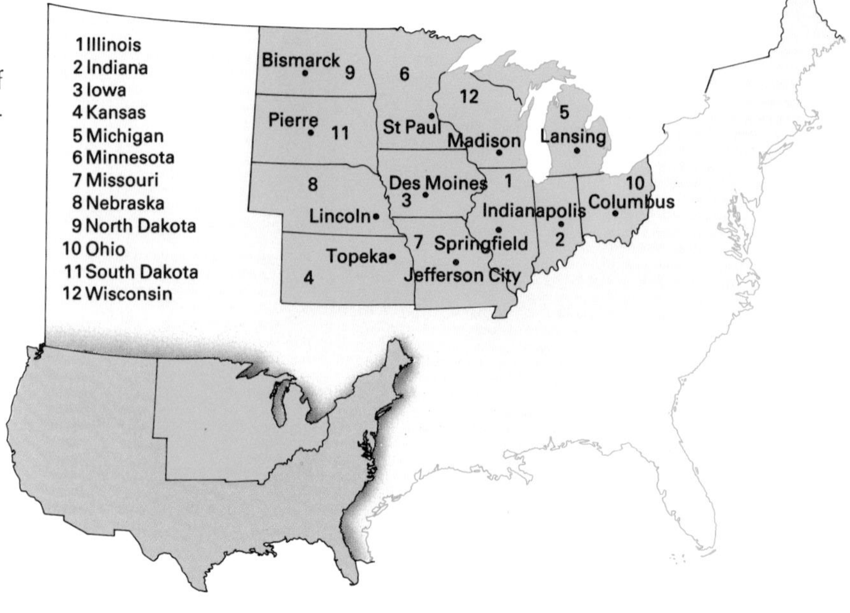

Wisconsin dairy farms, *far left,* with their well-kept outbuildings and green fields, make up a typical Midwest scene. Wisconsin's huge output of milk, cheese, and butter has earned this Midwest state the nickname *America's Dairyland.*

Downtown Chicago extends about 25 blocks along the west shore of Lake Michigan. The lakefront is lined with skyscrapers, parks, beaches, museums, and marinas. The John Hancock Center towers in the background.

Chemical carrier barges pass through a lock on the Mississippi River at Alton, Ill., *above.* The Mississippi River system, along with the Great Lakes and many railroads, gives the Midwest an excellent transportation network.

Farmers in Nebraska celebrate their corn harvest. Once called the "Great American Desert," Nebraska is now a leading farm state. Its official nickname is the *Cornhusker State.*

Southern States

The Mason and Dixon's line—an east-west boundary line separating Pennsylvania from Maryland—came to be considered the dividing line between the North and the South. Before the Civil War (1861–1865), the southern border of Pennsylvania was also the boundary between the antislavery states to the north and the proslavery states to the south.

The South is made up of the states of Alabama, Arkansas, Delaware, Florida, Georgia, Kentucky, Louisiana, Maryland, Mississippi, North Carolina, South Carolina, Tennessee, Virginia, and West Virginia. Here cotton and tobacco, grown on large plantations, led to an economy that depended on the labor of African slaves. In the North, however, the economy was based on trade and manufacturing. As a result, two very different cultures and life styles developed.

The North's opposition to slavery led to tension and eventually conflict. From 1860 to 1861, 11 Southern States broke away from the Union and formed a Confederacy. A bitter and bloody war followed, ending with the South's defeat. About 260,000 of its men had been killed, and its economy was nearly destroyed.

For decades, the South remained a fairly poor agricultural region. Not until the mid-1900's did its economy begin to change and grow stronger.

The land and people

The South is an area of rolling hills, mountains, and plains bordered by broad beaches along the Atlantic Ocean and the Gulf of Mexico. The Piedmont, which begins in New York, widens in Virginia and extends south into Alabama. Tobacco is widely grown in the Piedmont. The division between this gently rolling land and the Coastal Plain is the Fall Line, where rivers flowing from the west drop from higher, rocky ground to the sandy plain and then flow to the sea. Large cities have grown up along the Fall Line, such as Baltimore, Md.; Columbia, S.C.; Richmond, Va.; Washington, D.C.; and Wilmington, Del.

The Appalachians extend from the North into the South as the Blue Ridge Mountains and the Great Smoky Mountains. Mining is important in these mountain areas, especially coal mining in Kentucky and West Virginia. Lumber from this region is shipped to furniture factories in North Carolina. Many of the people in the Appalachians, as elsewhere in the South, are descended from early English, Irish, and Scottish immigrants.

Flat or gently rolling plains areas along the coasts and in parts of Kentucky and Tennessee are forested or farmed. At one time cotton was "king" in this Deep South land. Plantations spread over many acres, and slaves were numerous. Today, the descendants of those slaves form the largest minority group in the South.

The new South

The industrial boom that began in the 1950's and 1960's has greatly increased manufacturing in the region and raised the level of its economy.

The moist subtropical climate of the South brings thousands of tourists to the region each year, especially in winter, when the North is cold and snowy. In recent years, many new residents have come to live and work in this Sun Belt region, and many retired people move to Florida.

The lazy lower stretches of the Mississippi River break off into many small side channels as the river flows through bayous south of New Orleans. "Old Man River" is a major waterway for the South, linking the heartland of the United States with the rest of the world.

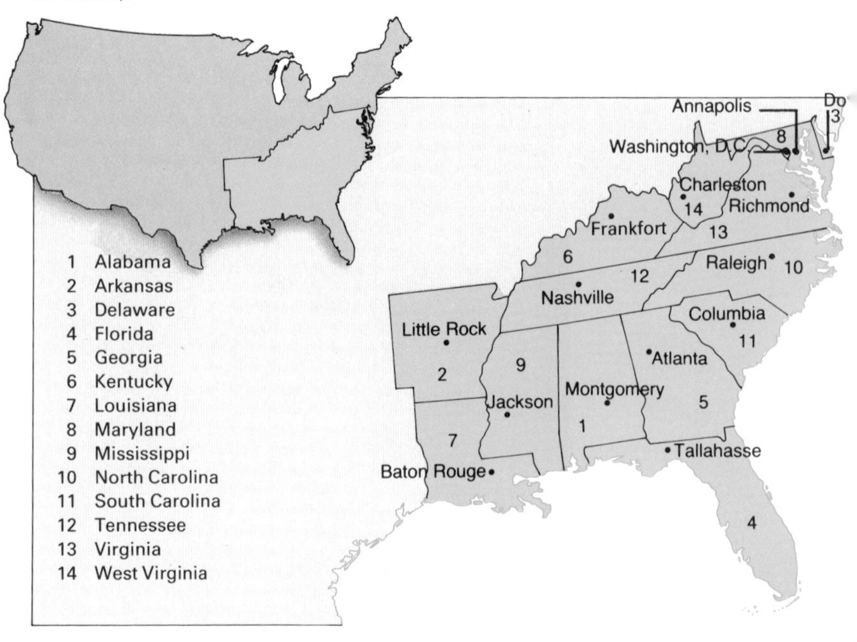

The South is a distinctive part of the United States. The bitter Civil War (1861–1865) badly damaged the South. Today, however, its population and economy are among the fastest growing in the country.

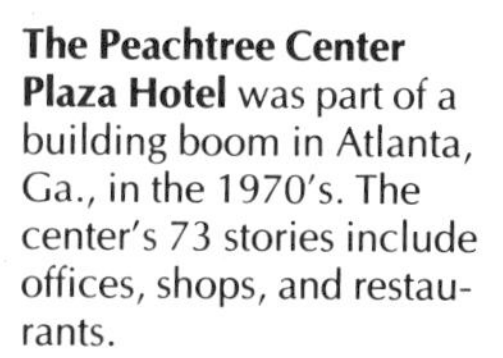

The Peachtree Center Plaza Hotel was part of a building boom in Atlanta, Ga., in the 1970's. The center's 73 stories include offices, shops, and restaurants.

A cruise ship pulls into the Port of Miami, Fla. Miami is a world-famous resort, and home to many Hispanics and retired people. It lies on Biscayne Bay, about 3-1/2 miles (5.6 kilometers) west of the Atlantic.

New Orleans, with its quaint streetcars, historic French Quarter, and annual Mardi Gras festival, attracts several million tourists each year. The city is also a major business, cultural, and shipping center of the South.

Western Interior States

The states in the Western interior contain some of the most spectacular scenery and natural wonders in the world.

The Western interior is made up of two regions: the Southwestern States of Arizona, New Mexico, Oklahoma, and Texas; and the Rocky Mountain States of Colorado, Idaho, Montana, Nevada, Utah, and Wyoming.

From the 1500's until the early 1800's, most of the Southwest was Spanish territory. The United States *annexed* (added) Texas in 1845, ten years after Texans had staged a revolt against Mexican rule. The country paid Mexico for the rest of its southwestern land in 1848 and 1853. The region's history is reflected in the Hispanic influences seen throughout the Southwest.

Both the Southwestern and the Rocky Mountain States were part of the Wild West. Although the West was not really as wild as legend and movies suggest, cowboys, miners, stagecoach drivers, sheriffs, and homesteaders all played a part in this region's history.

The Southwest

The Southwestern States spread out over a vast area that is sometimes called the "wide-open spaces." There, cattle graze on huge ranches. In some parts of the Southwest, vast fields of cotton and other crops soak up the abundant sunshine. In other areas, barren desert stretches as far as the eye can see.

In the 1900's, refineries and factories that make chemicals from petroleum products helped industrialize the Southwest. Petroleum has brought the region most of its wealth. Texas and Oklahoma are among the nation's leading producers of petroleum and natural gas.

Industrialization has led to a growing population, especially in urban areas where service industries are concentrated. Many of the fastest-growing U.S. cities are in the Southwest.

Many retired people move to the Southwest for its warm climate, while tourists come to enjoy its stunning natural beauty. The Grand Canyon draws about 3 million visitors each year. Arizona's Painted Desert, New Mexico's Carlsbad Caverns, and the Big Bend National Park in Texas are just a few of the area's tourist attractions.

Many people come to visit ancient Native American ruins and observe today's Native American culture. The Southwest is home to Apaches, Navajos, and Hopis and other Pueblos. Native American art, pottery, jewelry, and blankets are highly prized.

The Rocky Mountain States

The states of the Rocky Mountain region are named for the rugged, majestic range that cuts through the area. But the scenic landscape also includes deserts, plateaus, and plains.

Rich deposits of gold, silver, and other metals first attracted settlers to the Rocky Mountain region. Mining remains important, though manufacturing is now the chief source of income. Cattle and other livestock

Snow-dusted Boulder Valley in western Montana is Rocky Mountain country. Spruce, pine, and fir forests carpet the lower mountain slopes, but no trees grow above the timber line.

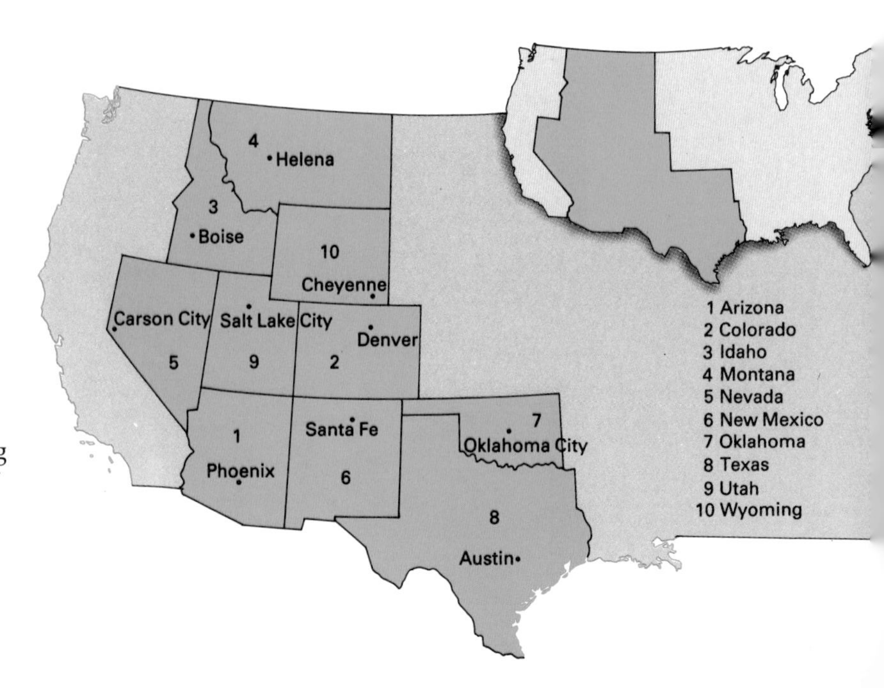

A cowboy herds cattle in New Mexico, *far left.* Cattlemen from Texas established ranches in New Mexico after the Civil War. Cattle are now the state's most important farm product.

The beautiful Cliff Palace in southwestern Colorado was built by Pueblos, probably in the 1200's. Now part of Mesa Verde National Park, the dwellings help preserve the Native American heritage of the Southwest.

graze on dry, grassy ranges. Farmers grow a variety of crops, such as wheat, hay, and potatoes. Many people are now employed in service industries, such as real estate and wholesale and retail trade.

As in the Southwest, tourism is important to the area. Some visitors come to ski in Idaho's Sun Valley and Colorado's Vail and Aspen. Others come to camp, fish, hike, and enjoy the mountain and desert scenery.

Valuable water

Water is scarce in this generally dry region. Part of Utah and almost all of Nevada, for example, are in the Basin and Range country, one of the driest areas in the nation. The Colorado River flows across 1,360 miles (2,189 kilometers) of the country and carves the Grand Canyon. A number of dams, including the Davis, Glen Canyon, Hoover, and Parker dams, stand along the river. They help prevent floods and erosion and provide electric power and water for much of the Southwest. So much water is stored in reservoirs and drained off by aqueducts and canals that the Colorado no longer reaches its mouth at the Gulf of California.

Glittering Las Vegas, with its big-name entertainment and casinos, is a major tourist attraction in the Nevada desert.

Pacific Coast States

The states that lie along the Pacific coast—California, Oregon, and Washington—are known for their dense forests, rugged mountains, and dramatic ocean shore. Their beauty and relatively mild climate—cooler and wetter in the north, warmer and drier in the south—encourage an outdoor life style enjoyed year-round by both residents and tourists.

Washington and Oregon were part of the Oregon Country, territory given to the United States by Great Britain in 1846. Settlers from the Midwest followed the Oregon Trail to this Pacific Northwest region.

California belonged to Spain and then to Mexico before the United States paid for it in 1848. The discovery of gold that same year brought thousands to the area in the Gold Rush. By 1850, California had enough people to be admitted to the Union as a state.

Land and people

Fertile valleys between the two parallel chains of Pacific Coast Ranges produce a large part of the nation's fruits, nuts, vegetables, and wine grapes. The Central Valley and Imperial Valley of California are especially productive farming areas.

The region also has abundant minerals, fish, and lumber—the Douglas fir is a leading timber tree. California's giant sequoias and famous redwood trees—the tallest living things on earth—attract tourists as well as lumber companies.

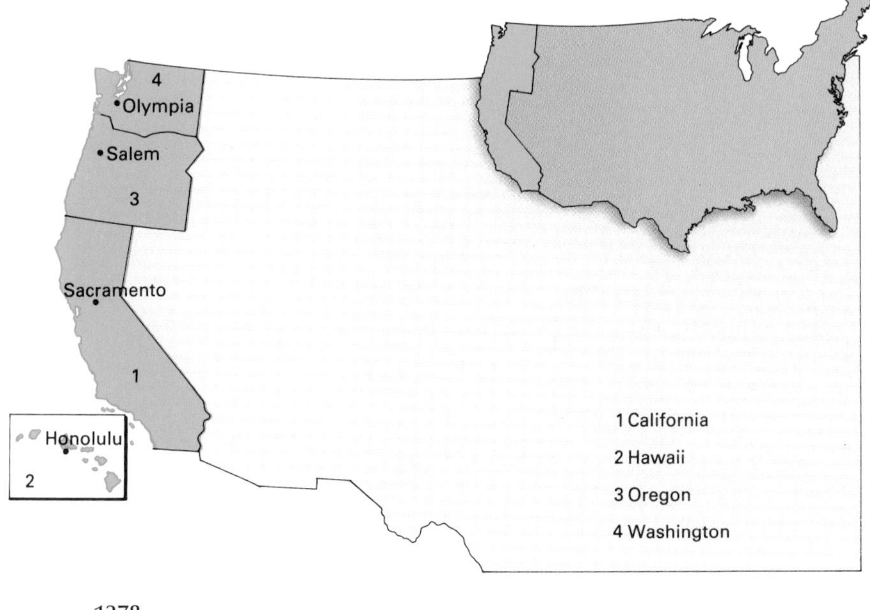

The fog-shrouded Golden Gate Bridge spans the entrance to San Francisco Bay. This city is also known for its picturesque cable cars, its bustling Chinatown—and its earthquakes.

Giant sequoias, *below,* reach for the sky in Sequoia National Park in California. The park's General Sherman Tree is the world's largest tree and one of the oldest living things on earth.

The breathtaking Olympic Peninsula lies in Washington's northwest corner. This area includes jagged peaks, lush rain forests, and more than 100 glaciers.

Visitors at Haleakala National Park, *left,* on the island of Maui, Hawaii, admire the rock formations of the world's largest inactive volcano. The name *Haleakala* means *House of the Sun.*

Manufacturing activities in the region include the building of transportation equipment in Washington, the processing of wood in Oregon, and the production of electrical equipment in California. Service industries are also leading economic activities. Hollywood, Calif., is known worldwide for its movies and television shows.

A stream of settlers to the Pacific Coast States began in the mid-1800's, and new residents have continued to pour in ever since. The California coast—from San Francisco through Los Angeles to San Diego—is a developing megalopolis.

Today, the region's population includes people of European ancestry, with African-American and Mexican-American minorities. In fact, more people of Mexican origin live in the Los Angeles area than in any other U.S. city. More people of Asian ancestry make their home in the Pacific Coast States than in any other part of the United States. A large number of Native Americans live there as well.

Hawaii

Hawaii can be considered a Pacific Coast State because its entire border is on the ocean. This state is a string of 8 main islands and 124 smaller ones. It lies in the middle of the North Pacific Ocean about 2,400 miles (3,860 kilometers) from the U.S. mainland. Hawaii is the 50th state, the last state to be admitted to the Union.

Hawaii is world famous for its tropical beauty and pleasant climate. The original settlers were Polynesians, but many other national and racial groups have also contributed to Hawaii's colorful way of life. Not surprisingly, tourism is a major Hawaiian industry.

Alaska

The name *Alaska* comes from a word used by native people meaning *great land* or *mainland.* Alaska is by far the largest state in the United States. Spreading across the northwest corner of North America, it is separated from Washington state by about 500 miles (800 kilometers) of Canadian territory. Alaskans often refer to the rest of the continental United States as the "lower 48."

The Pacific Coast Ranges extend from the lower 48 through Canada and into Alaska, where they become the Alaska Range. The Rocky Mountains reach into Alaska as the Brooks Range. Alaska has almost all the active volcanoes in the United States, as well as the 16 highest peaks in the country. Mount McKinley rises 20,320 feet (6,194 meters) above sea level, the highest point on the North American continent.

The Alaskan wilderness attracts many tourists who love the outdoors. Huge forests cover about a third of the state. The middle section has low, rolling hills and broad, swampy river valleys. The southern coast is cut by hundreds of small bays and narrow, steep-sided inlets called *fiords,* while thousands of glaciers fill Alaska's mountain valleys and canyons.

The far northern treeless plain is covered with grasses and flowers in summer, but permanently frozen ground called *permafrost* lies underneath. This land, called the *tundra,* is the summer grazing grounds of huge herds of caribou.

Other wild animals include polar bears, grizzly bears, deer, elk, moose, and mountain goats. The world's largest population of nothern fur seals live on the Pribilof Islands in summer.

The waters off Alaska's shores are rich in salmon, halibut, and crab. Alaskan fishermen catch about $700 million worth of fish every year.

Many people think of Alaska as very cold and snowy, but the state has a great variety of climates. Warm ocean winds give southern Alaska a fairly mild climate. Parts of the southeast, called the Panhandle, get heavy precipitation. Inland, Alaska has cold winters and cool summers and is fairly dry. The Alaskan Arctic has even colder winters, cooler summers, and less precipitation.

The climate and soil as far north as the Arctic Circle allow farmers to raise livestock

A tour boat, *top,* eases past Muir Glacier in Glacier Bay National Park. Many tourists take such cruises along Alaska's southeast coast.

Dog teams compete every March in the Iditarod Trail Sled Dog Race, *above.* The event honors a 1925 dog run, when medicine was rushed from Anchorage to Nome.

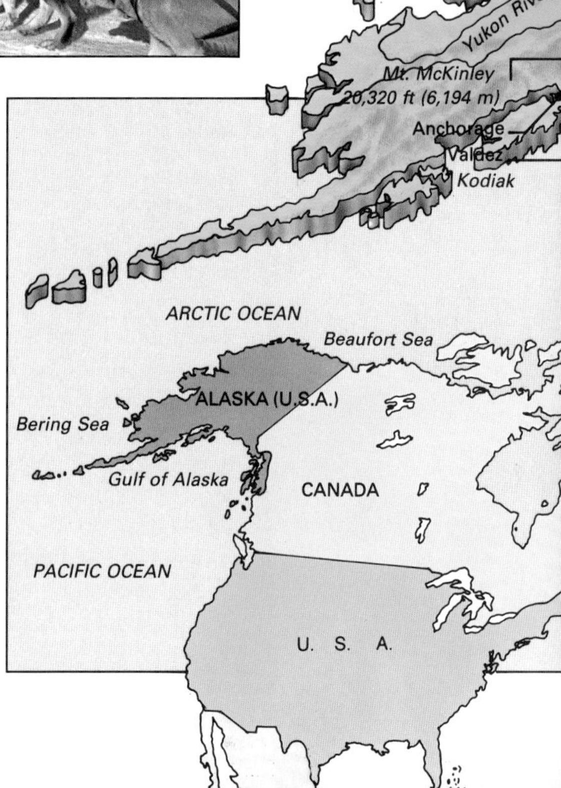

The Orthodox Church on Kodiak Island is a reminder of the time when Alaska was a Russian colony.

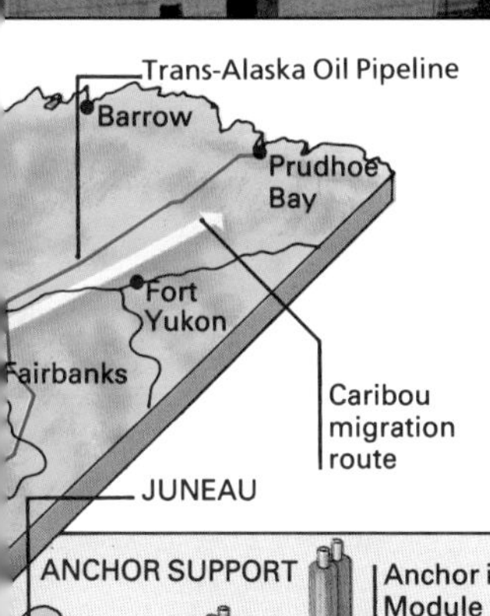

The Trans-Alaska Pipeline carries oil about 800 miles (1,300 kilometers), crossing the migration route of the caribou, *left*. Engineers designed different support systems to transport oil safely and efficiently over the rugged Alaskan terrain, *below*. A *conventional support* carries the pipeline over permafrost. An *anchor support* carries it through earthquake zones. *Conventional burial* ensures that the pipeline does not interfere with the caribous' migration.

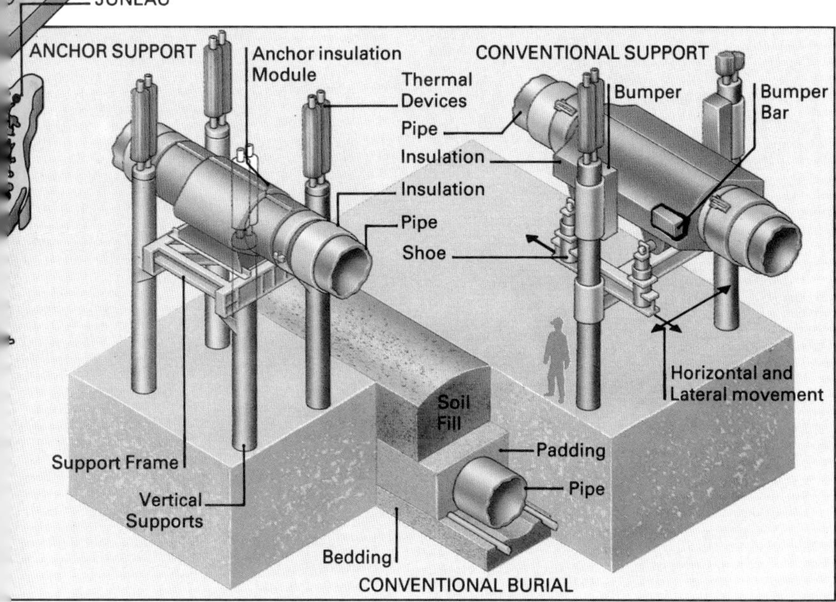

and grow barley, potatoes, and other hardy crops. Crops grow rapidly because the summer sun shines 20 hours a day. At Point Barrow in the Arctic, from May 10 to August 2, the sun never sets.

Eskimos, Russians, and Americans

When Europeans first arrived in Alaska in the 1700's, three groups of native people were living there. Eskimos lived near the coast in the far west and north, Aleuts lived on the Aleutian Islands and the Alaska Peninsula, and Native Americans lived on the southeastern islands, along the coast, and in the interior.

A Russian expedition in 1741 landed in Alaska and left with sea otter furs. Russian fur traders soon followed, and the area became Russian territory.

In 1867, however, Russia sold Alaska to the United States for $7.2 million. Some Americans thought the purchase was very foolish. They called Alaska *Seward's Folly* or *Seward's Icebox* after William Seward, the U.S. official who agreed to buy it.

Today, Alaska has an estimated population of more than 500,000. About a third were born in Alaska; many of those born elsewhere are members of the U.S. armed forces stationed in Alaska. Most of the people live in Anchorage (the largest city), Fairbanks, or cities on the southeast coast. Alaska is the most thinly populated state in the country.

The oil boom

One of the greatest oil discoveries of all time was made in 1968 at Prudhoe Bay on the Arctic Coast. In 1977, a pipeline was completed to carry the oil about 800 miles (1,300 kilometers) from Prudhoe Bay on the Arctic Ocean to Valdez on the southern coast, and oil production began.

Oil has boosted the state's economy and created many jobs, but oil production can cause problems too. In 1989, a tanker, the *Exxon Valdez*, struck a reef and caused a major oil spill in Prince William Sound. The oil killed wildlife and polluted beaches and fishing grounds.

National Parks

In 1807, an American trapper came across a wonderland in the northwest corner of what is now Wyoming. He and later trappers returned with stories of spouting geysers, deep gorges, thundering waterfalls, eerie hot springs, mineral deposits, and bubbling pools of mud.

In 1870, an expedition went into the area to see if the fantastic stories were true. By 1872, Congress had created a park out of the land. The park was named Yellowstone for the river that runs through it and for the yellow rocks that lie along the river.

Yellowstone became the world's first national park.

Natural wonders and monuments

The United States is rich in natural wonders like Yellowstone as well as famous historic places and recreation sites. Since 1872, the government has set aside more than 330 of these areas as national parklands. The parklands include parks, monuments, historic sites, memorials, cemeteries, seashores, lakeshores, and battlefields.

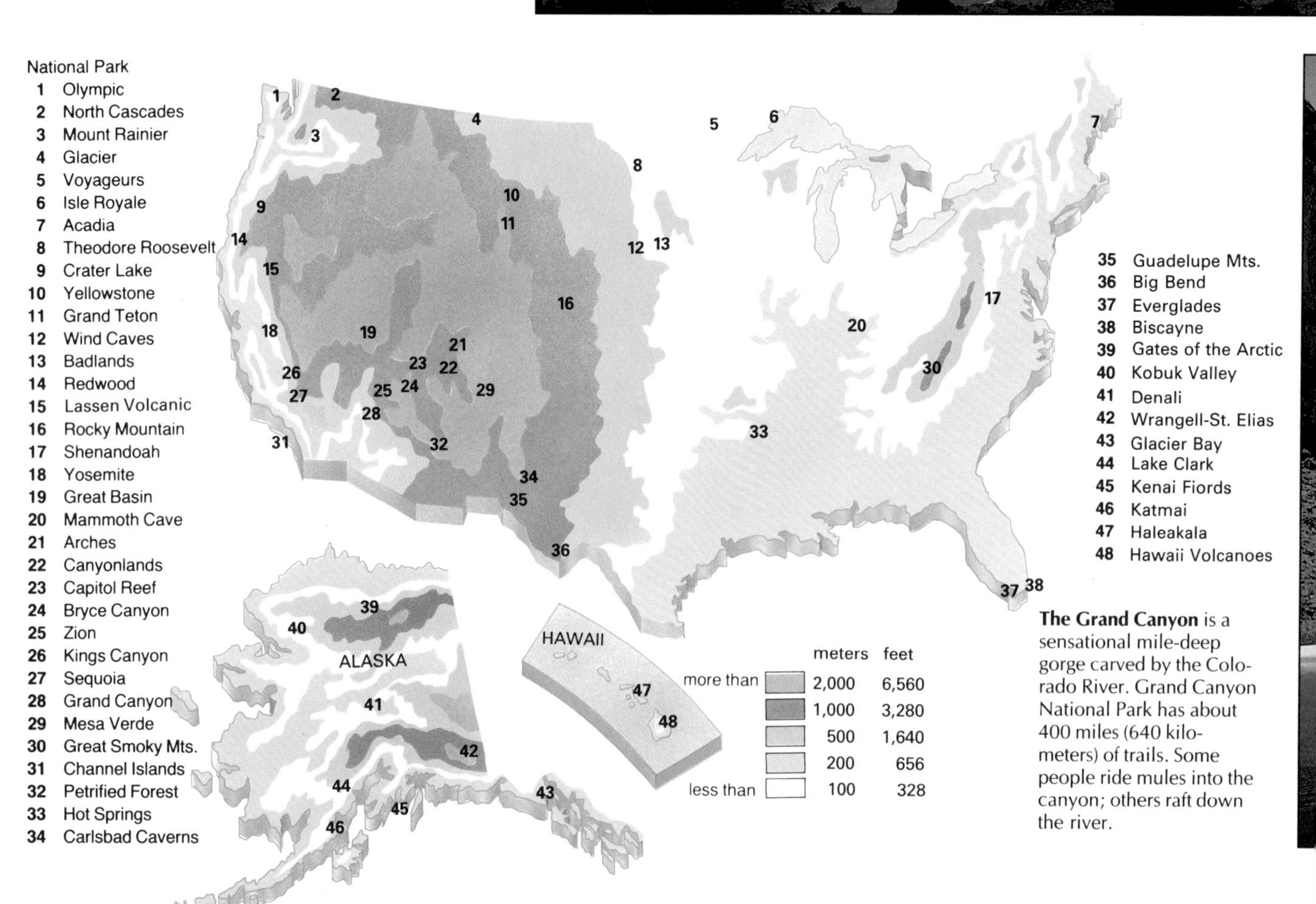

The Grand Canyon is a sensational mile-deep gorge carved by the Colorado River. Grand Canyon National Park has about 400 miles (640 kilometers) of trails. Some people ride mules into the canyon; others raft down the river.

In Carlsbad Caverns, *left,* rock formations called *stalactites* hang from the cave roofs, while *stalagmites* rise from the ground. Some passages in the caverns are still unexplored.

Castle Geyser is one of more than 200 geysers in Yellowstone. The park is also America's largest wildlife preserve. Bears, elk, and bison roam freely through Yellowstone's forests and meadows.

Most national parks have been set aside for their beauty or scientific importance. Acadia, in Maine, features a wild rocky coastline. Shenandoah, in Virginia, has the hardwood-forested Blue Ridge Mountains. In Grand Teton, south of Yellowstone, are rugged mountains and herds of elk. Crater Lake, in Oregon, features a deep-blue lake in a dead volcano and colorful lava walls almost 2,000 feet (610 meters) high.

Historic national monuments include ancient ruins, such as the towns and mounds built by ancient Native Americans at Ocmulgee in Georgia, as well as battlefields like Gettysburg in Pennsylvania. Abraham Lincoln's birthplace is a historic site, and so is the White House.

National recreational areas range from Lake Mead on the Arizona-Nevada border to Sleeping Bear Dunes in Michigan. These areas provide land and water resources for such outdoor activities as fishing, horseback riding, sailing, and water-skiing.

The National Park Service

Almost all the national parklands are managed by the National Park Service, a bureau of the U.S. Department of the Interior. Park rangers patrol the lands to protect them from damage and also provide services for tourists.

To preserve the parks, the balance of nature must be maintained, so plant and animal life is left as undisturbed as possible. Fishing is allowed, but hunting, lumbering, and mining are banned in most areas. The Park Service also lets many natural fires run their course.

The National Park Service encourages recreational activities in the parklands as long as the activities do not disturb the surroundings. Rangers try to teach people about the plant and animal life and the natural processes that shaped the land. In historic parklands, staff members sometimes restore old buildings and wear costumes that reflect America's colorful past.

The growing numbers of visitors are causing problems in some parklands. Overcrowding can result in too much car traffic, air pollution, dirty streams, and jammed campgrounds. Careful management is needed to meet visitors' demands without damaging the land.

History: 1492 to 1865

In 1497, five years after Columbus landed in America, John Cabot sailed from England across the North Atlantic. Like Columbus, Cabot was looking for a route to Asia; like Columbus, he failed. Instead, he found the east coast of North America.

More than 100 years passed before the first English colony was established, at Jamestown, Virginia, in 1607. The colonists raised and exported tobacco and prospered. In 1619, Virginians began self-government in America with the first representative legislature.

The English Pilgrims fled from religious intolerance at home and landed at Plymouth, Mass., in 1620. The Mayflower Compact of the Pilgrims also helped create a tradition of self-government. Other colonies—Maryland, Rhode Island, and Pennsylvania—were founded so that people of all faiths could practice their religion without persecution.

By 1754, 13 British colonies hugged the Atlantic coast. Then conflict between Great Britain and France in Europe spilled over into North America. Britain won the French and Indian War in 1763, and France lost Canada and all land east of the Mississippi except New Orleans.

The war for independence

Great Britain then tried to raise money to pay its war debts by taxing the colonists and limiting their trade. The angry colonists, demanding a voice in such matters, responded, "No taxation without representation!" Violent incidents like the Boston Massacre and acts of defiance like the Boston Tea Party followed.

Colonists and British soldiers finally clashed in 1775, the start of the Revolutionary War. In 1776, the colonists declared their independence from Britain, and—with help from the French—defeated the British in 1781. In 1783, Britain recognized the United States of America.

A young and growing country

The founders of the United States—men like George Washington, Thomas Jefferson, and Benjamin Franklin—met to draw up a plan

Southern troops attacked Fort Sumter in Charleston Harbor off Charleston S.C., on April 12, 1861, starting the Civil War. The map at the right shows the present-day states that were the original Thirteen Colonies.

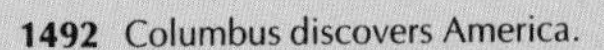

1492 Columbus discovers America.
1513 Ponce de León explores Florida.
1565 Spain founds St. Augustine, Fla.
1607 Jamestown colony founded.
1609 Henry Hudson reaches Hudson River.
1619 House of Burgesses, first representative legislature, established in Virginia.
1620 Pilgrims settle in New England.
1624 Dutch establish New Netherland colony.
1630 Boston founded by Puritans.
1636 Harvard College established.
1649 Maryland passes religious toleration act.
1664 British take over Dutch and Swedish colonies.
1681 Pennsylvania founded.
1718 France founds New Orleans.
1754–1763 French and Indian War.
1765 British pass Stamp Act.
1770 Boston Massacre.
1773 Boston Tea Party.
1775–1783 Revolutionary War.
1776 Declaration of Independence.
1781 British defeated at Yorktown.
1787 Constitution written.
1793 Eli Whitney invents cotton gin.
1800 Library of Congress established.
1803 Louisiana Purchase from France.
1804 Lewis and Clark explore the West.
1812–1814 War with Britain.
1819 Spain cedes Florida to United States.
1823 Monroe Doctrine set forth.
1825 Erie Canal opened.
1845 Annexation of Texas.
1846 Britain cedes Oregon Country.
1846–1848 Mexican War; Southwest ceded.
1848 Gold discovered in California.
1853 Gadsden Purchase from Mexico.
1861–1865 Civil War.
1863 Emancipation Proclamation frees slaves.
1865 President Lincoln assassinated.

George Washington was the first U.S. President.

Thomas Jefferson, *far left,* wrote the Declaration of Independence.

Benjamin Franklin helped found the United States.

for a new government. They argued over how powerful this government should be. After one unsuccessful plan, the Constitution was written in 1787. It is the law of the land to this day. George Washington was elected the first President of the United States in 1789, and the country started to develop and prosper. Britain had given land east of the Mississippi to the United States. When Jefferson, as President, made the Louisiana Purchase from France in 1803, a vast area of land west of the Mississippi was added to the country. The annexation of Texas in 1845, war with Mexico in 1848, and agreements with Spain and Britain added even more land.

By the mid-1800's, the United States stretched from the Atlantic to the Pacific. During the early and mid-1800's, thousands of pioneers spread across the Western frontier. The settlement of the West led to many wars with Native Americans, who were driven from their homelands.

A country divided

Also by the mid-1800's, the dispute over slavery between the North and the South threatened the Union. In 1860 and 1861, 11 Southern states withdrew and formed the Confederacy. President Abraham Lincoln declared that the Union must be saved, and the Civil War broke out. Lincoln freed the slaves in 1863. After a bitterly fought war, the North defeated the South in 1865, and the country remained united.

States in order of admission to the Union.

1 Delaware
2 Pennsylvania
3 New Jersey
4 Georgia
5 Connecticut
6 Massachusetts
7 Maryland
8 South Carolina
9 New Hampshire
10 Virginia
11 New York
12 North Carolina
13 Rhode Island

The Constitutional Convention met to draw up the Constitution of the United States in 1787. George Washington (standing at the right) was president of the convention.

History: 1866 to Present

The Civil War nearly ruined the South. During *Reconstruction,* a 12-year period following the war, plans were made to repair the region and return it to the Union.

Reconstruction laws gave rights to former slaves, and public schools were set up in the South. But Reconstruction also brought some corruption with it. Many Southerners deeply resented Reconstruction, especially the rights given to the freed slaves. In time, they regained control of their state governments and made new laws that denied former slaves and their descendants their rights. For many years, the South remained a poor, agricultural region.

Before the war, the North had been industrially and financially stronger than the South. But the typical American business was still small. After the war, however, industry changed dramatically.

Machines replaced hand labor as the major means of production. A nationwide network of railroads provided easy transportation of goods. Inventors like Thomas Edison created new products, and they were manufactured in large quantities. Big business grew, and the United States became an industrial giant.

The growing business activity attracted people from the country, who moved to the cities in record numbers. In addition, waves of immigrants came from other nations to work in U.S. factories and mines. More than 25 million immigrants entered the United States between 1870 and 1916.

In the West, meanwhile, homesteaders settled and farmed the Plains, miners flocked to boom towns, and ranchers spread throughout the Southwest. Native Americans were gradually forced onto reservations.

War and hard times

Industrialization brought wealth to a few powerful businessmen like John D. Rockefeller, Andrew Carnegie, and J. Pierpont Morgan. But most U.S. workers and farmers did not share in that wealth. Workers toiled long hours for little pay. Reformers tried to improve working conditions with new laws, and unions organized to fight for workers' rights.

Covered wagons head over the Rockies in this Currier and Ives engraving from the 1860's. The move west brought conflict with the Native Americans. Thousands of pioneers settled the West.

1867 Alaska purchased from Russia.
1869 Transcontinental railway completed.
1871 Chicago Fire.
1876 Battle of Little Bighorn.
1876 Alexander Graham Bell invents telephone.
1879 Thomas Edison invents electric light.
1884 First skyscraper begun in Chicago.
1886 American Federation of Labor founded.
1898 Spanish-American War.
1898 Annexation of Hawaii.
1906 San Francisco earthquake.
1917 United States enters World War I.
1920 Women get right to vote.
1920–1933 Prohibition (sale of alcohol banned).
1929 Stock market crash.
1933 Roosevelt's New Deal recovery plan.
1941 Japan attacks Pearl Harbor; United States enters World War II.
1945 United States drops atom bombs on Japan.
1945 United States joins the United Nations.
1950–1953 Korean War.
1961 Alan Shepard becomes first American in space.
1962 Cuban missile crisis.
1963 Nuclear test ban treaty signed.
1963 President Kennedy assassinated.
1964 Civil Rights Act enacted.
1965 United States enters the Vietnam War.
1968 Martin Luther King, Jr., assassinated.
1969 U.S. astronaut lands on moon.
1974 President Nixon resigns.
1976 U.S. Bicentenary celebrated.
1980 Mount St. Helens erupts.
1981 American hostages in Iran freed.
1986 Space shuttle *Challenger* explodes.
1988 Nuclear arms treaty in effect.
1989 Oil spill off Alaska.
1991 U.S.-led coalition liberates Kuwait from Iraqi forces.
1993 Bomb explodes at the World Trade Center in New York City, killing six people.
1995 Bomb destroys the Alfred P. Murrah federal building in Oklahoma City, OK, killing 167 people.

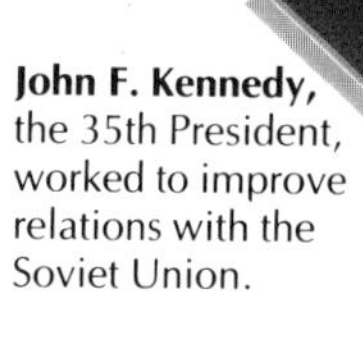

A space shuttle, *right,* one of three such craft in the U.S. space program, can make repeated flights. In 1969, U.S. astronauts landed on the moon, eight years after the first manned U.S. space flight.

Woodrow Wilson, the 28th President, guided the United States through World War I.

John F. Kennedy, the 35th President, worked to improve relations with the Soviet Union.

Franklin D. Roosevelt, *far left,* served as President from 1933 until his death in 1945.

The United States also began exercising its political and military power in Cuba and Central America. Nevertheless, when World War I (1914–1918) broke out in Europe, many Americans did not want to join the fight. By 1917, however, German attacks on U.S. ships led President Woodrow Wilson to declare war. By 1918, the United States had helped conquer Germany and win World War I.

A decade of good times followed in the 1920's. But although the economy seemed strong, it was actually on shaky ground. The 1930's brought the country's worst economic slump ever—the Great Depression. Many people lost their jobs, their homes, or their farms. President Franklin Roosevelt's New Deal program offered some relief. Then war broke out in Europe again.

World War II (1939–1945) was the most destructive conflict in human history. The United States entered the war against Nazi Germany and Japan in 1941, when Japan bombed the U.S. fleet at Pearl Harbor, Hawaii. The United States ended the war with Japan when it dropped two atomic bombs on Hiroshima and Nagasaki in 1945.

Postwar America

After the war, the United States was a world power, the leader of the non-Communist world. Over the next decades, it would fight a *Cold War*—one without large-scale fighting—with the Soviet Union, the leader of the Communist world.

The 1960's were a time of change and crisis. The civil rights movement gained power for African Americans, but riots and crime erupted in poor city neighborhoods. Students and others protested the country's involvement in the Vietnam War (1957–1975).

The 1970's brought periods of rising prices and high unemployment. The 1980's saw record budget deficits in the United States. Countries that had depended on U.S. aid became economic powers themselves.

January 1991 brought war to the United States, when the country led a United Nations coalition in massive air attacks against Iraq and its forces, which had occupied neighboring Kuwait since August 1990. In February 1991, after a short ground offensive, the coalition liberated Kuwait and restored its legitimate government.

A Multiethnic Society

The United States has been called a "nation of immigrants." No country has received more immigrants; no country has ever attracted people from so many other nations. With a few exceptions—particularly Native Americans, Alaskan Aleuts, and native Hawaiians—almost every resident of the United States has some immigrant ancestors. These immigrant groups make up nine of the ten largest ethnic groups in the United States. The ten largest ethnic groups are, in order of size, English, German, Irish, African American, French, Italian, Scottish, Polish, Mexican, and Native American.

Most white Americans trace their ancestry to Europe. Most black Americans are descendants of Africans who were forcibly brought to the United States as slaves. Most Hispanic Americans are immigrants or have immigrant ancestors who came from Latin America. A small percentage trace their ancestry directly back to Spain. Most Asian Americans trace their ancestry to China, India, Indochina, Japan, Korea, or the Philippines.

Waves of newcomers

The United States has had four great waves of immigrants. The first wave began in the 1600's, when immigrants from Europe settled on the east coast. Most were from the British Isles, but some came from the Netherlands, Germany, and other countries.

The second wave of immigrants started in the 1820's and lasted for about fifty years. About 7-1/2 million newcomers arrived, nearly all from northern and western Europe. Many Irish people settled in the East, while Germans came to farm in the Midwest. Some Chinese came to find work on the railroads and in the mines when gold was discovered.

The third wave of immigrants was the largest. From the 1880's to 1920, about 23-1/2 million people poured into the United States. After 1890, the majority were from southern and eastern Europe.

The fourth wave came after 1965, when immigration from Asia and the West Indies rose dramatically. Many were refugees fleeing from war, persecution, or famine, like the immigrants from Southeast Asia in the 1970's. Others came in search of a higher standard of living. Today, most immigrants come from Mexico, the Philippines, and Haiti.

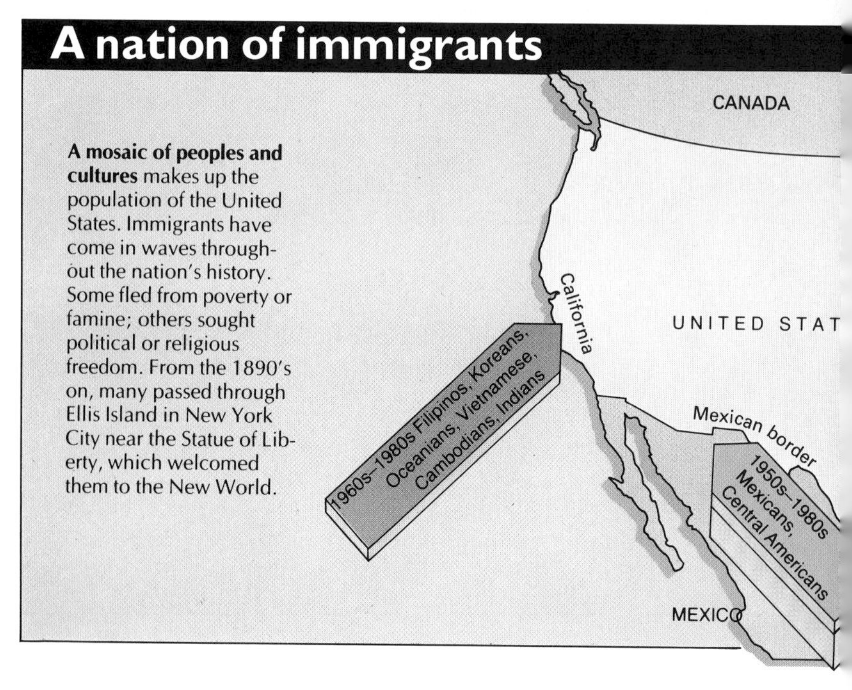

A nation of immigrants

A mosaic of peoples and cultures makes up the population of the United States. Immigrants have come in waves throughout the nation's history. Some fled from poverty or famine; others sought political or religious freedom. From the 1890's on, many passed through Ellis Island in New York City near the Statue of Liberty, which welcomed them to the New World.

An Italian delicatessen brings a taste of southern Europe to the United States. About 12 million Americans claim Italian ancestry, making this ethnic group one of the largest in the country.

The cheering crowd at a ticker-tape parade in New York City, *far left,* shows the ethnic diversity of the U.S. population.

New York City's Chinatown is an example of the ethnic neighborhoods found in many large U.S. cities. Here, Chinese celebrate the start of their new year with a parade, fireworks, and long paper dragons. San Francisco, where large numbers of Chinese also settled, has its own Chinatown—a popular tourist attraction.

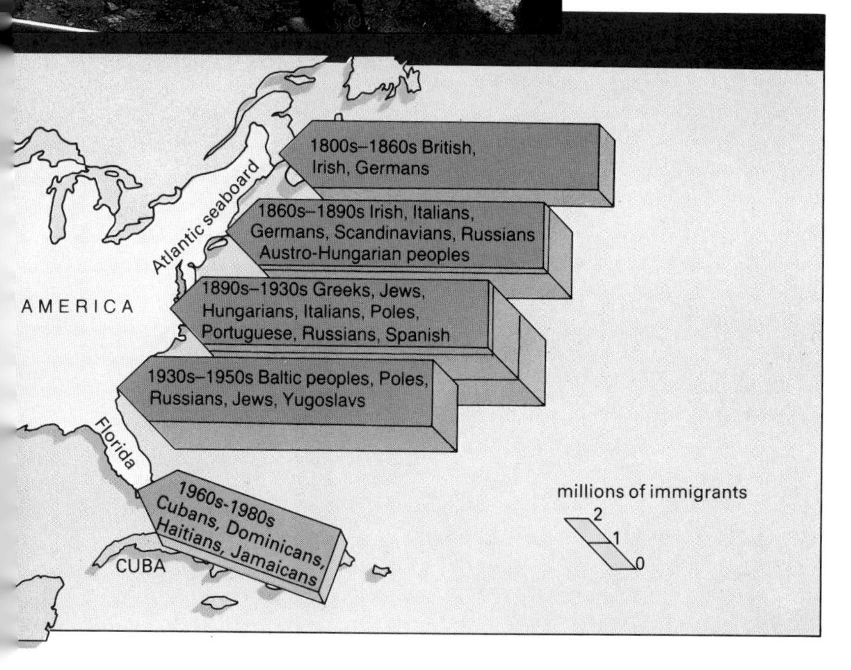

The American people

Some people call the United States a "melting pot." That term suggests a place where people from many lands have formed one unified culture.

Americans do have many things in common. Most speak English, wear the same kinds of clothing, and enjoy many of the same foods. Education, television, and radio have all helped shape an American identity.

But many things now considered American—or enjoyed by Americans—were actually introduced by immigrants, or created by them after they arrived. For example, favorite foods like hamburgers and hot dogs are German; pizza is Italian; and egg rolls are Chinese.

Jazz developed as a mixture of elements from West African and European music, African-American work songs, and spirituals. These last two forms of music also developed into blues music and, later, into rock music.

In other ways, the United States is not a melting pot but a *culturally pluralistic* society—that is, a society where large numbers of people keep part of the culture and traditions of their ancestors. Many Americans take special pride in their origins. They consider themselves Irish Americans or Mexican Americans or Greek Americans and keep their own customs and traditions. Many cities have ethnic neighborhoods, where people of one particular national or racial origin live. Ethnic restaurants, festivals, and parades reflect this cultural pluralism.

Some Americans have not accepted the idea of cultural pluralism, however. During the waves of immigration, some tried to stop the flow of newcomers. Discrimination and prejudice against certain groups caused many problems. To guarantee justice for all, Americans passed laws declaring that no one can be denied their rights on account of race, religion, color, or ethnic origin.

Native Americans

Native Americans, the first people in what is now America, lived there for thousands of years before Europeans came. They had no name for themselves as a people, but almost every Native American group had its own name—one that showed the pride the group had in its way of life.

The Native American tribes of eastern North America lived in small villages. The Algonquin lived in domed wigwams. The Iroquois built long houses. These eastern groups hunted, fished, and grew such crops as corn, beans, and squash.

The Plains tribes lived in villages of tepees along rivers, where land was fertile. The women tended crops, while the men hunted deer, elk, and buffalo. After the 1500's, when Spanish explorers brought horses from Europe, the Plains tribes rode horses into battle and on buffalo hunts.

The Pueblo tribes of the Southwest farmed along rivers where they could irrigate their crops. They built large, many-storied homes of adobe and rocks. Other Southwest tribes moved about in small bands in search of food. These warlike groups—the Apache and Navajo—often attacked the Pueblo people.

In the far Northwest, the Native Americans could catch plenty of fish, hunt game, and gather berries. They built plank houses with large wooden posts and beams, and carved totem poles depicting mythical beings.

California had a mild climate and an abundance of food. Modoc, Pomo, Maidu, and other California tribes lived in small villages and gathered wild plants, seeds, and nuts, especially acorns. They also hunted and fished.

The tribes that lived in the Great Basin east of California, however, had to adapt to a much drier climate. These people moved about in small bands searching for food.

Native Americans and whites

When Europeans first came to America's shores, most of the native peoples they met there were friendly. They taught the Europeans how to plant food and travel by canoe. They even joined the Pilgrims in their Thanksgiving feast celebrating their harvest and peace.

The Europeans brought useful things for the Native Americans too, such as guns and horses. But the two groups had widely different ways of life. Soon, the cultures began to clash and small battles became common.

As the European settlers moved westward, they took land from the Native Americans. Some battles grew into wars. The settlers made numerous treaties with them, but quickly broke most of them. In 1830, the U.S. government began forcing all the eastern tribes to move west of the Mississippi.

The battles and bloodshed continued, though, once settlers themselves began to move west. Many members of the California tribes died from diseases brought by the Europeans or were murdered by gold miners. By killing off almost all the buffalo, the whites robbed the Plains tribes of their way of life. The U.S. Army fought the Sioux and Cheyenne frequently, often unjustly. Many tribes were moved onto reservations. The Native Americans in the Southwest and Northwest met the same fate.

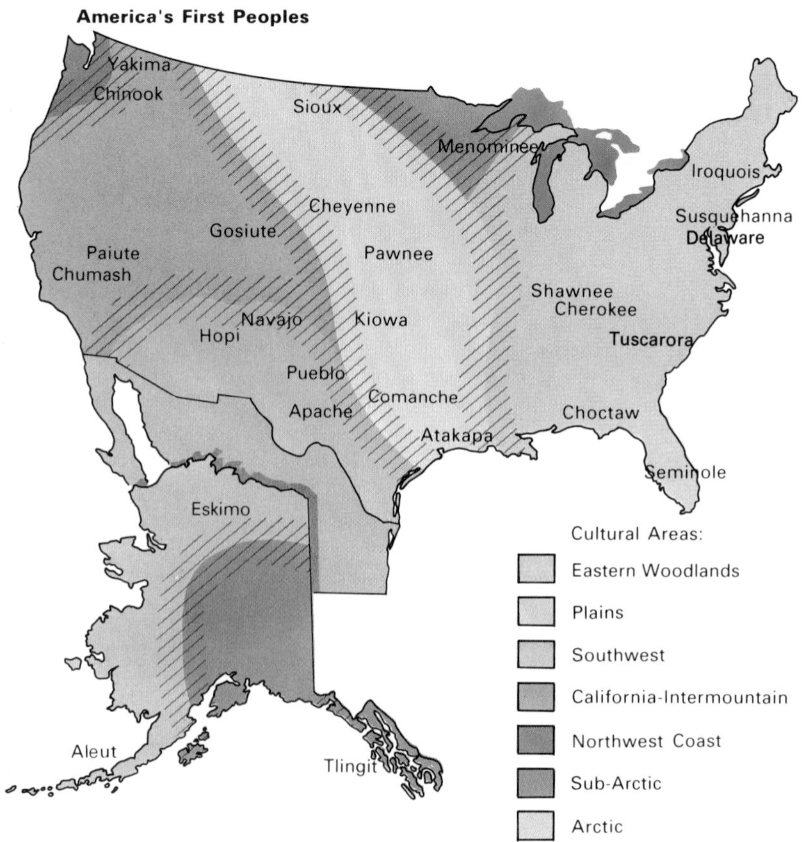

A Navajo shepherd, *far left,* guards her flock on the vast expanse of the Navajo reservation. Covering 16 million acres (6.5 million hectares), the reservation lies in three states—Arizona, New Mexico, and Utah.

A Mohawk construction worker treads a steel beam high above New York City.

Native American leader Jim Russell, *above* (left), has worked to block construction of a nuclear waste dump in the state of Washington. Many Native Americans have become active in social and political activities.

Navajo artists, like this one from Taos, N. Mex., draw on a rich heritage. Taos has popular art festivals, and nearby Taos Pueblo village also draws tourists.

Native Americans today

Today about 1.4 million Native Americans live in the United States. Native Americans, like all U.S. citizens, can live wherever they wish today, but many choose to make their homes on reservations. There they can practice and preserve their traditional ways of life.

Native Americans were granted full citizenship and voting rights in 1924. The Bureau of Indian Affairs is supposed to promote the welfare of Native Americans, especially those living on reservations. In recent years, however, Native Americans have taken more control over their lands, schools, and other resources. Some have sued the U.S. government over broken treaties and land that was illegally taken.

Hispanic Americans

In the years after Columbus discovered America, Spanish explorers, priests, and settlers created a region of Hispanic culture from South America to what is now the Southern United States. Florida and the Southwest became part of the United States long ago, but much of the Hispanic influence remains today.

More than 20 million people of Hispanic ancestry currently live in the United States. They make up the second largest and fastest-growing minority group. Hispanic Americans have a high birth rate, and many continue to immigrate to the United States, especially from Mexico and the Caribbean.

Hispanic Americans have various national origins. The three largest Hispanic groups in the United States are Mexican Americans (63 per cent of the Hispanic population), Puerto Ricans (12 per cent), and Cuban Americans (5 per cent). Others emigrated—or had ancestors who emigrated—from Central or South America or from Spain.

Hispanic Americans also have various racial origins—a blending of white European, Native American, and black African. Most Mexican Americans are *mestizos*—people of mixed European and Native American ancestry. Many Puerto Ricans are of mixed Spanish and African descent, while others have some Native American ancestry as well.

Hispanic communities

About 90 per cent of Hispanic Americans live in urban areas. Mexican Americans form the largest Hispanic group in most Southwestern cities, such as Los Angeles and San Antonio. Los Angeles also has small communities of Cubans, Guatemalans, and Puerto Ricans.

Miami, Fla., has the largest Cuban American population among U.S. cities. Many Cubans came to the United States in order to escape the Communist government in their homeland.

A few Northern cities also have sizable Hispanic populations. About half of all Puerto Ricans in the mainland United States live in New York City. New York also has communities of people from Colombia, Cuba, the Dominican Republic, and Ecuador. Chicago has large groups of Mexican Americans, Puerto Ricans, and Cuban Amer-

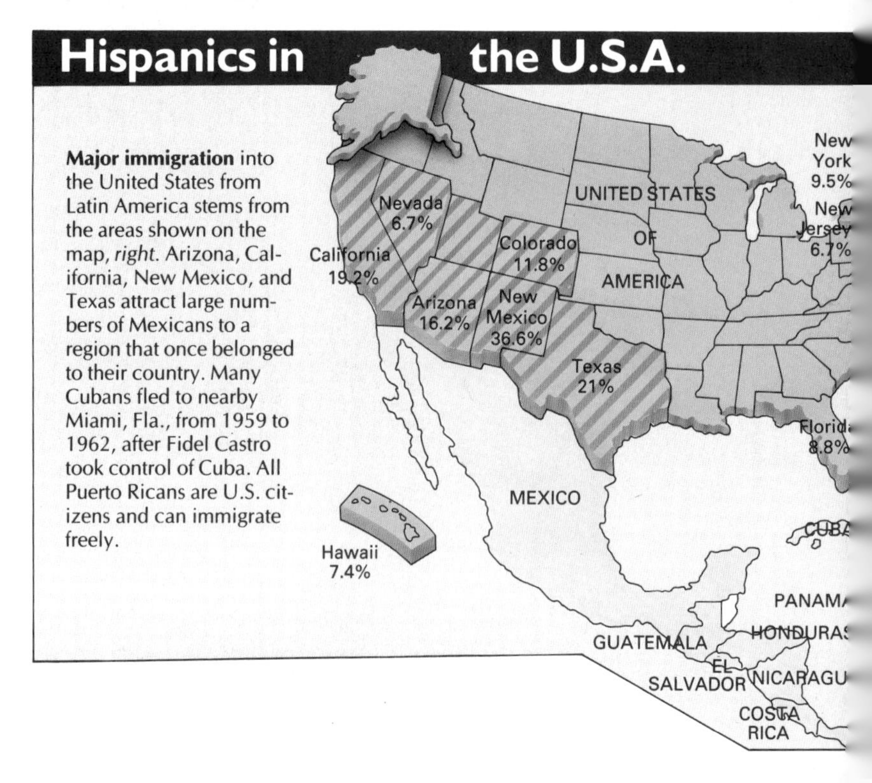

Hispanics in the U.S.A.

Major immigration into the United States from Latin America stems from the areas shown on the map, *right*. Arizona, California, New Mexico, and Texas attract large numbers of Mexicans to a region that once belonged to their country. Many Cubans fled to nearby Miami, Fla., from 1959 to 1962, after Fidel Castro took control of Cuba. All Puerto Ricans are U.S. citizens and can immigrate freely.

At a Cuban restaurant in Miami's Little Havana, workers serve traditional Cuban seafood dishes. Although Little Havana is the center of the Cuban-American population, many Cubans have settled in New York City; Jersey City and Newark, N.J.; Los Angeles; and Chicago.

A young Hispanic farmworker, *far left,* from Mexico harvests beans in California. Large numbers of migrant farmworkers in the West are Mexican Americans. Since the 1960's, labor leader Cesar Chavez has worked to organize farmworkers and improve their lot.

Katherine Davalos Ortega, shown here addressing the 1984 Republican National Convention, became treasurer of the United States in 1983.

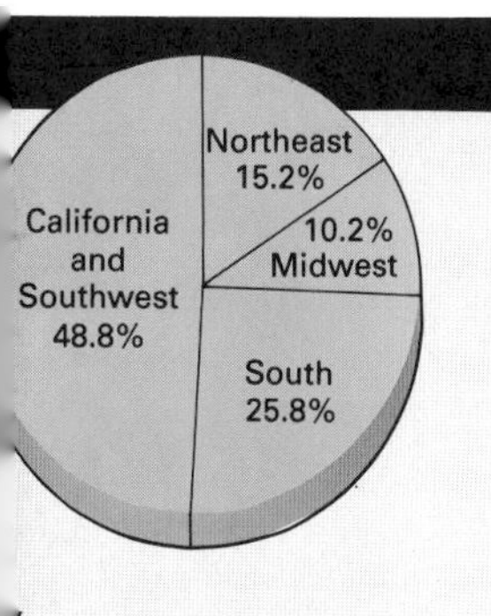

Spanish population LESS than national average (6.4%)
Spanish population MORE than national average (6.4%). Actual percentage shown
Part of Mexico until 1835, 1848, 1850, and 1853
Spanish-speaking Central America

icans. In recent years, Hispanic immigrants have begun to settle in smaller Northern cities too.

Hispanic culture

A majority of Hispanic Americans speak English, but most continue to use Spanish as well, especially at home. Many are proud of their heritage and feel they should not lose touch with it. They want to be bicultural as well as bilingual.

Hispanic Americans place a high value on family life. Religion is also a common cultural heritage among Hispanics. A large majority practice the Roman Catholic religion brought by the Spanish missionaries.

The Hispanic influence on American culture can be seen in many areas, including foods, music, and art. For example, tacos and enchiladas are popular Mexican foods. Latin and Cuban styles of music have "crossed over" into popular American culture.

Like other minorities, Hispanic Americans have suffered discrimination in employment, housing, and education. Such discrimination results in a high level of poverty. Some non-Hispanics are offended because some Hispanics cannot speak English. Others resent Hispanic people who have entered the United States illegally. These common problems unite Hispanic Americans just as their language and religion do.

African Americans

The 28 million African Americans living in the United States today make up its largest minority group. Most African Americans trace their origins to an area in western Africa that was controlled by three great and wealthy empires—the Ghana, Mali, and Songhai.

In the early 1500's, Europeans joined in the slave trade that had been carried on in Africa since ancient times. Over the next 300 years, millions of black Africans were enslaved and shipped to colonies in America. Until 1863, most of these Africans worked as slaves throughout the South.

Slavery was abolished in 1863, and the slaves were freed. In 1868, the 14th Amendment gave African Americans equal rights; in 1870, the 15th Amendment stated that African-American men could not be denied the right to vote because of their color. Reconstruction in the South also tried to improve the political power of the freed slaves.

The progress African Americans made was not allowed to last, however. Southern whites began to pass laws that discriminated against them. African Americans living in Southern States increasingly lost their voting rights and were *segregated* (kept apart from whites) in such public facilities as schools, buses, and restaurants. In 1896, the Supreme Court of the United States ruled that such segregation was legal as long as the public facilities were "equal."

In the 1900's, African Americans continued to suffer from discrimination. They had little opportunity to better their lives. Even those who moved to the North did not find answers to their problems. There, too, they were segregated, not by law but in practice. Because they were poor and poorly educated, African Americans had to live in run-down areas of the large Northern cities. These poor communities developed into slum ghettos.

The civil rights movement

In 1954, a historic ruling was handed down by the Supreme Court. In *Brown v. Board of Education of Topeka,* the high court reversed the 1896 decision that "separate but equal" public schools were legal. The Supreme Court justices ruled that an African-American student named Linda Brown should be allowed to attend an all-white school near her home.

African Americans began to strike out against discrimination. In Montgomery, Ala., in 1955, an African-American woman named Rosa Parks was arrested for refusing to give up her seat on a bus to a white person. A city law required African Americans to do so. African Americans boycotted the buses by refusing to ride in them until the city abolished the law. The boycott cast the nation's attention on its leader, Martin Luther King, Jr., a Baptist minister.

Voter registration became a chief goal among African-American leaders during the mid-1980's. These leaders stress the importance of political participation in helping solve the problems that face African Americans today.

With other civil rights leaders, King went on to lead boycotts and protest marches in the South and then the North. Riots in ghettos broke out during the 1960's, but King urged African Americans to use only peaceful means to reach their goals.

King was assassinated in 1968, but civil rights laws passed during the 1960's banned discrimination in voting, jobs, housing, and public places like hotels and restaurants.

African Americans today

African Americans have made great progress since the 1960's. Gains in education have

African-American businessmen review plans for a new shopping plaza. The number of African American-owned businesses has grown since the 1970's, but they still account for only a fraction of U.S. production.

been important. Although the dropout rate remains high, enrollment in high school and college has increased.

The number of African American-owned businesses has increased also—though most are small—and the African-American middle class is growing. Nevertheless, a large number of African-American families still live in poverty, and the rate of unemployment is much higher among African Americans than among whites.

Sports, entertainment, and the arts have been open to African Americans longer than other fields, and many have made great achievements in these areas. Baseball player Henry Aaron, football player Walter Payton, and basketball player Michael Jordan are all record-setting athletes. Entertainers like Bill Cosby and Michael Jackson are very popular. Novelists Alice Walker and Toni Morrison have written award-winning books.

African Americans also have played important roles in government, politics, and the military. African Americans who have served as mayors of major U.S. cities include Thomas Bradley of Los Angeles, David Dinkins of New York City, and Harold Washington of Chicago. Andrew Young served as U.S. ambassador to the United Nations as well as mayor of Atlanta. In 1990, L. Douglas Wilder took office as governor of Virginia—the country's first elected African-American governor. In 1984 and 1988, Jesse Jackson waged strong campaigns to become a candidate for President. In 1983, Guion Stewart Bluford, Jr., became the first African American to travel in space. Colin L. Powell became chairman of the Joint Chiefs of Staff in 1989.

A gospel group livens up a street festival in Los Angeles. Gospel groups sing *spirituals* (religious songs). Spirituals once were sung by slaves in the South and are now a well-known form of American music.

Urban Life

In 1790, when the first official U.S. census was taken, about 95 per cent of the nation's people lived in rural areas. Only 5 per cent lived in cities like Philadelphia, New York, and Boston.

Through the years, however, a dramatic shift occurred. When agricultural methods and equipment improved, farming became more efficient. From the 1800's on, far fewer workers were needed on farms.

About this time, the industrial boom created numerous factory jobs. As a result, a steady flow of people moved from rural areas to cities.

In addition, the wave of immigrants to the United States from the 1890's to 1920 swelled city populations. Many of these immigrants settled in tenements in New York City and other urban areas.

The fast-paced life of cities appealed to many rural people, especially younger ones. Large numbers of them left rural America for the excitement of the "big city."

Today, about 200 years after the first U.S. census, about 74 per cent of the American people are urban dwellers. Urban areas range in size from giant cities to small towns. For census purposes, an urban area is a community of 2,500 or more people. Such urban areas dot the U.S. landscape, taking up less than 2 per cent of the land, but housing about three-fourths of the people.

Most cities are not isolated communities but instead are surrounded by suburbs. Suburbs grew rapidly during the mid-1900's, as many people moved to these outlying areas and commuted to work in the cities. The automobile contributed to the growth of suburbs

City and country

In 1790, *below left,* the United States was an agricultural nation, with farms strung along the Atlantic. About 95 per cent of the people lived in rural areas.

By 1890, *below center,* waves of immigrants had swelled the population of the East, but most people still lived in rural areas.

By 1990, *below right,* 74 per cent of the U.S. population lived in urban areas on less than 2 per cent of the land.

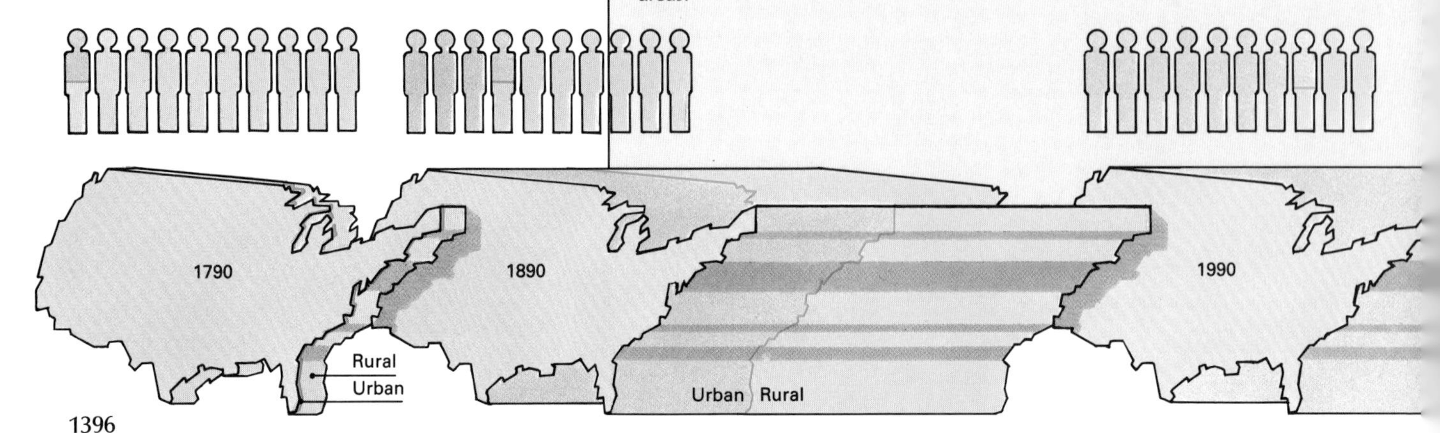

Residential areas, *far left,* spread outward from the skyscrapers of San Francisco, part of the continuing mushrooming of U.S. cities.

In this leafy suburb of Washington, D.C., large single-family homes and well-groomed yards are common.

The South Side of Chicago, *below,* is the city's largest section in both area and population. It includes an international port, sprawling industrial areas, spacious parks, pleasant residential communities, and poverty-stricken neighborhoods. This photo was taken from Sears Tower, the world's tallest building.

because suburbanites need transportation to work or shop, and mass transit, such as buses and trains, is limited or nonexistent.

The move to the suburbs was so massive that in 1980, for the first time, more Americans lived in suburbs than in cities. Now, most suburban residents work and seek entertainment in the suburbs instead of traveling to the city.

A *metropolitan area* consists of a city and the surrounding developed area. Some metropolitan areas have spread out so much that they blend with other metropolitan areas into one heavily populated region. Such a region is called a *megalopolis.* Three megalopolises that have developed in the United States are the Boston-New York City-Baltimore-Washington, D.C., area; the Milwaukee-Chicago-Pittsburgh area, and the San Francisco-Los Angeles-San Diego area.

Cities offer a wide variety of jobs, ranging from medical personnel and office workers to trash collectors and transportation workers. Cities also offer special services, shops, night life, and cultural events that rural areas lack. Concerts, art galleries, theaters, sporting events, and museums make cities exciting.

The variety of ethnic and racial backgrounds makes urban areas interesting too. Large cities are divided economically and often have several ethnic neighborhoods. Wealthy people live in large, luxurious apartments, condominiums, or single-family homes. The large urban middle class lives in similar but more modest housing. Most poor people live in small, crowded apartments or run-down single-family homes. Sometimes public housing is available, paid for in part by the government.

Poverty and substandard housing are just two of the many problems facing U.S. cities. Crime, noise, air pollution, and traffic congestion all come with the advantages urban areas in the United States offer.

Urban Rural

The Mississippi River

The Native Americans who lived in the upper Mississippi Valley chose the name for the river. They called it *Mississippi,* meaning *big river.*

The Mississippi is the longest river in the United States. It begins as a small, clear stream emerging from Lake Itasca in northwest Minnesota, then flows 2,348 miles (3,779 kilometers) to the Gulf of Mexico. As it flows, the Mississippi and its tributaries drain almost all the plains that lie between the Appalachian Mountains and the Rocky Mountains. This river basin includes the nation's most productive agricultural and industrial regions—more than 1 million square miles (3 million square kilometers) of land.

"Old Man River" is the nickname given to this mighty waterway. It forms part of the boundary of 10 states. The Illinois and Missouri rivers are two of the major northern tributaries. Because the Missouri River is muddy, its waters begin to turn the Mississippi muddy as well. In the South, the Mississippi is known for this muddy color.

The Ohio River, flowing into the Mississippi River at Cairo, Ill., doubles the amount of water in the river. This spot divides the upper Mississippi from the lower Mississippi. The flood plain of the lower Mississippi forms a broad, fertile valley where the river twists and turns in wide loops.

By the time the Mississippi nears its mouth, it is carrying large amounts of silt. The river deposits this fertile soil to form a huge delta. The Mississippi Delta is now about 13,000 square miles (33,700 square kilometers), and it is growing into the Gulf of Mexico about 1 mile (1.6 kilometers) every 16 years.

The Mississippi has played a key role in U.S. history. In 1682, the French explorer Sieur de La Salle traveled down the river to its mouth. He claimed the river and all the land it drained for the king of France. Later, France lost the land east of the Mississippi to England. In 1803, the French sold land west of the river to the United States in the Louisiana Purchase.

In the 1880's, steamboats turned the river into the great transportation and trade route it is today. The river carries about 400 million short tons (360 million metric tons) of freight every year. That tonnage represents about 60 per cent of all the freight carried on the nation's inland waterways.

Oceangoing cargo vessels can travel up the Mississippi as far north as Baton Rouge, La. These large ships transport such products as coffee, grain, and petroleum between the United States and about 60 countries throughout the world.

The Gateway Arch in St. Louis, Mo., reflects the city's historic location as the gateway to the West. St. Louis is the busiest inland port on the Mississippi River.

River barges pushed by tugboats carry most of this freight. On the upper Mississippi, southbound freight is mainly agricultural goods like corn, soybeans, and wheat. Coal and steel products from the Ohio River Valley are northbound freight.

South of Cairo, freight is doubled because of the additional goods coming from the Ohio. Southbound freight combines the agricultural goods from the upper Mississippi with the coal and steel products from the Ohio.

At Baton Rouge, La., petroleum, petrochemical products, and aluminum are added to the river traffic. From Baton Rouge south, the Mississippi deepens, and oceangoing ships can travel up from the Gulf of Mexico. The greatest volume of traffic on the Mississippi moves between New Orleans and the gulf.

Mississippi River wildlife

A White-tailed deer
B Water hyacinth
C Grass pink orchid
D Carolina mallow
E Slider turtle
F Black cherry
G Warbler
H Palmetto
I Night heron
J Otter
K Raccoon
L Alligator
M Nutria
N Monarch butterfly
O Fishing spider
P Snow goose

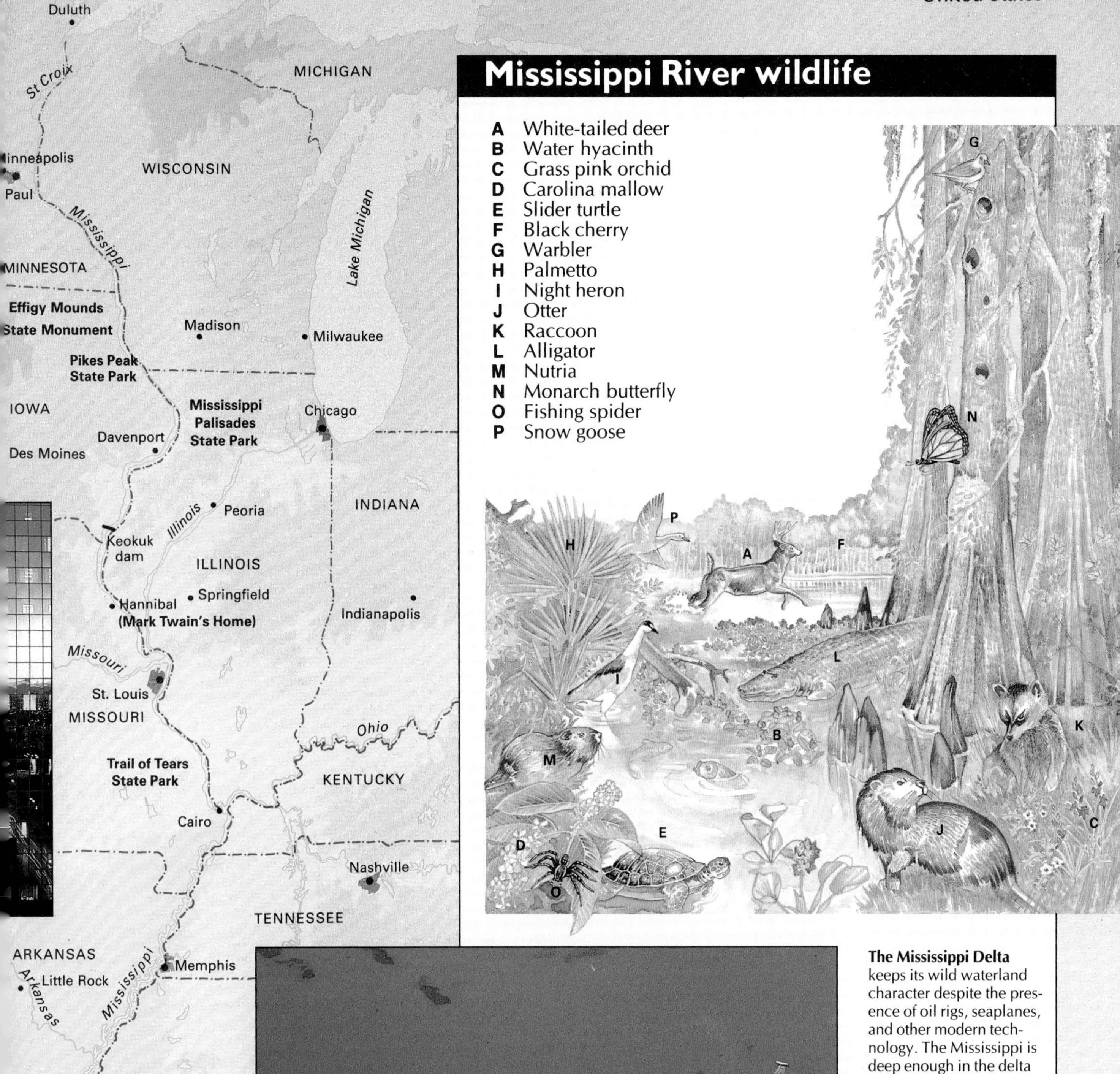

The Mississippi Delta keeps its wild waterland character despite the presence of oil rigs, seaplanes, and other modern technology. The Mississippi is deep enough in the delta region to carry ocean-going ships. Farm chemicals wash into the river, and industrial wastes are dumped into it. Since the 1970's, steps have been taken to prevent further pollution of the river.

Energy and Resources

In their homes and offices, cars and trucks, and farms and factories, the people of the United States use a vast amount of energy. On average, each person in America uses about five times as much energy as someone who lives in another part of the world. The country as a whole uses about one-fourth of all the world's energy.

Energy comes from various sources. Petroleum, or oil, provides about 40 per cent of the energy used in the United States. It is used to power cars, trucks, ships, and airplanes, and it heats millions of homes, offices, and factories.

Natural gas produces about 25 per cent of the energy used nationwide. Many industries burn natural gas for heat and power, and millions of people use it to heat their homes, cook their food, and dry their laundry.

Coal, which supplies about 25 per cent of U.S. energy, is used mainly to produce electricity and steel. The electricity in turn lights buildings and powers machinery for offices, factories, and farms.

Water produces about 5 per cent of America's energy, mainly in hydroelectric plants where electricity is produced for industries and homes. Nuclear power also produces about 5 per cent of the nation's energy, and, like water, nuclear power generates electricity for industries and homes.

But the United States is more than just a great consumer of energy. It is also a major producer of energy resources. America is second in the world in the production of petroleum and natural gas (after Russia), and second in the production of coal (after China).

The United States has many other natural resources as well. Besides the minerals used to produce energy, it has valuable deposits of copper, gold, iron ore, lead, phosphates, potash, silver, sulfur, and zinc.

Potash, *right,* a salt mainly used to make fertilizer, is extracted from evaporation ponds. Western states supply some potash, but most of the nation's supply is imported from Canada.

The steel town of Mingo Junction, *below right,* on the Ohio River, contrasts with the natural beauty of the land. Steel production requires two resources that are plentiful in the United States—coal and iron ore.

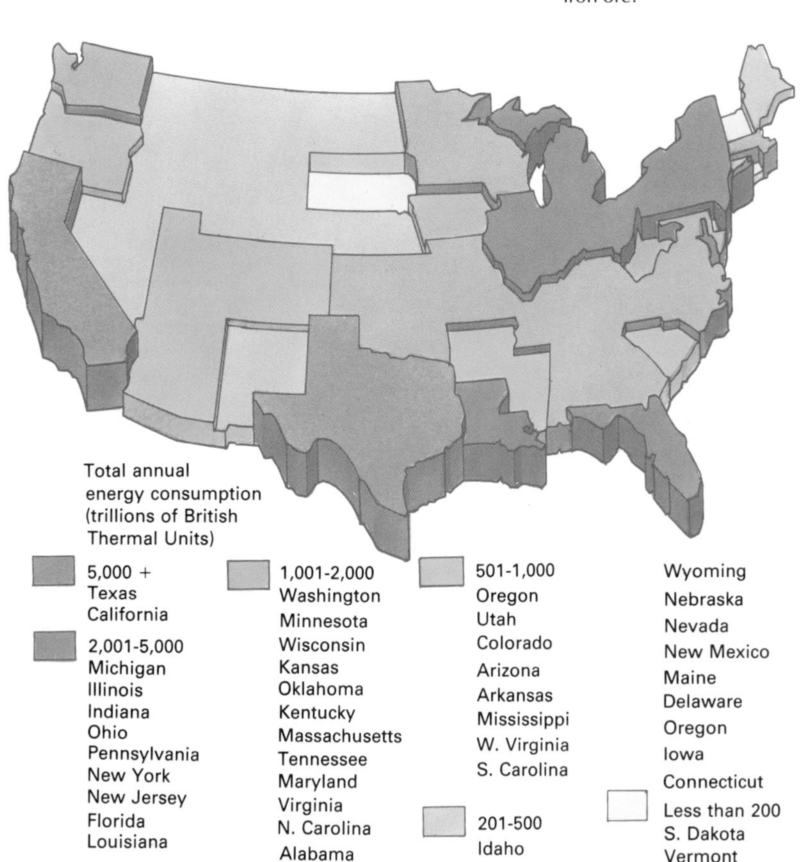

Total annual energy consumption (trillions of British Thermal Units)

5,000 +
Texas
California

2,001-5,000
Michigan
Illinois
Indiana
Ohio
Pennsylvania
New York
New Jersey
Florida
Louisiana

1,001-2,000
Washington
Minnesota
Wisconsin
Kansas
Oklahoma
Kentucky
Massachusetts
Tennessee
Maryland
Virginia
N. Carolina
Alabama
Georgia

501-1,000
Oregon
Utah
Colorado
Arizona
Arkansas
Mississippi
W. Virginia
S. Carolina

201-500
Idaho
Montana
N. Dakota
Wyoming
Nebraska
Nevada
New Mexico
Maine
Delaware
Oregon
Iowa
Connecticut

Less than 200
S. Dakota
Vermont
New Hampshire
Rhode Island

Fishermen haul in their net, brimming with menhaden from the North Atlantic. The American fishing industry produces about 4-1/2 million short tons (4 million metric tons) of seafood every year.

Glen Canyon Dam in Arizona, *above,* harnesses the Colorado River to produce electricity for businesses and homes. Water power helps meet the country's high level of energy consumption.

The rich soils of the land are another major resource. The most fertile lands include the dark soils of the Midwest and the *alluvial* soils containing water-deposited silt along the lower Mississippi River and in other river valleys.

Fresh water—in the country's lakes and rivers and under the ground—is also a precious natural resource. About 400 billion gallons (1,500 billion liters) of water is used every day in the United States, mainly to operate manufacturing and power plants, and to irrigate farmland. Homes use about 10 per cent of the total.

Fish in the coastal waters of the country are another valuable resource. The largest catches, including menhaden, oysters, and shrimp, are taken from the Gulf of Mexico. The Pacific Ocean has an abundance of cod, crab, herring, salmon, and tuna, while the Atlantic catch includes flounder, lobsters, and scallops.

Finally, the forests that cover almost one-third of the United States yield many valuable products. The forests of the Pacific Northwest supply about 40 per cent of all the nation's lumber. Southern forests also provide lumber, as well as wood pulp for making paper, turpentine, pitch, rosin, and wood tar. The Appalachian forests and areas around the Great Lakes produce fine hardwoods, such as hickory, maple, and oak, for making furniture.

The moderate climate enjoyed by much of the United States can also be considered a natural resource. It has allowed people to settle in most parts of the country and enabled farmers to grow a wide variety of crops.

Industry

The United States is first in the world in *gross national product (GNP)*—the total value of all goods and services a country produces in a year.

The growing service economy

Service industries, a general name for a large, varied category of economic activities that produce services rather than goods, account for 72 per cent of the U.S. GNP. Service industries include communications; community, social, and personal services; finance; government; and trade.

Service industries are of growing importance in the U.S. economy. In the mid-1960's, 56 per cent of all U.S. workers were employed in service industries. In the late 1980's, 74 per cent of the country's workers were employed in such industries.

Community, social, and personal services form the most important service industry in terms of percentage of the U.S. GNP. This category includes health care, legal services, nursery schools, and many other types of businesses.

The economic activity of the country needs money to operate. The finance industry supplies this money in the form of loans from banks. Two other kinds of financial institutions are (1) securities exchanges, where stocks and bonds are bought and sold to raise money for businesses, and (2) commodities exchanges where such goods as grains and precious metals are bought and sold.

The trade industry employs about 22 per cent of all U.S. workers. In *wholesale trade,* a buyer purchases products directly from a producer, and then sells the products to retailers. For example, a wholesaler for vegetables buys large amounts of vegetables from the growers and then sells them to grocers. In *retail trade,* goods are sold directly to the consumer. The grocers, who sell the vegetables, are in retail trade.

The government provides many services to the people of the country. Local and state governments and the federal government employ about a fifth of all American workers. They provide such services as police protection, education, and trash collection.

The communications industry includes publishing and broadcasting companies that provide news and entertainment. Phone service and mail delivery are also part of the communications industry.

Manufacturing and construction

While the service industries as a whole play the largest role in U.S. economic production today, manufacturing is the single most important economic activity. It accounts for about 19 per cent of the GNP and employs about 17 per cent of the working population.

Factories in the United States turn out a tremendous variety of *producer goods* (articles used to make other products), such as sheet metal and printing presses. They also manufacture *consumer goods* (products that people use), such as cars, clothes, and television sets. In order of their value, the leading kinds of manufactured products are transportation equipment, food products, chemicals, nonelectrical machinery, electrical machinery and equipment, printed materials, fabricated metal products, scientific instruments, and paper products.

The Midwest and Northeast have long been centers of manufacturing. Midwestern factories produce much of the nation's iron and steel, as well as cars. The Northeast has many clothing factories, food-processing

Construction of skyscrapers makes use of computer-operated cranes to hoist steel beams. Computers are the latest phase of *automation*—the use of machines to do work.

The New York Stock Exchange, *right,* is located in the city's Wall Street district. The selling of stocks and bonds is one of America's service industries. Service industries employ 74 per cent of the nation's workers.

Bell Laboratories, *left,* is part of AT&T, the largest communications company in the world. The company's research and development work led to many inventions, including the transistor and the *Telstar* satellite.

A steelworker operates a giant machine at the USX Corporation in Pittsburgh. Formerly called United States Steel, USX remains one of the largest steelmakers in the world.

plants, printing plants, and manufacturers of electronic equipment.

Since the mid-1990's, the fastest-growing manufacturing areas have been in California, the Southwest, and the South. California produces aircraft, aerospace equipment, computers and electronic components, and food products. In Texas and other Gulf States, petroleum refineries and petrochemical industries are major manufacturers.

The construction industry provides jobs for 5 per cent of all U.S. workers. Architects, engineers, contractors, bricklayers, carpenters, and electricians build homes, offices, and factories across the country.

According to many observers, a new era for American economic growth dawned on August 12, 1992, when the U.S., Canada, and Mexico formally announced a plan known as the North American Free Trade Agreement. The plan was designed to make American industry more competitive by lowering labor costs. It would also provide U.S., Mexican, and Canadian consumers with a wider variety of goods at lower prices. The agreement was ratified by all three nations in 1993.

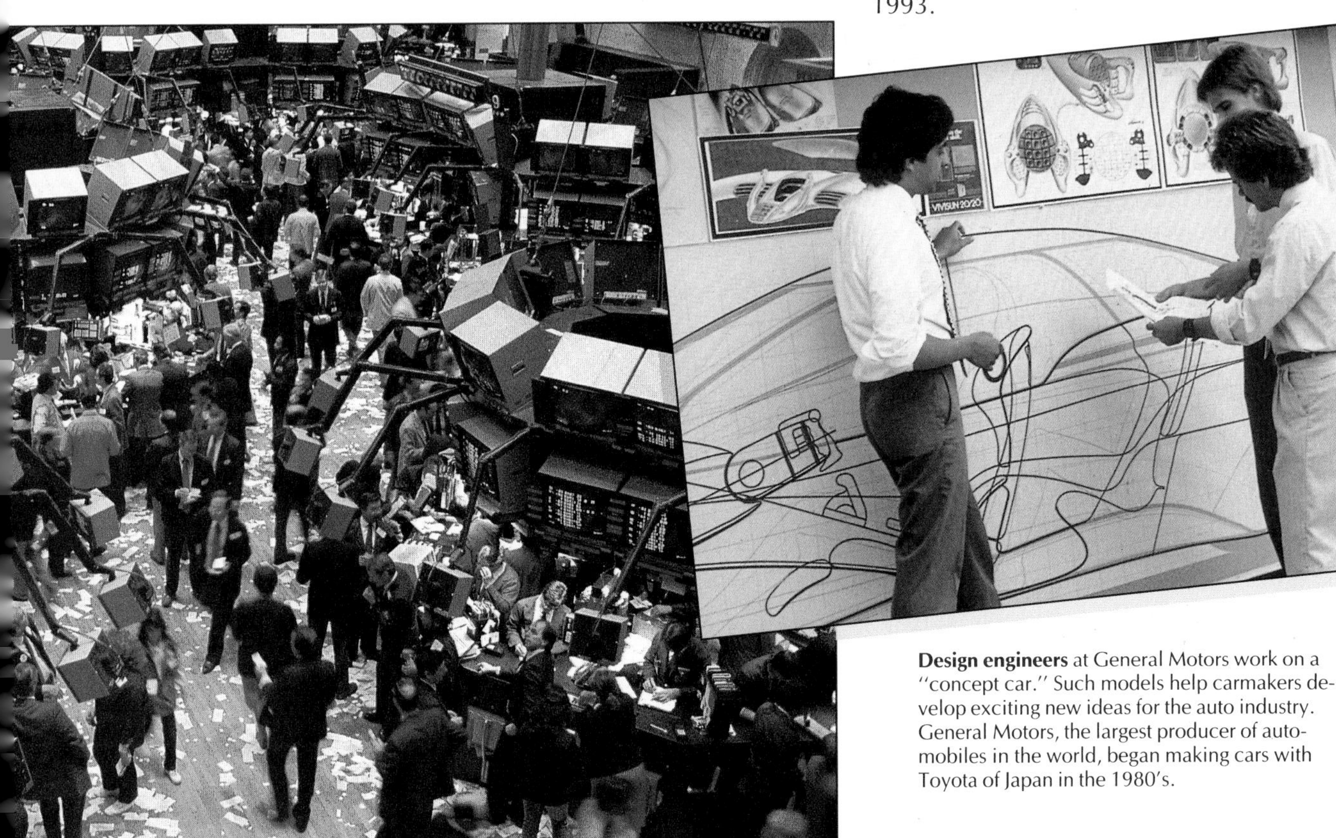

Design engineers at General Motors work on a "concept car." Such models help carmakers develop exciting new ideas for the auto industry. General Motors, the largest producer of automobiles in the world, began making cars with Toyota of Japan in the 1980's.

Agriculture

The United States not only leads the world in agricultural production, but it also helps feed the world. Every year, the average U.S. farmer produces enough food to feed almost 80 people. Since the nation's total agricultural output is more than enough to feed its people, the United States exports large amounts of food. In fact, about a sixth of all food exports in the world come from the United States.

The most valuable farm product is beef cattle, followed by milk, corn (also called *maize*), soybeans, hogs, wheat, chickens and eggs, and cotton. Other farm products include hay, tobacco, potatoes, turkeys, sorghum, oranges, tomatoes, peanuts, grapes, and apples.

Farmers throughout the country raise dairy cattle for milk, cheese, and other products, but dairy production is especially concentrated in a northern zone running from Minnesota to New York. Millions of beef cattle are raised on huge ranches in the West, and large numbers are also found in the Midwest and South. The Midwest is noted for its hogs and the South for its chickens.

The Midwest, the country's Corn Belt, also accounts for much of America's soybean production. The Wheat Belt stretches across the Great Plains. Almost all the country's cotton is grown in California, the Southwest, and the South. And farmers throughout the nation produce poultry, eggs, fruits, vegetables, nuts, and many other crops.

During the 1900's, the number of farms in the United States decreased, but the size of the individual farm increased. The United States today has about 2 million farms, compared with about 6.5 million in the 1920's. The average size of a farm today is 460 acres (186 hectares), compared with about 153 acres (62 hectares) in the 1920's.

America's farms produce more now than ever before, largely for two reasons: the use of modern farm machines and agricultural methods, and efficient management. American inventors devised the harvesting machine and steel plow. American scientists have helped develop improved livestock breeds and plant varieties, as well as chemicals for fertilizing soil and controlling weeds and insects.

An aerial view of farmland near Denver, Colo., *below,* shows the geometric patterns that result from modern farming practices. U.S. farms produce enough food for the country and much of the world.

Agriculture in California, *right,* produces more than 200 crops, including chili peppers, and brings in more income than agriculture in any other state.

A cattle rancher, *far right,* feeds his stock hay in winter when natural forage is scarce. The United States produces more beef than any other country. The U.S. cattle industry is centered in the Western states.

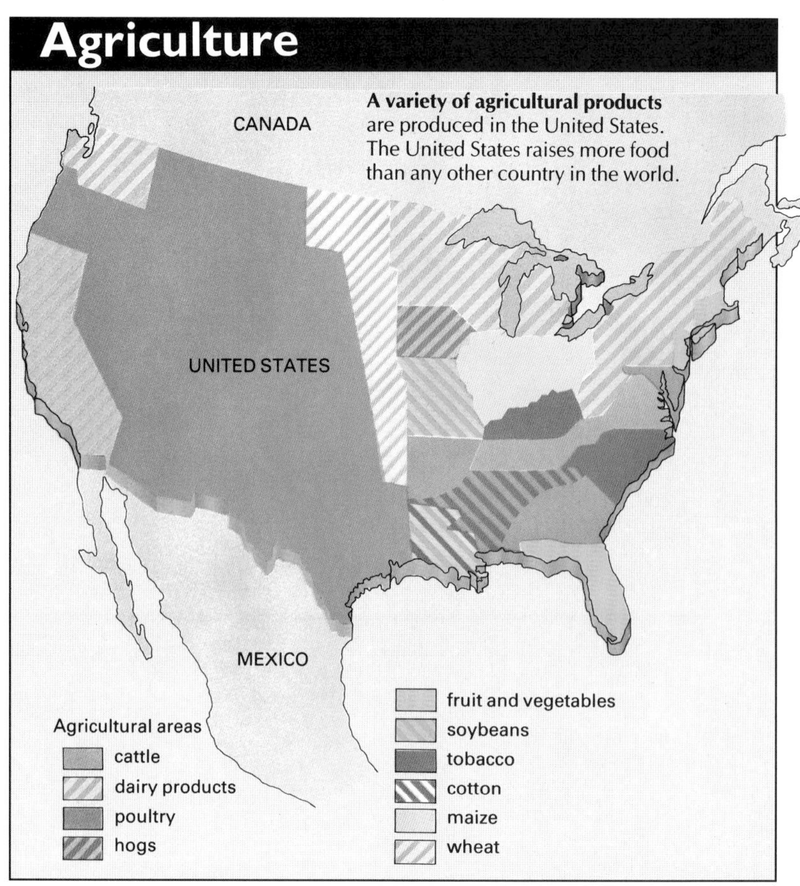

A variety of agricultural products are produced in the United States. The United States raises more food than any other country in the world.

Kansas grain is loaded onto barges on the Missouri River, *below*. Kansas lies in the Wheat Belt and leads the nation in producing this grain. Wheat is ground into flour to make such foods as bread and pasta.

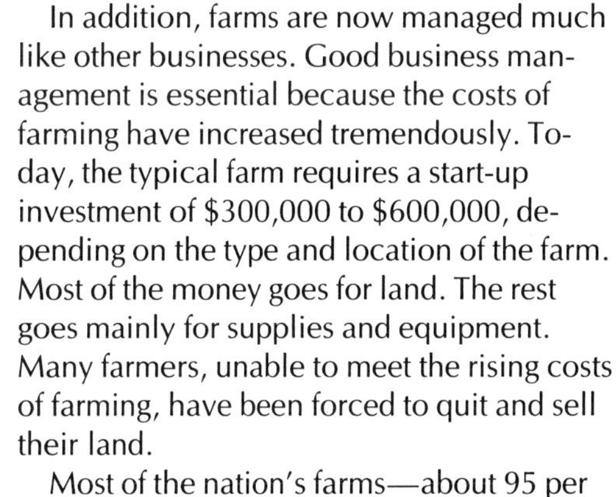

In addition, farms are now managed much like other businesses. Good business management is essential because the costs of farming have increased tremendously. Today, the typical farm requires a start-up investment of $300,000 to $600,000, depending on the type and location of the farm. Most of the money goes for land. The rest goes mainly for supplies and equipment. Many farmers, unable to meet the rising costs of farming, have been forced to quit and sell their land.

Most of the nation's farms—about 95 per cent—are owned by individuals or by partnerships or corporations made up of family members. In many cases, the owners operate the farms, but some owners rent land to other farmers. More than half of all farmland in the United States is rented. Some of the largest farms in the country are owned by such corporations as food-processing companies or feed manufacturers, who hire managers to run them.

American farmers today lead very different lives from those of their grandparents. Machines, such as tractors, harvesters, and conveyor systems, have eliminated much backbreaking work, and the homes of farm families have the same comforts and conveniences as those of urban people.

American Way of Life

The United States was built by brave and freedom-loving people who came from almost every part of the world. Through the years, they and their descendants learned to live and work together, and to be proud of being Americans. This cooperation and shared pride made the country the powerful and wealthy nation it is today.

The United States may be a nation of cultural pluralism, where many people keep some of the traditions of their ancestors, but there is also an American culture—a style and a special way of looking at life that Americans share.

At a family reunion in Raleigh, N.C., relatives enjoy a picnic buffet. American family life has changed greatly since the mid-1900's as people adopt new roles for family members and develop new kinds of family structures.

Americans enjoy sports, both as spectators and as players. Football, *right,* draws millions of people to stadiums each year to watch their favorite professional, college, and high school teams. Millions more watch football games on television.

American values

Most immigrants came to the United States seeking political or religious freedom or economic opportunity. Today, Americans still value these ideals highly. Freedom of speech, freedom of the press, and freedom of religion are guaranteed by the Constitution and guarded jealously. *Civil rights*—equal treatment for all people, including equal opportunity in jobs—are guaranteed by laws.

Equal economic opportunity enables people in the United States to move from one social class to another. As in many other societies, the values of the middle class are the nation's most widely held values. Middle-class Americans stress self-improvement and economic success. They believe it is important to work hard, make a good living, and follow the community's standards of morality. They also value education, and many send their children to college.

Athough every religious group is free to worship as it chooses, a majority of the American people are Christians, and the Christian religion has a stronger influence on American life than any other faith. For example, most people do not work on Sunday, the Christian day of worship. About 60 per cent of the people are members of a religious group, and about 92 per cent of these Americans belong to Christian religions.

The American family

Traditionally, the American family has consisted of a mother, a father, and several children. This kind of family structure is called a *nuclear family.*

Today, many people have turned away from this traditional family pattern. Now, on the average, married couples have only one or two children. Some couples decide to have none. Others get divorced; about half of the marriages that take place in the United States end in divorce. Divorced or widowed parents sometimes choose not to remarry. They and their children live together in *single-parent families.*

The growing number of working wives and mothers has also changed the pattern of family life in many ways. This dramatic increase has rapidly advanced the ideal of the *equalitarian family,* in which each member is respected and neither parent tries to be "head" of the family.

Recreation

Many Americans have a great deal of leisure time, and they spend it in a variety of ways. They pursue hobbies; take part in sports activities; attend sporting and cultural events; watch movies and television; listen to records, tapes, and radios; and read books and

magazines. They enjoy trips to museums, beaches, parks, playgrounds, and zoos. They take weekend and vacation trips, eat at restaurants, go on picnics, and entertain friends at home. These and other activities contribute to the richness and diversity of American life.

Hobbies occupy much of the leisure time of many Americans. Large numbers of people enjoy raising flower or vegetable gardens or indoor plants. Other popular hobbies include stamp collecting, coin collecting, and photography. Since the mid-1900's, interest in such crafts hobbies as needlepoint, pottery making, quilting, weaving, and woodworking has increased sharply.

The Stars and Stripes—the U.S. flag—flies outside a house on Long Island.

A roadside diner in Dubois, Wyo., displays a huge skull and an oversized moose to catch travelers' attention. Such facilities, which offer a variety of services, are found along U.S. interstates and cater to out-of-town motorists.

Arts and Entertainment

The first American artists were Native Americans. They used their skills in pottery, weaving, and carving to make everyday objects beautiful as well as useful. The first major American works of art, however, were probably houses built by the colonists shortly after their arrival from Europe. *Colonial style* houses date back to the 1600's.

During the 1700's, American craft workers began producing outstanding examples of furniture and silver work. John Singleton Copley and other American painters of the period created excellent portraits.

American literature first gained recognition in Europe in the early 1800's. Washington Irving combined the styles of the essay and the sketch to create a new literary form, the short story. Irving's "Rip Van Winkle" and "The Legend of Sleepy Hollow" are probably his best-loved works. James Fenimore Cooper's series of five novels, *The Leather-Stocking Tales,* contained the first serious portrayal of American frontier characters and scenes.

During the late 1800's, American architects began designing skyscrapers that revolutionized urban architecture throughout the world. William Le Baron Jenney designed the first metal-frame skyscraper, completed in Chicago in 1885.

The late 1800's and early 1900's saw the birth of two uniquely American art forms—jazz and musical comedy. Motion pictures and modern dance soon followed.

Painting

By the mid-1800's, many U.S. artists had come to feel that the country's landscape was the perfect subject for a truly American style of painting. New York's Hudson River Valley and the West inspired many artists.

The American public got its first look at modern art in 1913 at a famous exhibit called the Armory Show. Many American artists then adopted the European modern style, but in the 1930's, some returned to American themes. Grant Wood painted Midwest scenes, and Edward Hopper depicted urban life.

Since World War II (1939–1945), the United States has largely replaced Europe as the center of Western painting. Modern painting has produced abstract art, like that of Jackson Pollock; realistic art, like that of Andrew Wyeth; and pop art, like that of Andy Warhol.

Dance and theater

Modern dance, which developed in the early 1900's, has centered on U.S. dancers and dance companies since the 1940's. America's famous modern choreographers include Twyla Tharp, Alvin Ailey, and Martha Graham, who formed her own dance company and created dances for ballets such as *Appalachian Spring.*

Today, all across the United States, more theater groups than ever before are producing plays. Broadway in New York City is the best-known center of theater in the country, but cities around the nation have their own acting companies. Most towns of more than 30,000 people have community theaters.

American playwrights have produced masterpieces of serious drama as well as musical comedy. Arthur Miller's *Death of a Salesman* deals with a salesman who fails to realize the American dream of success; the play has been performed around the world. *A Chorus Line*, a musical about dancers, was the longest-running show in the history of Broadway theater.

Movies and music

Motion pictures are one of the most popular and influential art forms in the United States, ranging from early silent classics like *The Birth of a Nation* to such "blockbuster" movies of the 1970's and 1980's as *Star*

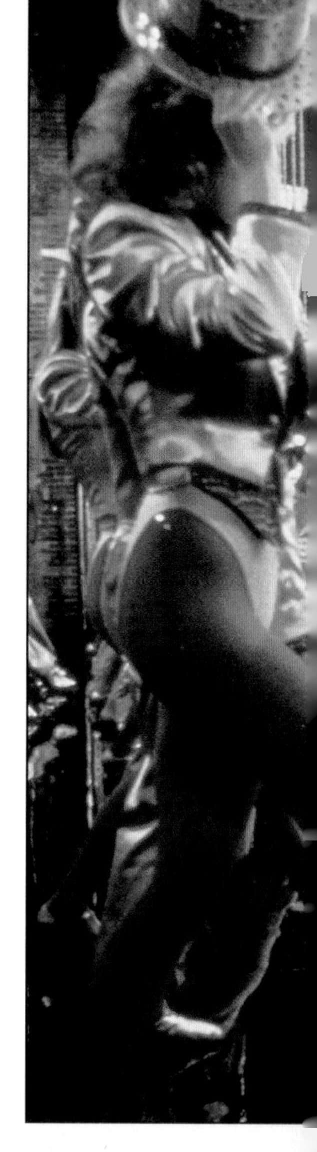

Wars, *E.T.*, and *Batman*. Walt Disney's *animated* (cartoon) films are internationally acclaimed for their artistic merit as well as their entertainment value.

Popular music has taken many forms in the United States. Blues sprang from the songs of slaves. Jazz first became popular about 1900 among African Americans. Louis Armstrong, a trumpeter, was the first great jazz soloist.

George Gershwin combined elements of jazz with serious and popular music to produce musical comedies, popular songs, symphonic works, and opera. His *Rhapsody in Blue* is probably the best-known orchestral piece written by an American.

Country music, once the folk music of Southern whites, is now popular nationwide. Rock music is a mixture of blues, jazz, and American country music. Singers Elvis Presley and Chuck Berry helped make rock music the leading type of popular music since the 1950's.

A Broadway chorus line embodies the spirit and sparkle of American musical comedy, *center*.

The Guggenheim Museum, *left*, in New York City houses an important international art collection. The building itself, designed by Frank Lloyd Wright, is an impressive work of art.

Walt Disney World, *far left*, near Orlando, Fla., uses themes and characters from Disney's animated films to entertain millions each year.

At Mann's Chinese Theater in Los Angeles, *bottom center*, many movie stars have made a lasting impression by setting their handprints in the sidewalk's wet cement.

An outdoor concert at Chicago's Grant Park bandshell offers classical music in a casual setting.

Uruguay

On the southeastern coast of South America lies the continent's second smallest independent nation—Uruguay. A land of gently rolling plains and beautiful sandy beaches, Uruguay is bordered by Argentina on the west, Brazil on the north and east, and the Río de la Plata and Atlantic Ocean on the south. Uruguay's economy relies heavily on agriculture, with farm products providing most of the country's export income.

Most Uruguayans are descended from Spanish settlers who came to the country in the 1600's and 1700's and Italian immigrants who arrived during the 1800's and early 1900's. Nearly all Uruguayans speak Spanish, the country's official language. It is generally spoken with an Italian accent. Many Uruguayans also speak a second language, usually English, French, or Italian.

Uruguay's people reflect a wide range of personalities and occupations. Free-spirited gauchos herd cattle on huge ranches in the interior of the country, while hard-working farmers grow corn, tomatoes, and other crops in the fertile valleys of the Uruguay River and the Río de la Plata. Urban dwellers in Montevideo, the nation's capital, hold government or professional jobs or work in business and industry.

In their leisure time, people crowd the shops and cafes along the city's treelined boulevards. And in cities and towns throughout the country, young soccer fans play their favorite sport with boundless energy and high spirits.

These are the modern-day Uruguayans—people who generally enjoy a comfortable standard of living, unlike many other South Americans. During the early 1900's, Uruguay developed into one of the most wealthy and democratic nations in South America. However, a decline in the economy during the 1950's and 1960's led to widespread political unrest, terrorism, and military rule. Today, Uruguay is once again ruled by an elected civilian government, but many of its economic problems remain unsolved.

Early history

Long before the first Europeans arrived in what is now Uruguay, the region was inhabited by Indian tribes. The largest of these tribes were the fierce, warlike Charrúas. In

A ranch hand gathers up an armful of wool that has just been shorn from a sheep and will soon be shipped to a factory in Montevideo. Woolen textile manufacturing is an important industry in Uruguay, and textiles are a leading export.

A group of Uruguayan students, *below,* enjoy a break during afternoon recess. The government provides free public schooling through the university level, and the law requires children from ages 6 through 15 to attend school.

A Uruguayan enjoys his *yerba maté* (tea)—the country's national beverage—in the traditional way, sipped through a silver straw from a gourd. This refreshing drink is made by pouring hot water onto the dried leaves of a holly tree.

A cheerful waiter serves his customers in a crowded city cafe, a typical social center for middle-class city dwellers. Most of the people who live in Montevideo and other Uruguayan cities belong to the middle class.

Young soccer players, *below,* are so enthusiastic about their game that they risk the bruises that can come from playing on hard city streets. Soccer is by far the most popular sport in Uruguay, and many children begin playing soccer as soon as they can walk. The first World Cup championship games were played in Montevideo in 1930. Today, soccer games draw huge crowds to city stadiums. Uruguayans also enjoy basketball and rugby. Gaucho rodeos, called *domos,* are also popular events.

1516, when the Spanish explorer Juan Díaz de Solís sailed into the Río de la Plata, he and his expedition were attacked and killed by the Charrúas.

When later Spanish explorers found that Uruguay lacked deposits of precious metals, the region was all but forgotten for more than a century. But in 1680, Portuguese soldiers from Brazil established the town of Nova Colonia do Sacramento (now Colonia) on the Río de la Plata, across from the Spanish settlement of Buenos Aires.

To prevent the Portuguese from expanding any farther into Spanish territory, the Spaniards founded the town of Montevideo in 1726. By the 1770's, the Spanish had settled most of Uruguay, and in 1776, the region became part of the Spanish colony called the Viceroyalty of the Río de La Plata, also called the Viceroyalty of La Plata. The Portuguese formally gave up what is now Colonia in 1777.

Artigas and the Tupamaros

During the early 1800's, a Uruguayan soldier named José Gervasio Artigas organized an army to fight for independence from Spain. Just as Artigas' army was about to defeat the Spaniards at Montevideo, the Portuguese attacked both the Uruguayan and Spanish troops.

Rather than submit to either Spanish or Portuguese rule, Artigas led his army and thousands of Uruguayans across the border to Paraguay and Argentina. Spanish control over Uruguay ended in 1814, and in 1815 Artigas and his troops took control of Montevideo.

In 1816, Portuguese troops again attacked Uruguay. After four years of bitter fighting, the Portuguese annexed Uruguay to Brazil and forced Artigas into exile.

In 1825, the battle for Uruguayan independence was renewed under the leadership of a group of patriots called "The Immortal Thirty-Three." Following Great Britain's diplomatic intervention, Brazil and Argentina recognized Uruguay as an independent nation. The country's first Constitution was adopted in 1830.

Uruguay Today

The popular resort city of Punta del Este, *right,* lies on the southeastern tip of Uruguay. Its beautiful sandy beaches draw throngs of vacationers from both Uruguay and neighboring Argentina. Uruguay has many magnificent beaches along its Atlantic coast.

For most of its history as an independent nation, Uruguay has had a democratic government. However, conflict between its two major political parties—the Colorados and the Blancos—has caused much internal political strife.

Most of the members of the Colorado Party come from the cities, while the Blanco Party represents the interests of the rural people and the landowners. For many Uruguayans, party membership is a matter of family tradition.

The Colorados and the Blancos

Throughout the mid-1800's, the Colorados and the Blancos fought for control of the government. During this time, foreign governments often interfered in Uruguay's affairs by supporting one of these groups. By 1870, the Colorados had become the dominant political party, mainly because a huge wave of immigration dramatically increased Montevideo's population.

In 1903, José Batlle y Ordóñez, a strong believer in democratic principles and social justice, was elected president of Uruguay. Under his leadership, the ruling Colorado Party passed wide-ranging laws that made Uruguay a model of democracy, social reform, and economic stability.

A new Constitution

Economic problems began to develop for Uruguay in the 1950's. Foreign trade decreased, while the cost of social programs increased. In 1951, Uruguay ratified a new Constitution that abolished the presidency and established a nine-member National Council of Government.

Although the council allowed the Colorados and the Blancos to share political power, it proved inefficient in dealing with the nation's economic problems. In 1967, a new Constitution reestablished a presidential government.

As Uruguay's economic problems worsened, public unrest increased. Terrorist violence erupted, and one of the antigovernment groups, the Tupamaros, kidnapped and murdered Uruguayan and foreign officials. In 1973, military officers took over the government and forced President Juan Maria Bordaberry to dissolve the national legislature. Three years later, they removed Bordaberry from office and named Aparicio Mendez to the presidency. General Gregorio Alvarez succeeded Mendez in 1981.

Despite the bitter protests of the Uruguayan people, military rule continued during the early 1980's. Negotiations between military and party leaders led to

FACT BOX

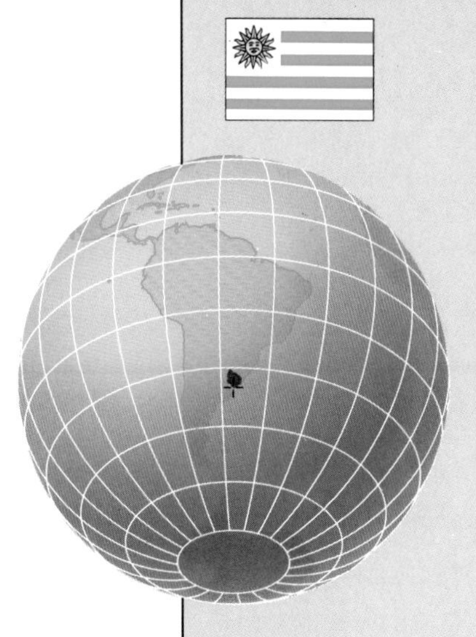

THE COUNTRY
Official name: República Oriental del Uruguay (Eastern Republic of Uruguay).
Capital: Montevideo.
Land regions: Coastal plains, interior lowlands.
Area: 68,500 sq. mi. (177,414 km^2).
Climate: Mild and humid, with regular rainfall.
Main rivers: Uruguay, Negro.
Highest elevation: Mirador Nacional, 1,644 ft. (501 m).
Lowest elevation: Sea level.

THE GOVERNMENT
Form of government: Republic.
Head of state: President.
Head of government: President.
Administrative areas: 19 departments.
Legislature: General Assembly consisting of a 30-member Senate and a 99-member Chamber of Deputies, members of both elected to 5-year terms.
Court system: Supreme Court, appeals courts, lower courts, justices of the peace.
Armed forces: 24,000 troops.

THE PEOPLE
Estimated 1996 population: 3,204,000.
Official language: Spanish.
Religion: Roman Catholic (66%).

THE ECONOMY
Currency: Peso.
Gross national product (GNP) in 1992: $10.4 billion U.S.
Real annual growth rate (1985–92): 2.9%.
GNP per capita (1992): $3,340 U.S.
Balance of trade (1992): Imports and exports equal at $1.7 billion U.S.

democratic elections and a return to civilian government in 1984. Julio Maria Sanguinetti—leader of the Colorado Party—took office as president in 1985.

With the return of democracy to Uruguay, its new leadership must now deal with rebuilding the country's economy. Export income dropped sharply during the early and middle 1980's. As a result, the amount of money available for social programs has decreased. The country's foreign debt has skyrocketed. Luis Alberto Lacalle, who was elected president in 1989, promised to introduce reforms that would strengthen Uruguay's financial position by reducing government spending, selling some government-owned businesses, and improving the country's financial relationship with other nations.

Uruguay lies at the mouth of the Río de la Plata. Once one of the wealthiest countries in South America, Uruguay now has serious economic problems, including a skyrocketing foreign debt. High inflation and unemployment, along with less money available for social programs, have hurt many Uruguayans.

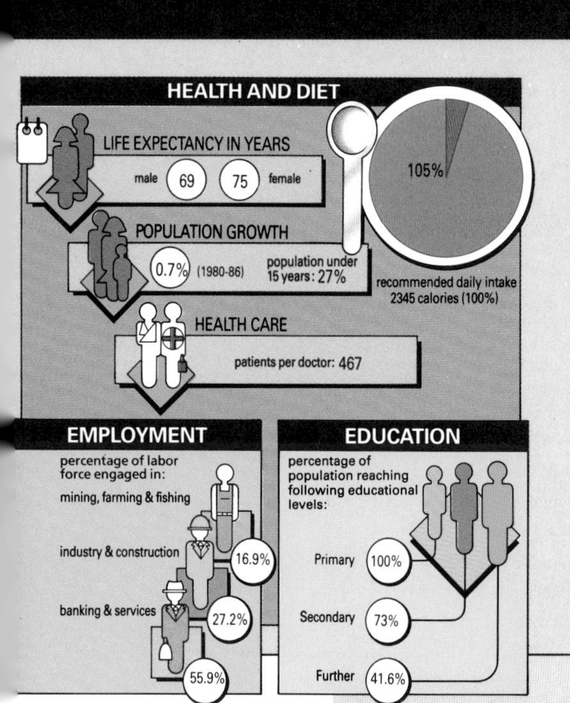

Goods exported: Beef, hides, live cattle and sheep, vegetable products, wool, and woolen textiles.
Goods imported: Appliances, chemical products machinery, metal goods, and petroleum.
Trading partners: Argentina, Brazil, France, Great Britain, Italy, Mexico, the Netherlands, and the United States.

Land and Economy

Uruguay can be divided into two land regions: the coastal plains; and the interior lowlands, which make up about four-fifths of the country. Unlike many other South American countries, Uruguay features no dramatic contrasts in its landscape, but it is a lovely, scenic country. Miles of sandy white beaches stretch along its coast, and sparkling rivers flow through the gently rolling grasslands of the interior.

The coastal plains

The coastal plains extend in a narrow arc along the Uruguay River, the Río de la Plata, and the Atlantic Ocean. The Uruguay River forms the country's western border with Argentina. Although the coastal plains cover only about a fifth of Uruguay, most of the nation's population is concentrated in this region, especially along the southern coast.

The capital city of Montevideo, located on the southern coast, is also the nation's commercial, political, and intellectual center. About two-fifths of Uruguay's people live there. Montevideo is a bustling city with many lovely parks, impressive monuments, treelined avenues, and beautiful beaches. Montevideo offers a variety of cultural and recreational opportunities.

Most of the people who live in Montevideo—and throughout Uruguay—are descended from Spanish and Italian immigrants who settled in Uruguay during the 1800's and early 1900's, but other groups include people of English, French, German, and Eastern European descent. *Mestizos* (people of mixed European and Indian ancestry) make up between 5 and 10 per cent of Uruguay's population. Under 3 per cent are blacks. The inhabitants of pure Indian ancestry disappeared almost entirely by the late 1700's.

Many people in Montevideo work in service industries, such as banks, health care facilities, schools, transportation, and communications. Others work in factories, or as laborers or household servants. Along the Atlantic coast, many Uruguayans are employed by hotels, restaurants, and resorts that serve the tourist industry.

The western and southwestern coastal plains have Uruguay's richest soil. In this region, family farms and large plantations produce enough corn, linseed, potatoes, rice, sugar beets, sugar cane, sunflowers, and wheat to feed Uruguay's large urban population. The rest of the land—about 85 per cent of Uruguay's total area—is taken up by huge cattle and sheep ranches.

The interior lowlands

The interior lowlands cover most of Uruguay. The grass-covered plains and hills of the interior lowlands make ideal pastureland for livestock. As a result, sprawling cattle and sheep ranches as large as 5,000 acres (2,024 hectares) cover the countryside. The production costs of raising livestock are low in this region, and the quality of the product is high.

An Uruguayan vineyard worker shows off the luscious grape harvest. Grapes are grown mainly on the coastal plains of Uruguay, where the crop produces enough wine to meet the country's domestic needs.

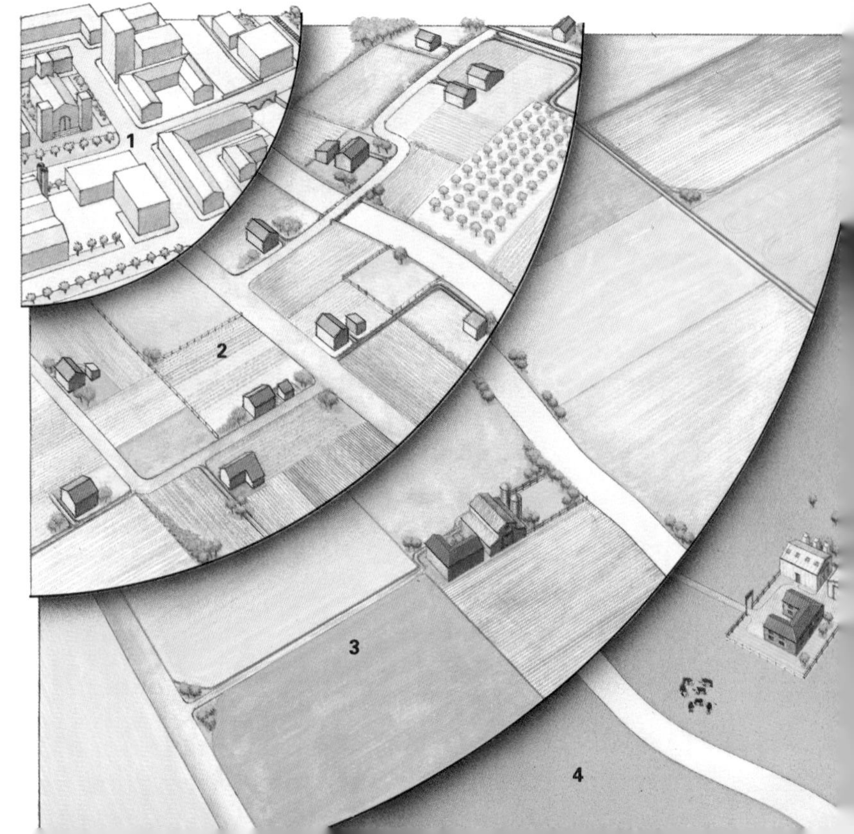

A mixture of crops and livestock forms the basis of Uruguay's farming economy. Market gardens predominate near the cities, while larger farms grow grain. Agriculture employs 16 per cent of Uruguay's workers.

Workers in a tannery process the skins and hides that form one of Uruguay's most valuable exports. Most working-class people in Uruguay enjoy a comfortable standard of living, with decent housing and good medical care.

Because livestock production is Uruguay's leading source of farm income, the grasslands are considered the country's most important natural resource.

The mighty Uruguay River, which gives the country its name, rises in southern Brazil and flows west, then south, along Uruguay's border with Argentina before it empties into the Río de la Plata. The Río Negro is the largest river in the interior. It flows southwestward through the heart of the lowlands. A dam on the Negro created Lake Rincón del Bonete, Uruguay's only large lake.

Uruguay has no mountains, but a long, narrow chain of highlands curves across the interior from the Brazilian border almost to the southern coast. These highlands are named *Cuchilla Grande* (Big Knife) for the knifelike formations of rock that jut through the soil on many of the ridges. The highest point in Uruguay, Mirador Nacional, also called Cerro de las Animas, rises 1,644 feet (501 meters) in the Cuchilla Grande.

Gauchos work hard at roundup time on a sheep ranch deep in the interior of Uruguay. Many gauchos still wear at least part of the traditional costume, which includes baggy trousers tucked into boots, a poncho, and a wide-brimmed hat. Most other Uruguayans today dress much as people do in the United States and Canada.

1. Urban center (85% of Uruguayans live in cities)
2. Market gardens: most less than 12 acres (5 hectares)
3. Grain-growing region: farms average 120-247 acres (50-100 hectares)
4. Grasslands: large ranches averaging 2,471 acres (1,000 hectares)

Uzbekistan

Uzbekistan is an independent country and a member of the Commonwealth of Independent States (CIS), which was formed in late 1991. It was formerly a republic of the now-defunct Soviet Union.

Uzbekistan lies in the foothills of the Tian Shan and Pamir mountains and extends to the Aral Sea. The region is bordered by Afghanistan in the south, Turkmenistan in the southwest, Kazakhstan in the west and north, and Kyrgyzstan and Tajikistan in the east. The Kyzylkum desert covers a large part of northwest Uzbekistan.

Uzbekistan covers 172,742 square miles (447,400 square kilometers) and has about 20,453,000 people. The country became a member of the Commonwealth of Independent States, *above*, in December 1991. (For a more detailed map of Uzbekistan, see the Commonwealth of Independent States article in volume 1 of this series.)

History

Two major rivers—the Amu Darya and Syr Darya—flow through Uzbekistan. The fertile valleys of these rivers once served as oases for caravans along the great Silk Road, a major trade route between the East and West opened by Kushan emperors about A.D. 50.

The cities of Tashkent, Samarkand, and Khiva—where the routes between Europe and the Middle East and between China and India crisscrossed—were centers of world trade during ancient times. The colorful markets, where silk, spices, and other luxury goods—as well as ideas and customs—were once traded, remain today.

The area that is now Uzbekistan was the ancient Persian province of Sogdiana, one of the world's oldest civilized regions. During the 300's B.C., it was conquered by Alexander the Great. Turkic nomads took control of the region in the A.D. 500's, and in the 700's, the Arabs arrived and introduced the people to the religion of Islam.

FACT BOX

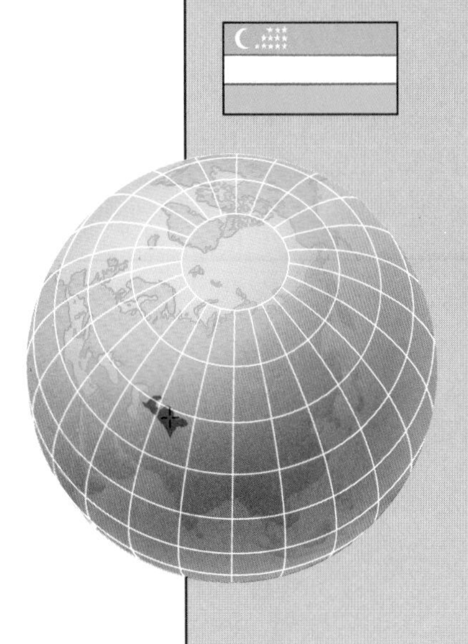

THE COUNTRY
Official name: Uzbekiston Respublikasi (Republic of Uzbekistan).
Capital: Tashkent.
Land regions: Aral-Caspian Lowland; Tian Shan and Pamir mountains in the southeast; plains and desert (Kyzylkum) regions.
Area: 172,742 sq. mi. (447,400 km²).
Climate: Continental, with long, dry, hot summers and cold winters.
Main rivers: Amu Darya, Syr Darya, Zeravshan.
Highest elevation: Peak in Gissar mountain range, 15,233 ft. (4,643 m).
Lowest elevation: Sarykamysh Lake, 65 ft. (20 m) below sea level.

THE GOVERNMENT
Form of government: Republic.
Head of state: President.
Head of government: Prime minister.
Administrative areas: 11 regions, 1 autonomous republic.
Legislature: Cabinet of Ministers.
Court system: Supreme Court, lower courts.
Armed forces: Undecided.

THE PEOPLE
Estimated 1993 population: 20,453,000.
Main language: Uzbek.
Religion: Muslim.

THE ECONOMY
Currency: Ruble.
Gross national product (GNP) in 1991: $28 billion U.S.
Real annual growth rate (1991): 3.4%.
GNP per capita (1991): $1,340 U.S.
Balance of trade (1990): −$2 billion U.S.
Goods exported: Cotton, fertilizer, gold, textiles, and vegetable oil.
Goods imported: Foods, grain, machinery, and parts.
Trading partners: Russia and Ukraine.

The Seljuk Turks gained control of the region in the 1100's but were driven out by the Mongols in the 1200's. Then, in the 1300's, a descendant of Genghis Khan named Tamerlane made Samarkand the center of his vast empire. In the early 1500's, a group of people from the Golden Horde—a once-powerful region of the Mongol Empire—swept down from the northwest and established the Uzbek Empire. Their leaders claimed to be descendants of Uzbeg Khan, so the people called themselves *Uzbeks.*

During the 1600's, the Uzbek Empire broke up into separate states, which were taken over by Russia in the late 1800's. In 1924,the region became the Uzbek Soviet Socialist Republic.

Uzbekistan remained under the strict control of the Soviet central government until 1991. In the midst of political upheaval following an attempted coup in August 1991, Uzbekistan declared its independence.

In December 1991, Soviet President Mikhail Gorbachev and Russian President Boris Yeltsin agreed to dissolve the Soviet Union by the end of the year and replace it with a new association called the Commonwealth of Independent States (CIS). The CIS had been established the previous week as a loose confederation of former Soviet republics. Uzbekistan agreed to join the CIS.

A marketplace in Bukhara is reminiscent of the ancient bazaars that once stood on this site. One of the largest cities in Uzbekistan today, Bukhara was once a stopping place for caravans along the ancient trade route known as the Silk Road.

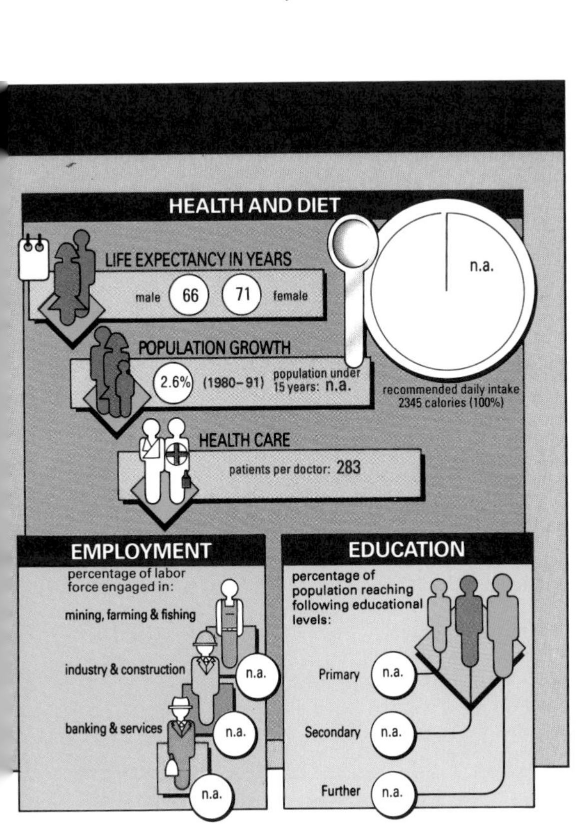

Land and people

Although much of Uzbekistan is desert, the region is rich in mineral resources, including coal, copper, gold, sulfur, and zinc. In addition, oil fields stand in the Fergana Valley, a populous area along the upper part of the Syr Darya, and western Uzbekistan has large natural gas deposits. Hydroelectric power stations along the rivers supply energy for the large-scale irrigation systems used in agricultural production.

About 70 per cent of the people who live in Uzbekistan are Uzbeks and follow the religion of Islam. The remaining population consists mainly of Russian people. Today, Uzbekistan is a unique blend of ancient Asian and modern European cultures.

Vanuatu

Eighty islands in the southwest Pacific Ocean make up the country of Vanuatu. The islands form a Y-shaped chain that extends about 500 miles (800 kilometers) from north to south. Most of the islands have narrow coastal plains and mountainous interiors, and several have active volcanoes. Vanuatu has a tropical wet climate—always hot and wet, with heavy precipitation throughout the year. Many houses, in fact, have thatched roofs to keep rain from dripping in. Savanna grassland and bush are prevalent in the southern islands, while tropical rain forests cover much of the northern islands.

Melanesians, like this man blowing on a conch shell, are the largest ethnic group in Vanuatu. Asians, Europeans, and Polynesians make up only about 10 per cent of the population.

Way of life

More than 90 per cent of Vanuatu's people are Melanesians. Asians, Europeans, and Polynesians make up the rest of the population. About three-fourths of the people live in rural villages. Many village houses are made of wood, bamboo, and palm leaves.

More than 100 languages are spoken in Vanuatu. Bislama, a type of Pidgin English that combines English words and Melanesian grammar, is widely used.

Agriculture is the country's chief economic activity. Rural families produce nearly all their own food, and some families produce copra for sale. They grow fruits and vegetables, raise chickens and hogs, and catch fish. Tourism is also important to the economy. Visitors and residents alike enjoy boating on the sparkling blue water near the islands' sandy shores.

The only urban communities in Vanuatu are Port-Vila, the capital, on the island of Efate, and Santo, on the island of Espiritu Santo. There are few good roads and no railroads. Small ships and airplanes are the primary means of transportation among the islands.

Vanuatu has about 300 elementary schools and several high schools. Over 85 per cent of the people are Christians, and most of the rest practice local religions.

Vanuatu is a republic. The country's laws are made by a Parliament, whose members are elected by the people to four-year terms. A prime minister, who heads the majority party in Parliament, runs the government with the aid of a Council of Ministers. The Parliament and regional council presidents elect a president, whose role is chiefly ceremonial. The government publishes a newspaper and operates a radio station.

History

Melanesians have lived in what is now Vanuatu for at least 3,000 years. In 1606, the commander of a Spanish expedition from

FACT BOX

THE COUNTRY
Official name: Vanuatu.
Capital: Port-Vila.
Land regions: 80 mountainous, volcanic islands.
Area: 4,700 sq. mi. (12,200 km^2).
Climate: Tropical wet.
Highest elevation: Mt. Tabwemasana, 6,165 ft. (1,879 m).
Lowest elevation: Sea level.

THE GOVERNMENT
Form of government: Republic.
Head of state: President.
Head of government: Prime minister.
Administrative areas: Local administration by 11 local government councils and 2 municipal councils.
Legislature: Parliament with 46 members elected to 4-year terms.
Court system: Supreme Court, Court of Appeal, magistrates' courts.
Armed forces: 300-member paramilitary force.

THE PEOPLE
Estimated 1992 population: 156,000.
Languages: Bislama, English, and French.
Religions: Protestant (55%), Roman Catholic (17%), Anglican (15%), local religions (8%).

THE ECONOMY
Currency: Vatu.
Gross national product (GNP) in 1989: $100 million U.S.
Real annual growth rate (1980–89): 0.7%.
GNP per capita (1989): $860 U.S.
Balance of trade (1988): –$50 million U.S.
Goods exported: Copra, coffee, cocoa, fish, meat, and wood.
Goods imported: Food, industrial goods, fuels.
Trading partners: Australia, France, Japan, the Netherlands, and New Zealand.

The peaceful town of Port-Vila, *above,* is Vanuatu's capital. A fierce typhoon struck in 1987, leaving behind damage and death, *left.*

Peru became the first European to see the islands. The British explorer James Cook mapped the region in 1774 and named the islands the *New Hebrides* after the Hebrides Islands of Scotland.

British and French traders, missionaries, and settlers began coming to the islands during the 1820's. Settlers established vast plantations on the fertile land and grew coconut palms, coffee, and cocoa. They also set up large beef cattle farms.

In 1887, Great Britain and France set up a joint naval commission to oversee the area. In 1906, the commission was replaced by a joint British and French government called a *condominium*. English and French interests clashed, however. Each nation had its own colonial administrator and its own police force on the islands, and insisted on using its own currency and language.

During World War II (1939–1945), the New Hebrides became an important Allied military base. U.S. troops built many roads, bridges, and airstrips there. In 1945, foreigners owned more than a third of the land area, but during the 1960's islanders began a movement for independence, and the New Hebrides became the independent nation of Vanuatu on July 30, 1980.

In 1987, a typhoon struck the islands, causing much loss of life and property damage.

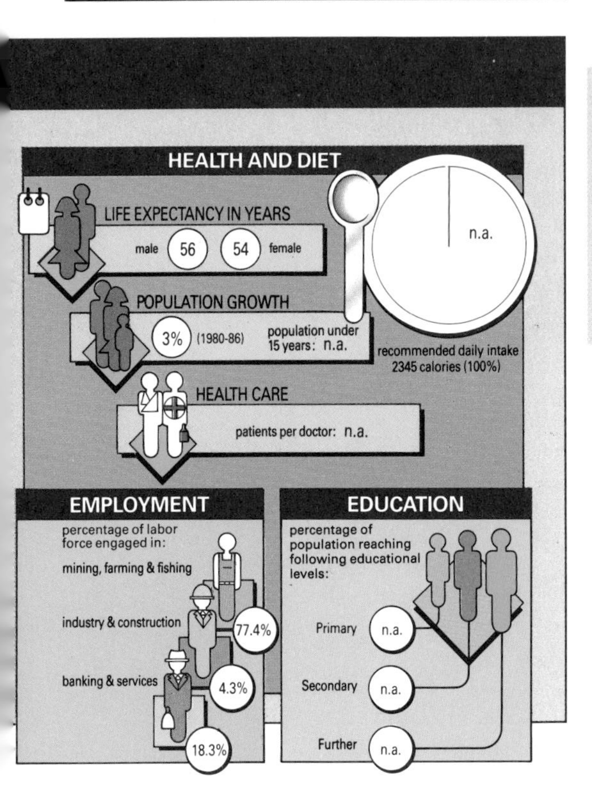

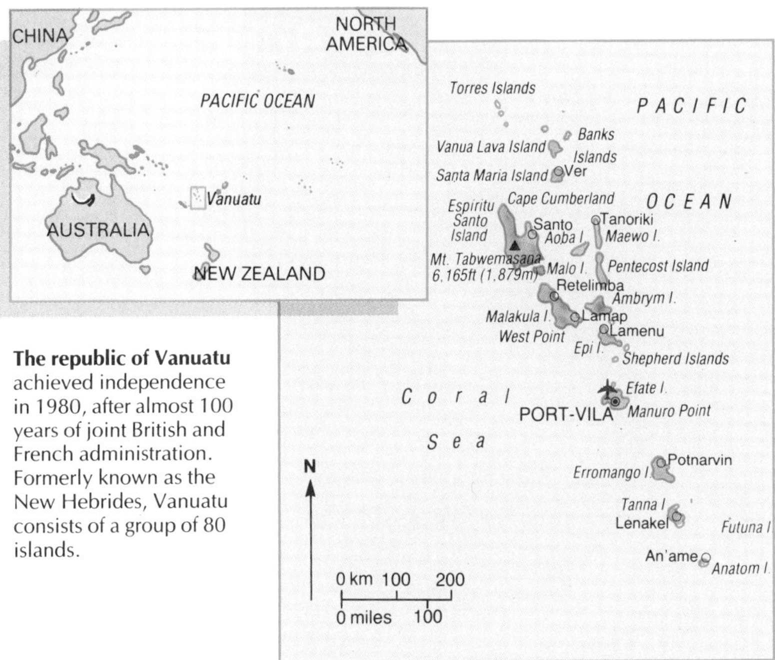

The republic of Vanuatu achieved independence in 1980, after almost 100 years of joint British and French administration. Formerly known as the New Hebrides, Vanuatu consists of a group of 80 islands.

Vatican City

The State of Vatican City is the smallest independent country in the world. It occupies only 109 acres (44 hectares) on Vatican Hill, entirely within the city of Rome. Although it is only about the size of an average city park, Vatican City influences millions of people all over the world. It is the spiritual and governmental center of the Roman Catholic Church, the world's largest Christian church.

Vatican City is situated in northwestern Rome, just west of the Tiber River. Most of the Vatican is surrounded by high stone walls. Within these walls stand a number of lovely buildings, courtyards, landscaped gardens, and quiet streets. Most of the area is taken up by St. Peter's Church.

Pope John Paul II, the first Pole to hold this office, was elected in 1978. The pope is head of the Roman Catholic Church and Bishop of Rome, as well as head of the Vatican's legislative, executive, and judicial affairs.

Origins of the Vatican

According to tradition, Saint Peter was crucified on Vatican Hill and buried nearby. The early popes erected Vatican City on the site of a shrine thought to have marked Saint Peter's tomb.

In the A.D. 300's, the Christian emperor Constantine the Great built a *basilica* (a church with certain ceremonial privileges) where the shrine stood. Gradually, the Vatican Palace and other buildings were constructed around the basilica. Beginning in the 1500's, St. Peter's Church was built on the site of the Old Basilica of Constantine.

During the Middle Ages, the popes gained control over much of central Italy, an area once known as the Papal States. But in 1870, after Pope Pius IX lost his power over the Papal States, the popes retreated to the Vatican and refused to deal with the Italian government.

It was not until 1929 that the Treaty of the Lateran resolved the status of Vatican City. By this treaty, the pope gave up all claim to the Papal States, and Italy recognized the independence of the State of Vatican City.

The buildings of Vatican City

Vatican City includes a number of important buildings. The Vatican Palace, with well over 1,000 rooms, is a group of connected buildings clustered around several open courts. The palace, which includes various chapels, apartments, museums, and other rooms, is also the residence of the pope.

Among the palace buildings are the Vatican Museums—a vast collection of priceless art treasures. The many rooms and chapels of the museums are decorated with masterpieces created by the world's greatest artists, including Fra Angelico, Pinturiccio, Raphael, Titian, and Leonardo da Vinci.

In the famous Sistine Chapel, Michelangelo's ceiling frescoes tell the Biblical stories of the creation of the world, the fall of hu-

FACT BOX

THE COUNTRY
Official name: Stato della Città del Vaticano (The State of Vatican City).
Area: 109 acres (44 hectares).

THE GOVERNMENT
Head of state: Pope.
Head of government: Pontifical Commission for the State of Vatican City (for internal affairs); Cardinal Secretary of State (for external affairs).
Court system: Supreme Tribunal of the Apostolic Signature; Tribunal of the Sacred Roman Rota; lower courts and civil courts.
Armed forces: None. A military corps called the Pontifical Swiss Guard acts as the pope's personal bodyguards.

THE PEOPLE
Estimated 1992 population: 1,000.
Official language: Italian.
Religion: Roman Catholic (100%; official).

THE ECONOMY
Currency: Vatican lira/Italian lira.
No data are available for gross national product, annual growth rate, trade balance, goods exported, goods imported, or trading partners.

The colorful uniforms of the Swiss Guard, the pope's personal bodyguards, are thought to have been designed by Michelangelo.

manity, and the Flood. The famous statues *Apollo Belvedere* and the *Laocoön* are part of the museums' collection of ancient sculpture.

Administering the Vatican

The population of Vatican City consists mainly of nuns and priests who work in administrative positions in the Roman Catholic Church. The pope is the absolute ruler of Vatican City, but the day-to-day affairs are the responsibility of the Pontifical Commission for the State of Vatican City, whose members are appointed by the pope. A governor, whose duties resemble those of a mayor, directs the city's administration.

The pope delivers an Easter message from a balcony above St. Peter's Square, *top*. St. Peter's Square was completed in 1667 and contains an *obelisk* brought from Egypt about A.D. 37.

Cardinals and bishops gather in the Sistine Chapel during the bishop's *synod*, an assembly called together to discuss church affairs. Cardinals from all over the world elect the pope.

Vatican City, an independent state since the Treaty of Lateran was signed in 1929, lies entirely within the city of Rome. In addition to a number of important church buildings, Vatican City includes large blocks of apartment buildings for its citizens—mostly the nuns and priests who work there. Gardens cover the western half of the Vatican, while the famous Sistine Chapel and St. Peter's Church lie in the southeastern corner.

Venezuela

Venezuela, a land of sprawling, modern cities, spectacular scenery, and gushing oil wells, lies on the north coast of South America. Once one of the poorer nations of South America, with an agriculture-based economy, Venezuela has been transformed by its petroleum industry. Now it is one of the continent's wealthiest and most rapidly changing countries.

Although the face of Venezuela is changing in many ways, reminders of this nation's long history can still be seen. The remarkable story of this South American country is written in the faces of its people—from the Indian tribes in the southern forests to the residents of Spanish colonial buildings in the northern city of Coro and those in the high-rise apartment buildings of the capital city of Caracas.

Spanish conquest and colonial rule

Christopher Columbus was the first European to reach Venezuela. He landed on Venezuela's Paria Peninsula in 1498, during his third voyage to the New World. Later, in the northwest region of the country, Spanish explorers discovered Indian houses built on stilts over the waters of Lake Maracaibo and the connecting gulf that opens northward to the Caribbean Sea. These houses reminded the Spaniards of the villas lining the canals of Venice, so the explorers named the region *Venezuela,* which is Spanish for *Little Venice*.

Long before the Spaniards arrived, the land was inhabited by two groups of Indian tribes—the Carib and the Arawak. But even their bravest warriors were no match for the ruthless *conquistadores* (conquerors), and the Spanish invaders took over the land in the early 1500's. Many Indians were killed in battle or died of diseases brought by the Europeans. Others starved or were worked to death as laborers.

Although the coastal areas of Venezuela provided pearls and salt, the new colony did not prosper under the Spanish. Its agricultural economy made it one of Spain's poorest colonies. The Spaniards did not find in Vene-

zuela the incredible hordes of gold and silver which Hernando Cortés found in Mexico and Francisco Pizarro found in Peru.

Struggle for independence

In 1730, Spain gave the Royal Guipuzcoana Company of Caracas all rights to trade in Venezuela. The colonists, who bitterly resented the company's activities, began to long for independence from Spain.

The colony declared its independence on July 5, 1811, but Spanish forces continued to occupy much of the country. In 1819, Simón Bolívar, one of the chief leaders of the independence movement, set up a republic called Gran Colombia, which eventually included what are now Venezuela, Colombia, Ecuador, and Panama. Not until 1821 did Venezuela gain true independence from Spain. In that year, Bolívar defeated the Spanish at Carabobo, near Valencia.

By 1831, Venezuela had broken away from the republic of Gran Colombia and elected General José Antonio Páez as the nation's first president.

A series of civil wars broke out in 1846 and lasted until 1870, when the dictatorial *caudillo* (leader) Antonio Guzmán Blanco seized power. Guzmán Blanco brought order to Venezuela and encouraged investment in the development of the country, but he was overthrown in 1888. The nation was then ruled by a series of other caudillos.

Although reformist political parties were founded in Venezuela in the mid-1930's, democracy was slow to come. In 1947, the people elected Rómulo Gallegos of the Acción Democrática (AD) party as president, but Gallegos was overthrown by the army in 1948. Since 1958, every president of Venezuela has come from either AD or the nation's other major political party—the Comité de Organización Política Electoral Independiente (COPEI), also known as the Social Christian Party.

Today, Venezuela's primary struggle is to lessen its dependence on petroleum and the economic instability caused by price changes in this important resource.

Venezuela Today

Once valued for little more than the salt mines on the Araya Peninsula and pearls along the north coast, Venezuela has become one of South America's wealthiest and most progressive nations. But the wealth is not distributed evenly among the people, and poverty is a major problem in some areas. Another difficulty is the economic instability created by changes in the price of petroleum.

Economy

Since the 1920's, when the nation's oil industry began to boom, Venezuela's leaders have used the income from petroleum exports to pay for massive industrial and modernization programs. A nationwide network of paved roads was built. The skyline of Caracas, Venezuela's capital and largest city, reflects the changes funded by the petroleum profits. High-rise buildings, wide boulevards, and multilaned expressways have transformed Caracas. What was once a quiet colonial city is now a bustling and crowded metropolis.

Although profits from the oil industry have created a well-to-do middle class, the steel and glass towers of Caracas cannot hide the dreadful poverty of the city's slums. Since the 1960's, the government has tried to improve the conditions of the poor through public housing and other programs. But government services have had difficulty keeping up with the swelling population, and many unskilled laborers still crowd into squatter settlements along the outskirts of Caracas and other Venezuelan cities.

Today, Venezuela's leaders face the challenge of reducing the nation's dependence on income from petroleum.

Rising prices led to riots in 1989, and three years later an attempted coup against President Carlos Andrés Pérez failed. The leader of the coup, Colonel Hugo Chaves Frías, was jailed but pardoned in 1994. President Pérez was removed from office in May 1993 on charges of embezzling public funds.

In January 1994, Venezuela's second largest bank failed, causing a financial panic. In February, Rafael Caldera Rodríguez was elected president, a post he had held from 1969 to 1974. Caldera assumed extraordinary powers in June to deal with the financial crisis. A total of 18 banks closed, and economists put the cost of a bailout at $6.1 billion.

Social progress

Compared with some other Latin-American countries, which have a strict class system based on ancestry, Venezuela has an open society. In general, the people are not rigidly

FACT BOX

THE COUNTRY
Official name: República de Venezuela (Republic of Venezuela).
Capital: Caracas.
Land regions: Maracaibo Basin, Andean Highlands, Llanos, Guiana Highlands.
Area: 352,145 sq. mi. (912,050 km^2).
Climate: Tropical. Average temperature varies, depending on altitude.
Main river: Orinoco.
Highest elevation: Pico Bolívar, 16,411 ft. (5,002 m).
Lowest elevation: Sea level along the coast.

THE GOVERNMENT
Form of government: Republic.
Head of state: President.
Head of government: President.
Administrative areas: 20 states, 2 federal territories, 1 federal district, and 72 offshore islands as federal dependencies.
Legislature: National Congress consisting of a 203-member Chamber of Deputies and a 49-member Senate, each elected to 5-year terms.
Court system: Supreme Court of Justice, each state has a superior court and secondary courts.
Armed forces: About 70,500 troops.

THE PEOPLE
Estimated 1996 population: 20,490,000.
Official language: Spanish.
Religion: Roman Catholic (95%).

THE ECONOMY
Currency: Bolívar.
Gross national product (GNP) in 1992: $58.9 billion U.S.
Real annual growth rate (1985–92): 1.1%.
GNP per capita (1992): $2,900 U.S.
Balance of trade (1992): +$1.6 billion U.S.
Goods exported: Aluminum, iron ore, petroleum, and petroleum products.

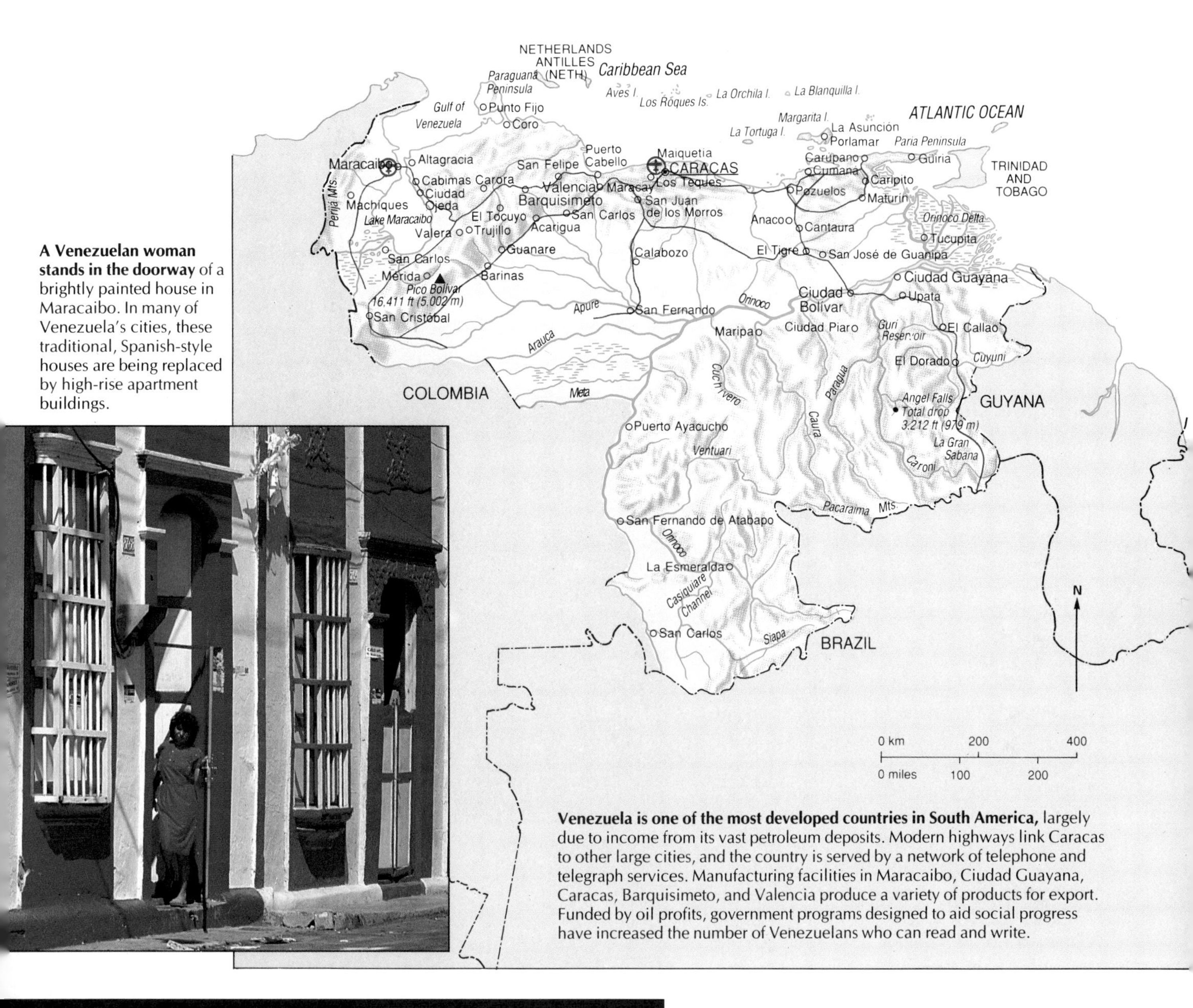

A Venezuelan woman stands in the doorway of a brightly painted house in Maracaibo. In many of Venezuela's cities, these traditional, Spanish-style houses are being replaced by high-rise apartment buildings.

Venezuela is one of the most developed countries in South America, largely due to income from its vast petroleum deposits. Modern highways link Caracas to other large cities, and the country is served by a network of telephone and telegraph services. Manufacturing facilities in Maracaibo, Ciudad Guayana, Caracas, Barquisimeto, and Valencia produce a variety of products for export. Funded by oil profits, government programs designed to aid social progress have increased the number of Venezuelans who can read and write.

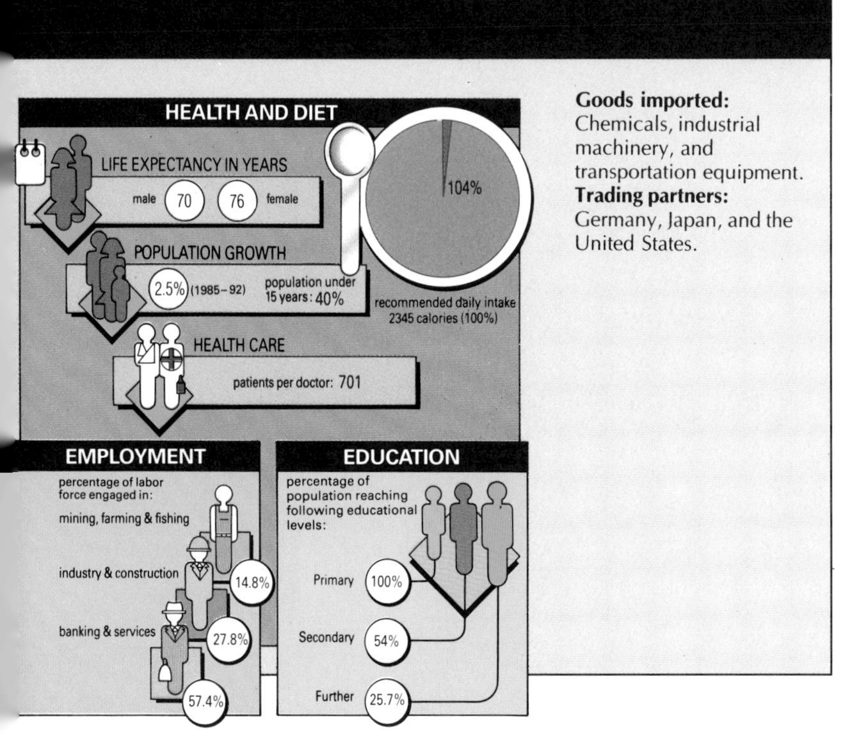

Goods imported: Chemicals, industrial machinery, and transportation equipment.
Trading partners: Germany, Japan, and the United States.

segregated on the basis of racial or class differences.

Although poverty remains a widespread problem, Venezuela has a growing middle class made up of business people, government workers, and doctors, lawyers, teachers, and other professionals. Most middle-class Venezuelans enjoy comfortable lives with many modern benefits, such as Western-style clothing, cars, and vacations.

Since the 1960's, government programs have not only established a social security system, but also improved public health and education. Children between the ages of 7 and 13 must attend school, and free university education is available. But in the early 1990's, Venezuelans endured high inflation, rising unemployment, and worsening crime.

Land and Economy

In addition to its mainland territory, Venezuela has 72 islands off its northern coast in the Caribbean Sea. The nation also claims a large part of Guyana, its neighbor to the east. The Guyanese territory in question includes more than 50,000 square miles (130,000 square kilometers) of land west of the Essequibo River.

A farmer leads his horse to pasture in a lush valley nestled in the Andean Highlands. The two parallel ranges of the Central Highlands enclose many such valleys, where small farms thrive.

Angel Falls, the world's highest waterfall, *above,* creates a magnificent spectacle as the waters plunge 3,212 feet (979 meters) into the Churún River. The falls are named for American pilot Jimmy Angel, who became the first known white person to see them when he flew over them in 1935.

Landscape

A nation of extraordinary natural beauty, Venezuela boasts spectacular waterfalls, swift-flowing rivers, soaring snow-capped mountain peaks, and broad, fertile valleys. Its four land regions reflect the country's scenic variety.

The Maracaibo Basin is located in northwestern Venezuela. It consists of Lake Maracaibo—the largest lake in South America—and the lowlands surrounding it.

The Andean Highlands form a natural boundary between the Maracaibo Basin and the gently sloping plains of the *Llanos.* Most of Venezuela's people live in the Andean Highlands, which include the Mérida Range, the Central Highlands, and the Northeastern Highlands. The capital city of Caracas lies close to the north-central coast, where the Andean Highlands meet the Caribbean Sea.

Huge, sprawling cattle ranches dot the open prairies of the Llanos, where cowhands known as *llaneros* herd their livestock. The region also has some farmland, but the dry climate makes irrigation necessary for such crops as rice and sesame.

The Guiana Highlands, which rise south of the Llanos, cover nearly half of Venezuela and are almost empty of people. Tropical rain forests blanket much of the southern part of the region. The Orinoco River, Venezuela's major waterway, rises in the Guiana Highlands near the Brazilian border.

An abundance of wildlife

Wildlife is plentiful in Venezuela. A variety of mammals, birds, and reptiles—including more than 30 species of eagles—live far from human activity in the forests, mountains, and along the riverbanks. Venezuela's magnificent forests are home to such exotic creatures as tapirs, sloths, anteaters, and a variety of monkeys, as well as such colorful tropical birds as caciques, parrots, and macaws. Puma, deer, and vampire bats live high in the mountains, while crocodiles bask in the lowland rivers.

Economy

Venezuela, one of the world's largest oil producers, gets about 80 per cent of its export earnings from oil. In an effort to reduce its

Huge oil tankers lie at the loading wharfs in the busy port of Barcelona, *right,* which serves the oil fields of the eastern Llanos. The petroleum industry provides about 80 per cent of Venezuela's export earnings.

Venezuela's abundant wildlife, *right,* includes the capuchin (1), the red howler monkey (2), the sloth (3), the tamandua (4), the oilbird, or guacharo (5), the black spider monkey (6), the ocelot (7), the scarlet ibis (8), the anaconda (9), the puma (10), the skunk (11), a reptile called the cayman that is related to the alligator (12), the boat-billed heron (13), the jaguar (14), the anteater (15), the bushmaster, or rattlesnake (16), and the salamander (17).

dependency on oil income, the government has encouraged the growth of manufacturing. In fact, the Guri Dam hydroelectric project spearheaded the construction of one of the largest industrial zones in all of Latin America, at Ciudad Guayana. Today, in addition to petroleum-refining plants in Maracaibo, aluminum and steel are produced in Ciudad Guayana. Venezuelan factories also produce cement, processed foods, and textiles.

Although rich in deposits of petroleum, natural gas, bauxite, coal, diamonds, gold, gypsum, iron ore, and phosphate rock, Venezuela has few areas of very fertile soil. Only about 15 per cent of Venezuela's workers are farmers. They raise bananas, coffee, corn, oranges, and rice. The most highly developed agricultural region is the basin of Lake Valencia.

People

The people of modern Venezuela are the descendants of three very different ethnic groups: the native Indians, the Spanish colonists, and the black slaves brought from Africa during colonial times. Almost all Venezuelans speak Spanish, the country's official language, and follow the Roman Catholic religion. Some Indians in remote regions have preserved their tribal languages and carry on their traditional religious practices.

Today, about two-thirds of Venezuela's population are of mixed ancestry, and the remainder are people of unmixed black, white, or Indian ancestry. The native Indian population of Venezuela was almost completely wiped out during the Spanish conquest of the 1500's. Thousands died in battle, and many others starved to death or fell victim to European diseases. Most of the survivors intermarried with the colonists. As a result, people of unmixed Indian ancestry make up only about 1 per cent of the population.

Since the end of World War II (1939–1945), many Europeans and Colombians have moved to Venezuela. Europeans—mainly from Italy, Spain, and Portugal—were attracted to the country's booming, petroleum-based economy. About 3 million refugees from Colombia have increased Venezuela's already swelling population since the 1970's.

Indians living along Venezuela's rivers travel from village to village in small canoes. Houses on stilts, built by native Americans of the 1500's on Lake Maracaibo, were the inspiration for the name *Venezuela*, which is Spanish for *Little Venice*.

City life

About 90 per cent of Venezuela's people live in cities and towns. In the country's large urban areas, located mainly in the northern valleys and basins of the Andes near the Caribbean, many people live in terrible poverty. About one-third of the entire population of Caracas live in the *barrios* (slum neighborhoods) on the outskirts of the city. Their tumbledown shacks, called *ranchos,* stand in stark contrast to the modern skyscrapers and high-rise apartment buildings that dominate the city's skyline.

The Venezuelans are a sociable people who find much to enjoy in a variety of activities. Colorful fiestas brighten the streets at Easter and Christmas. Baseball and soccer games attract multitudes of fans to the city stadiums. And Venezuelans love music and dancing—from the rhythmic *salsa* dance to the exciting, foot-stamping *joropo,* the national folk dance.

The forest Indians

Far from the sunny sidewalk cafés and crowded streets of Caracas, a small group of Venezuelans live much as their ancestors lived thousands of years ago. They are the nomadic tribes of the Guiana Highlands—wanderers who roam the forests and jungles in small bands—hunting game, fishing for turtles, and gathering fruits, nuts, and berries.

The face of a Venezuelan mestizo, *right,* reveals her mixed white and Indian ancestry. The Venezuelan civil code extended the rights of women in 1982, but women still do not participate fully in the nation's political and economic activities.

An overcrowded shack, *above,* is typical of living conditions in the city *barrios.* In an effort to discourage people from moving to the already overcrowded cities, the government has improved housing and public health facilities in rural areas.

These Indians are one of the few groups of Venezuelans who have resisted modern life and rejected contact with the industrializing outside world.

In the far northwest corner of Venezuela, on the land stretching from the western shore of Lake Maracaibo to the green slopes of the Perija Mountains, stand the small villages of the Motilones. The Motilones, a small, fine-featured people, retreated into the swamps and tropical forests during the Spanish conquest. For 450 years, they kept outsiders at bay with 6-foot (1.8-meter) arrows shot from remarkable black palm bows, which they held between their toes while lying on their backs.

Like the nomadic tribes, the Motilones live much as their ancestors did, cultivating a little land and hunting and fishing for most of their food. As many as 70 people may live in one huge oval hut, its wooden frame held together by rattan cord.

Vietnam

Vietnam, a tropical country on the eastern coast of the Southeast Asian peninsula, is bounded by China on the north, Laos and Cambodia on the west, and the South China Sea on the east. Hanoi is the capital of Vietnam, and Ho Chi Minh City is its largest city and a leading industrial center.

Almost 90 per cent of the country's population are Vietnamese. Other ethnic groups living in Vietnam include the Chinese, the Khmer, and the Montagnards.

Most Vietnamese live in villages on the fertile lands of the coastal plain and on deltas formed by rivers, where they make their living as farmers, raising rice and a few other crops. Some Vietnamese fish for a living, particularly those who live near the coast.

Thousands of years ago, people moved from China to the north and from islands to the south and settled in what is now northern Vietnam. The Vietnamese people, who probably developed out of these two groups, date their history from around 200 B.C., when the Chinese general Zhao Tuo established the independent kingdom of Nam Viet.

Early history

The kingdom of Nam Viet, which stretched from central Vietnam into parts of southeastern China, was conquered by China in 111 B.C. and renamed Jiao Zhi. Then, in A.D. 679, the Chinese changed the name to *Annam,* meaning *pacified south.*

China controlled the northern part of the kingdom, but by the A.D. 100's the kingdoms of Funan and Champa had developed in what is now southern and south-central Vietnam. Funan was conquered by Khmer people during the 500's and 600's, but Champa remained independent until the late 1400's.

In 939, the Chinese withdrew from Annam, and the Vietnamese established an independent state called Dai Co Viet that endured as an empire for over 900 years. The Ly family ruled Dai Co Viet from 1009 until 1225.

In 1225, the Tran family seized power from the Ly rulers and governed the country until 1400. China invaded Dai Co Viet in 1407, but the Vietnamese drove them

out in 1427. The Le family, which had led the fight against China, came to power and renamed the country *Dai Viet* (Great Viet).

Le rulers held the throne until 1787, when they were removed by the Tay Son brothers. The Tay Son also overthrew two other powerful families, the Nguyen and the Trinh, but Nguyen Anh, a member of the conquered Nguyen family, defeated the Tay Son in 1802. Nguyen Anh then declared himself Emperor Gia Long of all Dai Viet, which he renamed Vietnam.

French rule

Roman Catholic missionaries from France began to arrive in Dai Viet in the 1600's. However, Dai Viet's rulers became suspicious of the missionaries and persecuted them through the early 1800's.

In 1858, French military forces began to attack parts of southern Vietnam, partly to stop the persecution of the missionaries and partly because France wanted to become a colonial power in Vietnam. By 1883, the French forced the Nguyen ruler to sign a treaty that gave France control of all Vietnam, and the country was divided into three areas—*Cochin China* (southern Vietnam), *Annam* (central Vietnam), and *Tonkin* (northern Vietnam)—as part of French Indochina.

During World War II (1939-1945), Vietnam was under Japanese control, but after Japan's defeat in August 1945, no single group held power in Vietnam. At that time, Ho Chi Minh, a Vietnamese Communist leader, returned to Vietnam from China as head of the Revolutionary League for the Independence of Vietnam, commonly called the Vietminh. The Vietminh took control of much of northern Vietnam.

In September 1945, Ho proclaimed himself head of the independent Democratic Republic of Vietnam (DRV). The French reestablished control of Cochin China, but they were unable to put down all resistance. On Dec. 19, 1946, fighting broke out between France and the Vietminh—the first battles in a series of wars that would go on almost continuously for nearly 30 years.

Vietnam Today

In April 1975, the Communists gained control of South Vietnam, and in 1976 Vietnam was reunified under Communist rule. The new government initiated a number of programs designed to rebuild the war-torn country. To relieve urban overcrowding and unemployment, large numbers of people were moved from cities to rural areas. The government also sent many southerners to "reeducation" camps, which were essentially concentration camps for political prisoners.

Widespread opposition to these programs led about a million people to leave Vietnam as refugees. In addition, thousands of Chinese were expelled. Many refugees left Vietnam in small boats, risking drowning and pirate attacks in the South China Sea. A large number of these refugees, who became known as *boat people,* eventually settled in the United States.

After the end of the Vietnam War in 1975, Vietnam had troubles with neighboring countries. In 1978, Vietnamese troops helped the Cambodian Communists overthrow the Khmer Rouge and establish a new pro-Vietnamese government in Cambodia. Vietnamese troops then occupied Cambodia for 11 years.

In 1979, China, which had supported the Khmer Rouge, invaded and occupied Vietnam's northern border in retaliation. Continuing friction between Vietnam and China led to border clashes from time to time.

Vietnam depended on the Soviet Union for economic assistance, but by 1988, the Soviet Union had begun to reduce its aid to Vietnam. In an effort to attract investment and aid from Western nations, the government introduced reforms that allowed some private enterprise.

Vietnamese leaders hoped that their

The tomb of Ho Chi Minh, president of North Vietnam from 1954 until his death in 1969, overlooks a street in Hanoi, once the capital of North Vietnam and now the capital of unified Vietnam. Saigon, the former capital of South Vietnam, was renamed Ho Chi Minh City.

FACT BOX

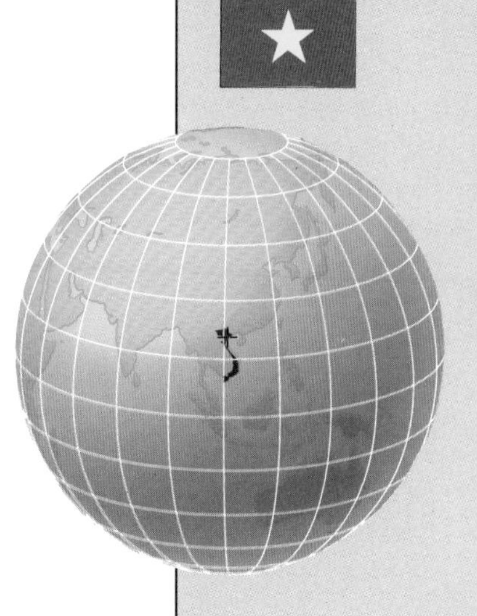

THE COUNTRY
Official name: Cong Hoa Xa Hoi Chu Nghia Viet-nam (Socialist Republic of Vietnam).
Capital: Hanoi.
Land regions: Northern Highlands, Red River Delta, Annamite Range, Coastal Lowlands, Mekong Delta.
Area: 128,066 sq. mi. (331,689 km²).
Climate: Tropical, with monsoons throughout the year. Most of Vietnam has two seasons: a wet, hot summer and a drier, slightly cooler winter. Some northern areas have four seasons.
Main rivers: Mekong, Red.
Highest elevation: Fan Si Pan, 10,312 ft. (3,143 m).
Lowest elevation: Sea level along the coast.

THE GOVERNMENT
Form of government: Communist state.
Head of state: Chairman of Council of State.
Head of government: Chairman of Council of Ministers (Premier).
Administrative areas: 36 provinces, 3 cities independent of provinces, 1 special zone.
Legislature: National Assembly, with 496 members elected to five-year terms.
Court system: People's Supreme Court, local people's courts, and military courts.
Armed forces: About 1,100,000 regular troops and 2,000,000 paramilitary troops.

THE PEOPLE
Estimated 1996 population: 75,280,000.
Official language: Vietnamese.
Religions: Buddhism (55%), New religionism (11%), Roman Catholicism (4%).

The Republic of Vietnam is called a "republic and a dictatorship of the working class" by the country's leaders, but the government is rigidly controlled by the Communist Party. Government efforts to improve the economy have not succeeded, and Vietnam is an extremely poor nation.

withdrawal from Cambodia in September 1989 would open the way for foreign assistance. But the United States maintained the trade embargo imposed on Vietnam in 1975 following the Communist take-over.

In August 1990, the United Nations (UN) negotiated a peace plan calling for a supervised cease-fire in Cambodia and the establishment of a new coalition government. In 1991, U.S. officials outlined a four-step plan for normalizing relations with Vietnam. The U.S. embargo on trade was lifted in February 1994, and the two countries agreed to open liaison offices in Hanoi and Washington, D.C.

Also in 1994, many Vietnamese people who had emigrated after the Communist take-over returned. They brought expertise and money with them, and Vietnam's economy expanded by 10.5 per cent in the first half of the year. But summer floods in the Mekong Delta Valley killed 300 people and reduced the nation's important rice crop. Foreign investors, particularly from Taiwan and Hong Kong, began to invest in Vietnam. In mid-1995, Vietnam was expected to join the Association of Southeast Asian Nations (ASEAN), a group of countries that promotes cooperation among its members.

HEALTH AND DIET

LIFE EXPECTANCY IN YEARS: male 63, female 67

POPULATION GROWTH: 2.3% (1985–92); population under 15 years: 39%

Recommended daily intake 2345 calories (100%): 106%

HEALTH CARE: patients per doctor: 3,067

EMPLOYMENT

percentage of labor force engaged in:

mining, farming & fishing 70.2%

industry & construction 14%

banking & services 15.8%

EDUCATION

percentage of population reaching following educational levels:

Primary 100%

Secondary 42%

Further 2.3%

THE ECONOMY
Currency: Dong.
Gross national product (GNP) in 1992 (est.): $16 billion U.S.
Real annual growth rate 1992 (est.): 7.4%.
GNP per capita (1992 est.): $230 U.S.
Balance of trade (1992): +$400 million U.S.
Goods exported: Bamboo and rattan products, coal, peanuts, refined petroleum products, rice, rubber, and tea.
Goods imported: Food, machinery, medicines, military supplies, petroleum, and vehicles.
Trading partners: Hong Kong, Japan, and Singapore.

The Vietnam Wars

When World War II ended in 1945, Communist leader Ho Chi Minh and the Revolutionary League for the Independence of Vietnam (Vietminh) quickly took control of many areas of Vietnam, particularly the north, and established the Democratic Republic of Vietnam (DRV). The new government was also supported by many non-Communists who did not want to return to French colonial rule. Meanwhile, France regained control of Cochin China in southern Vietnam, but was unable to put down all resistance. In December 1946, Vietminh forces attacked the French in Hanoi and the Indochina War began.

Although the French retained control of the cities in Vietnam, they were unable to gain power in the countryside. The Vietminh waged a guerrilla war in the hills and forests, shooting at French soldiers and escaping before the French could mobilize their forces.

In 1953, France established a base at the village of Dien Bien Phu in northwestern Vietnam to disrupt Vietminh operations. However, in 1954, about 50,000 Vietminh soldiers destroyed the French base, and France's defeat at the Battle of Dien Bien Phu ended its claim to the area.

The Geneva Accords, held between May and July 1954, arranged a cease-fire that ended the war between the French and the Vietminh. The agreements temporarily divided Vietnam into North Vietnam and South Vietnam and called for elections in 1956 to reunify the country. These elections were never held, however. President Ngo Dinh Diem of South Vietnam, fearing a Communist victory, would not let them take place. Both sides violated the cease-fire, and in 1957 South Vietnamese Communist guerrillas called the Viet Cong began the fighting that grew into the Vietnam War.

By 1960, the Viet Cong had about 10,000 troops and threatened to overthrow Diem's government. In support of the South Vietnamese government, the United States increased its military advisers in the country from about 900 in 1961 to more than 16,000 by 1963.

Then in 1964, President Lyndon B. Johnson announced that two U.S. destroyers had been attacked in the Gulf of Tonkin, off the coast of North Vietnam. As a result, Congress approved the Gulf of Tonkin Resolution, which allowed the President to take any action necessary against further aggression. Although the United States never declared war on North Vietnam, the 1964 resolution was used as the legal basis for increased U.S. military involvement, and by 1969 the United States had more than 543,000 troops in Vietnam. The U.S. forces fought alongside about 800,000 South Vietnamese troops and some 69,000 allied soldiers.

The United States relied mainly on massive bombing raids in North Vietnam and ground missions in South Vietnam to defeat the enemy. In contrast, the Communist

North Vietnamese soldiers carry portraits of Ho Chi Minh through Saigon following the Communist victory in April 1975. Saigon, the capital of South Vietnam, was renamed Ho Chi Minh City after the take-over.

South Vietnam's countryside was scarred by U.S. bombing raids and by the spraying of plant-killing chemicals such as Agent Orange. The United States used these chemicals to reveal Communist hiding places in the jungle and to destroy their crops.

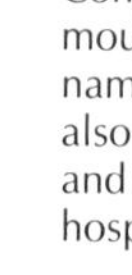

American combat helicopters landed troops on "search and destroy" missions to seek out Viet Cong in the jungles and mountains of South Vietnam. Helicopters were also used to carry supplies and take the wounded to hospitals.

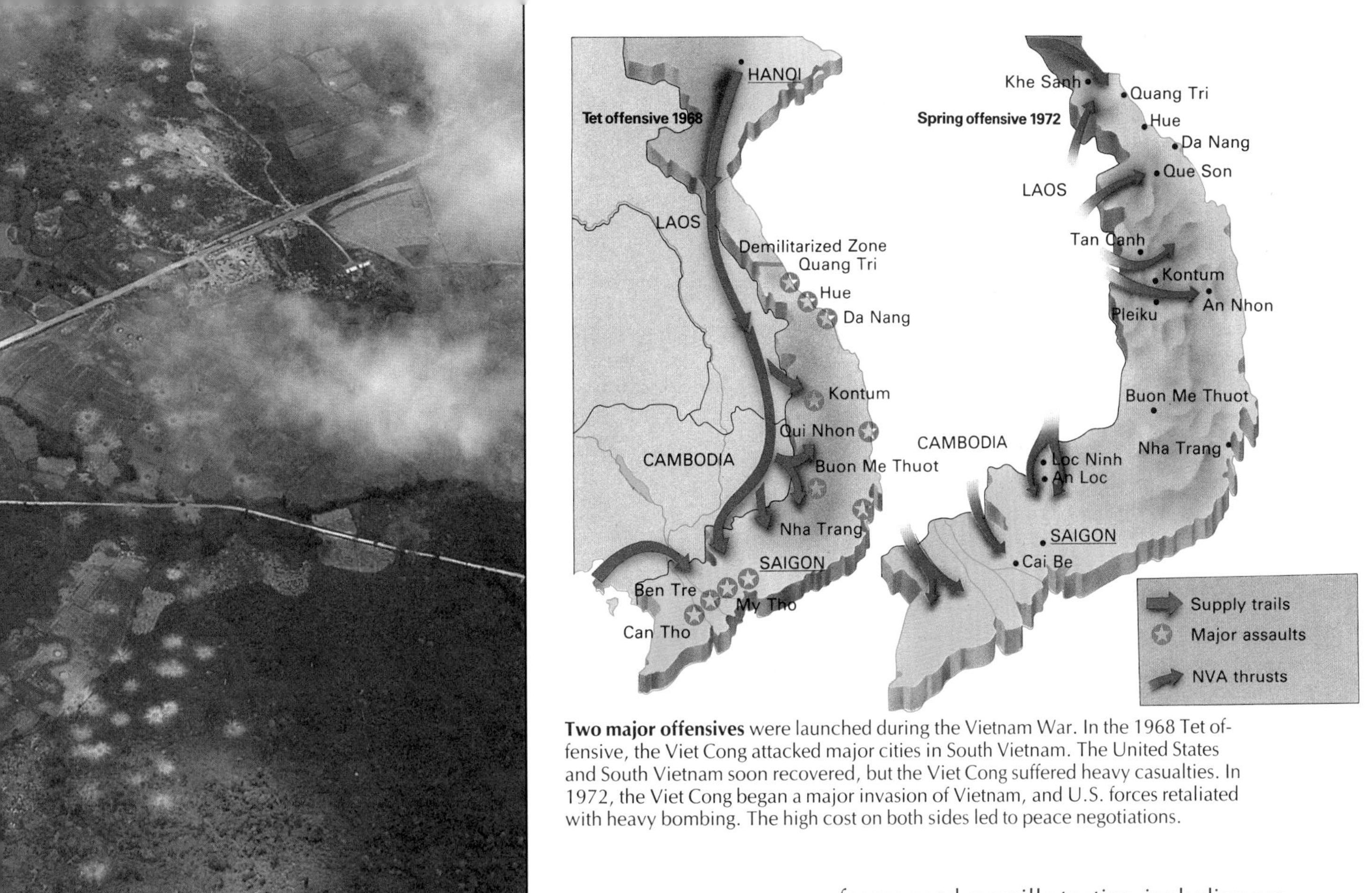

Two major offensives were launched during the Vietnam War. In the 1968 Tet offensive, the Viet Cong attacked major cities in South Vietnam. The United States and South Vietnam soon recovered, but the Viet Cong suffered heavy casualties. In 1972, the Viet Cong began a major invasion of Vietnam, and U.S. forces retaliated with heavy bombing. The high cost on both sides led to peace negotiations.

forces used guerrilla tactics, including ambushes and hand-laid bombs. Their knowledge of the terrain, along with plentiful war supplies from the Soviet Union and China, aided this strategy.

As the fighting dragged on, many Americans—seeing the horrors of war revealed on television—began to oppose U.S. involvement in Vietnam. Antiwar demonstrations took place throughout the United States in the late 1960's and early 1970's, and opposition grew even more intense in 1970 when National Guard units killed four students and wounded nine others during a demonstration at Kent State University.

Heavy fighting and casualties on both sides led to peace negotiations in 1972, and in 1973, a cease-fire agreement was signed. North Vietnamese and Viet Cong troops resumed attacking South Vietnam, however, and the war continued—but without U.S. involvement. On April 30, 1975, when South Vietnam surrendered to North Vietnam, the war that had taken the lives of about 58,000 Americans and wounded 365,000 more finally ended. Nearly 2 million North Vietnamese and South Vietnamese soldiers were killed in the fighting, as well as countless Vietnamese civilians.

South Vietnamese refugees left the country in large numbers after the war. Fleeing poverty and government oppression, the so-called boat people risked pirate attacks as well as the treacherous waters of the South China Sea.

An orphaned Vietnamese baby rides in a basket carried by an American soldier, *left*. Ground operations in South Vietnam killed many civilians.

Land and People

Vietnam's outline has reminded some people of two rice baskets hanging from opposite ends of a farmer's carrying pole. The Red River Delta in the north represents one "basket," and the Mekong Delta in the south represents the other, while the narrow stretch of land in central Vietnam forms the "pole." The long, narrow land of Vietnam can be divided into five main land regions—the Northern Highlands, the Red River Delta, the Annamite Range, the Coastal Lowlands, and the Mekong Delta.

The Northern Highlands in northwestern Vietnam extend into China and Laos. Forests and jungles cover most of this thinly populated region, and the country's highest peak, Fan Si Pan, soars 10,312 feet (3,143 meters) in the highlands.

Most of the Red River Delta on the Gulf of Tonkin lies only 10 feet (3 meters) or less above sea level, and the Red River, which flows through northern Vietnam into the gulf, floods much of the delta almost every year. This densely populated region is northern Vietnam's chief farming area.

The Annamite Range in western Vietnam runs from the Northern Highlands to about 50 miles (80 kilometers) north of Ho Chi Minh City. Forests cover most of this thinly populated mountain chain.

The Coastal Lowlands, a densely populated region in east-central Vietnam, stretch from the Red River Delta to the Mekong Delta and slope from the mountains to the South China Sea. At their narrowest point, the lowlands are only about 30 miles (48 kilometers) wide. Rice is raised in this area, and many people along the coast fish for a living.

The Mekong Delta was formed by the Mekong River, which flows from China through Southeast Asia into the South China Sea. The Mekong Delta extends over much of southern Vietnam and, like the Red River Delta, lies 10 feet (3 meters) or less above sea level. This region is the nation's chief agricultural area, and more than 50 per cent of southern Vietnam's people live there.

The Vietnamese people, who make up almost 90 per cent of the country's population, are generally small in stature, with broad faces, high cheekbones, and straight black hair. Most of the Vietnamese people live in the deltas and on the coastal plain.

Much of the rest of the population is made up of Chinese, Khmer, and Montagnards peoples. Most of the Chinese live in Vietnam's cities, though thousands were expelled at the end of the Vietnam War and many left the country as refugees. Most of the Khmer farm the southwestern areas bordering Cambodia, while the Montagnards, who are divided into many tribal groups, live in the mountains.

Most of the people in Vietnam live in villages and farm the land. Rural life has

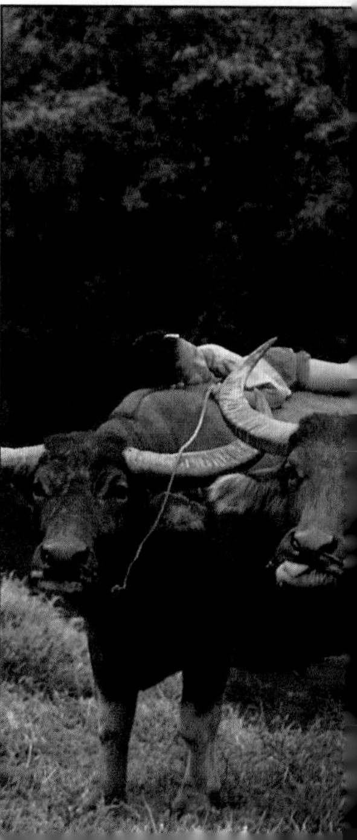

Workers harvest rice, Vietnam's staple crop, *far left.* About 35 per cent of the country's land is suitable for farming, but only about 15 per cent is cultivated.

Street vendors sell vegetables in Ho Chi Minh City. The market places are crowded with peddlers who often display their goods on the sidewalks.

Rafting goods down the Mekong River is an age-old method of transportation still carried on in Vietnam. The Mekong and its branches are important waterways throughout Southeast Asia.

The music of a bamboo flute lightens the tasks of farm children as they tend gentle water buffaloes. These powerful animals can plow a field even when they are knee deep in mud, and are highly valued by rice farmers.

traditionally been built on strong family ties where people set family interests above their own. The eldest male was head of the family, parents chose their children's marriage partners, and families honored their ancestors in special ceremonies.

This way of life began to change in the late 1800's when the French gained control of Vietnam and brought industry to the country. Many Vietnamese left the farms to work in the city factories.

However, the Vietnam War and its aftermath brought the most radical changes to Vietnamese life. To begin with, the war broke up families, as fathers, husbands, and sons left home to fight. In addition, the bombing of the countryside often drove rural people into the cities, where they learned Western customs from U.S. soldiers stationed there. After the war, the Communist government controlled every aspect of the people's lives. They urged women to perform the same jobs as men, and discouraged religion and the traditional honoring of ancestors.

The Vietnam War also disrupted the nation's educational system, and the government has been unable to provide the funding required to restore it. Nevertheless, most of the Vietnamese people can read and write.

Virgin Islands, The British

Together with the U.S. Virgin Islands, the British Virgin Islands form the group known collectively as the Virgin Islands. The British Virgin Islands consist of more than 60 islands, including Anegada, Jost van Dyke, Tortola, and Virgin Gorda islands, and their surrounding islets.

The British Virgin Islands are far less developed than their U.S. counterparts. This may be partly due to the more favorable geographical position of the U.S. islands, which face the Caribbean Sea. The British Virgin Islands, on the other hand, look outward toward the vast Atlantic Ocean.

The culture of the British Virgin Islands also contrasts with the distinctive blend of African, Danish, and American influences found on the U.S. islands. Many qualities of the British way of life are preserved on these tiny Caribbean islands.

In the British Virgin Islands, cars are driven on the left side of the road, as in Great Britain. Like most British people, most islanders are Protestants. They celebrate the birthdays of Queen Elizabeth II and the Prince of Wales as national holidays, and hotels serve afternoon tea—a long-standing British tradition. In the heat of the tropics, though, the tea is usually iced.

An islander wears a straw hat for protection against the tropical sun as he rides his donkey into town. In the rural areas of the islands, most people live in small wooden huts with thatched roofs.

Island life

The British Virgin Islands have been under the British flag since 1672. Only 16 of the more than 60 islands in the group are inhabited, and about 80 per cent of the people live on Tortola, the largest island. Many islanders work in the tourism industry, the backbone of the islands' economy.

Despite a steady stream of vacationers arriving from all corners of the globe, the tourism industry has so far left the islands relatively undisturbed. Resort developers have worked hard to prevent the destruction of natural habitats as they build hotel and restaurant facilities.

Most of the British Virgin Islands are hilly. The only exception of significant size is Anegada, a flat coral and limestone island surrounded by outstanding diving areas. And in the underwater world of Horse Shoe Reef, adventurous divers can see more than 300 shipwrecks, as well as a variety of colorful marine life.

Tortola and Virgin Gorda

Tortola has a number of magnificent beaches, including those at Apple Bay and Belmint Bay. From the Road Town marina, studded with sleek and stylish yachts, many tourists take a boat to Dead Chest to see the famous coral reefs, or to Norman Island, said to be the inspiration for Robert Louis Stevenson's novel *Treasure Island.*

Nature lovers seeking peace and quiet often visit Virgin Gorda, the second largest of the British Virgin Islands. Beautiful beaches stretch along Virgin Gorda's southern coast, while steep cliffs line the north coast. Virgin Gorda also has magnificent natural caves. At Copper Mine Point, tourists may visit abandoned mines where Spaniards dug for copper, gold, and silver more than 400 years ago.

Hills covered by lush tropical vegetation form a backdrop for the sparkling blue water and palm-shaded beach at Deadmans Bay on Peter Island. The climate in the British Virgin Islands is warm and pleasant throughout the year.

This tiny island near Beef Island, *bottom left,* can be reached only by boat. The British Virgin Islands' main airport is on Beef Island.

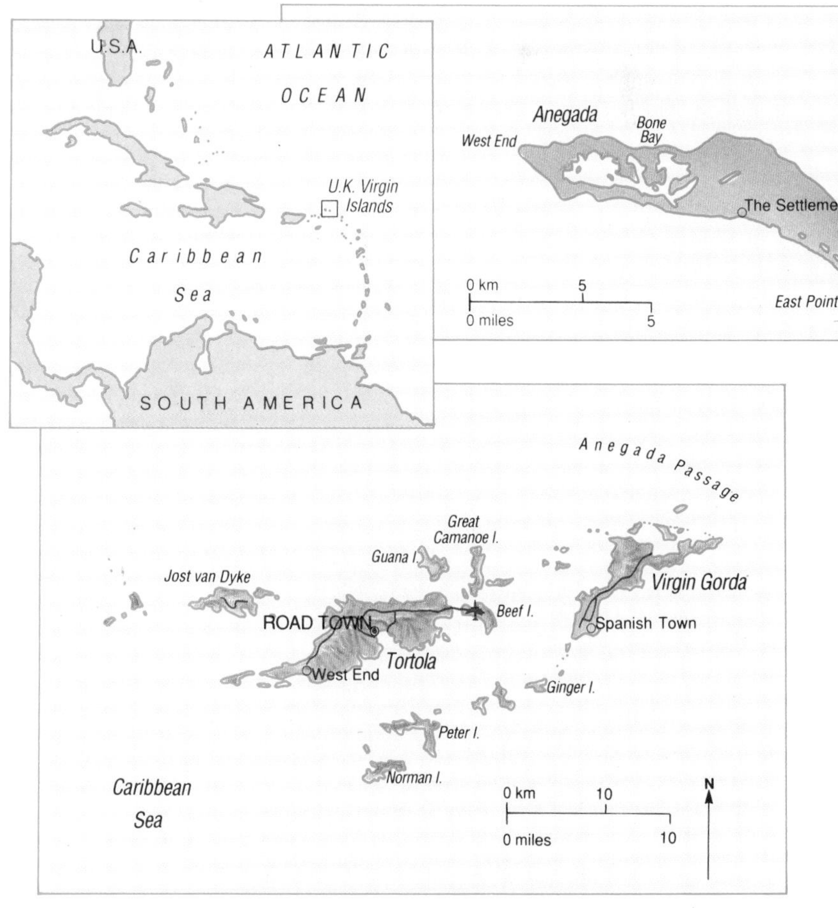

The British Virgin Islands lie near the western end of the Lesser Antilles and cover a land area of 59 square miles (153 square kilometers). A channel called *The Narrows* separates the group from the U.S. Virgin Islands.

Virgin Islands, The U.S.

The easternmost possession of the United States, the U.S. Virgin Islands include St. Croix, St. John, and St. Thomas islands, along with many nearby islets. Together with the British Virgin Islands, they are part of the Leeward Islands group of the Lesser Antilles.

The U.S. Virgin Islands are a self-governing territory of the United States. The people elect a governor, who serves a four-year term, and a one-house legislature of 15 senators, elected for two-year terms. The islanders also elect one delegate to the U.S. House of Representatives, but the delegate may vote only in House committees.

Christopher Columbus was the first European to discover the great natural beauty of the Virgin Islands, sighting the islands on his second voyage to the New World in 1493. Columbus was so captivated by the unspoiled appearance of the many hills rising from the sea that he named the group the Virgin Islands, in memory of the 11,000 maidens who, according to legend, were guided by St. Ursula, a Roman Catholic saint.

St. Croix is the largest of the U.S. Virgin Islands, making up about two-thirds of the island group's area. St. Thomas is the second largest island, and St. John, the third largest. Fossils of ancient animals show that the islands were covered by the sea until volcanoes pushed the land up from the ocean floor. Except for St. Croix, the islands are rugged and hilly.

Cruise ships and yachts crowd the harbor of Charlotte Amalie on the island of St. Thomas. Beautiful scenery, fine beaches, and a warm, tropical climate make the U.S. Virgin Islands a favorite with vacationers, who spend more than $400 million there annually.

The composition of the rocks that form much of the land on the U.S. Virgin Islands, *right,* suggests that volcanoes pushed the islands up from the ocean floor.

Early history

Although Columbus claimed the Virgin Islands for Spain, the Spaniards did not settle there, but they used the islands as places to hide their treasure ships from pirates. It was not until 1625 that British and Dutch colonists established settlements on St. Croix. By then, the Carib Indians—the islands' original inhabitants—had either died or left the islands.

In the mid-1600's, Spaniards from Puerto Rico drove out the British and Dutch settlers, but the French defeated the Spaniards within 20 years. The French controlled St. Croix until 1733, when they sold it for $150,000 to the Danes, who had formally claimed St. Thomas in 1666. The Danish West Indies, which then included St. Croix, St. John, and St. Thomas, remained mainly under Danish control until 1917.

On Jan. 17, 1917, Denmark formally transferred ownership to the United States, who paid $25 million for the islands. Ten years later, the U.S. Congress passed a law making the people of the Virgin Islands citizens of the United States.

Tourism

The U.S. Virgin Islands attract more than 1 million vacationers a year, making tourism the islands' major industry, with more than half the islanders employed in tourist-related jobs. Others work in government jobs and in

the rum distilleries, while some make their living as farmers.

On St. Croix, tourists enjoy exploring the towns of Christiansted and Frederiksted, where the charm of old Denmark can still be seen in pastel-colored buildings with red tile roofs. On St. Thomas, tourists enjoy duty-free shopping for imported luxury goods in the bustling port of Charlotte Amalie. St. John is a natural paradise where more than 250 species of trees, flowers, and other plant life flourish in the Virgin Islands National Park, which covers about three-fourths of the island.

The total area of the U.S. Virgin Islands is 132 square miles (342 square kilometers). St. Croix, the largest island, covers 82 square miles (212 square kilometers); St. Thomas covers 27 square miles (70 square kilometers); and St. John is 19 square miles (49 square kilometers). Charlotte Amalie, on St. Thomas, is the capital of the U.S. Virgin Islands.

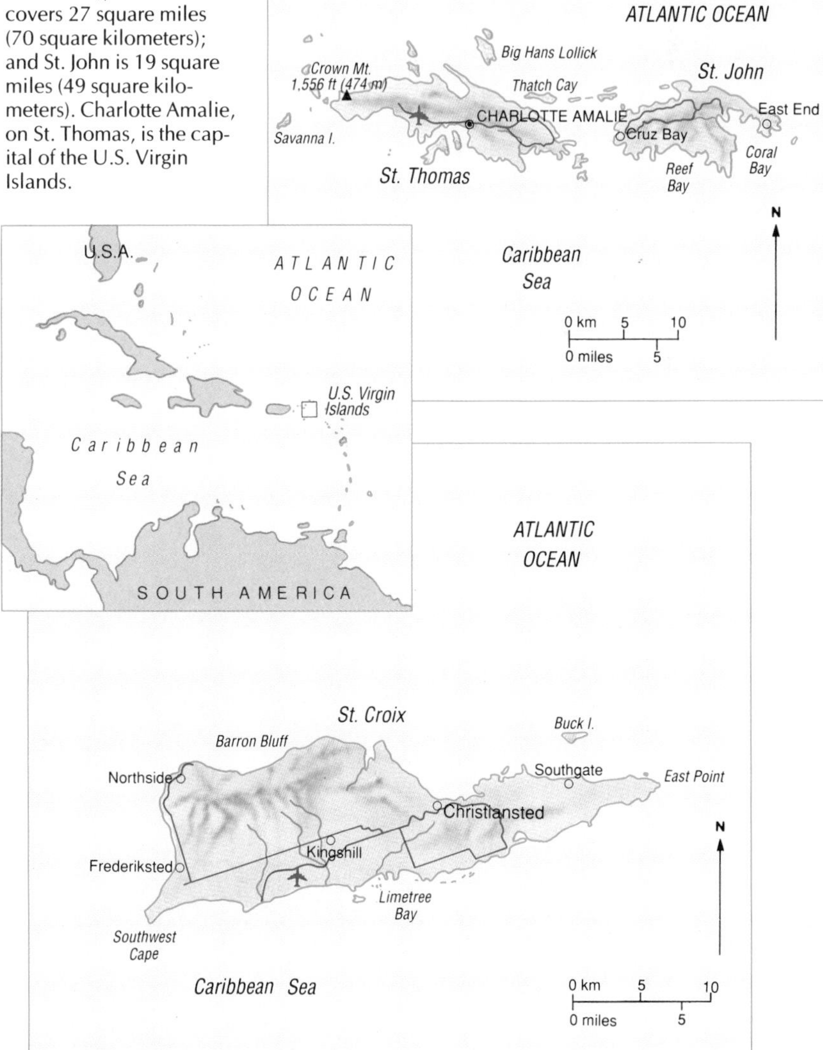

Western Sahara

Western Sahara is a desert land on the northwestern coast of Africa. It lies between Morocco to the north, Algeria to the east, Mauritania to the east and south, and the Atlantic Ocean to the west.

Western Sahara is exactly what its name implies—the western end of the vast Sahara, a barren, rocky desert. Plant life is sparse except for patches of coarse grass and low bushes near the coast.

About 180,000 people live in Western Sahara—mainly Arabs and Berbers. The exact population is hard to determine because most of the people are nomads who move around the area in search of water and pasture for their herds of camels, goats, and sheep.

Western Sahara is rich in phosphates. These valuable chemicals are used as fertilizers and in making some detergents. Large deposits of phosphates have been found near Bu Craa. Fish are plentiful off the Atlantic coast and provide a second valuable export.

The fight for Western Sahara

Today, possession of the territory of Western Sahara is disputed. Morocco claims the region, but its claim is opposed by some of the people who live in Western Sahara, as well as by Algeria.

The land was claimed by foreign powers as far back as 1509, when Spain claimed the area. Morocco then ruled the region from 1524 until Spain regained control in 1860—a period of almost 350 years. In 1958, Spain declared the area one of its provinces and called it the Province of Spanish Sahara.

In 1975, tens of thousands of Moroccans crossed their southern border into Spanish Sahara in support of King Hassan II of Morocco, who claimed the northern portion of Spanish Sahara for his country. Spain relinquished its claim to Spanish Sahara in 1976 and gave control of the region to both Morocco and Mauritania. The area then came to be called Western Sahara.

Morocco claimed northern Western Sahara, and Mauritania claimed the southern portion of the land. However, the country of Algeria and a group of Western Saharans called the Polisario Front protested these claims and demanded independence for the region.

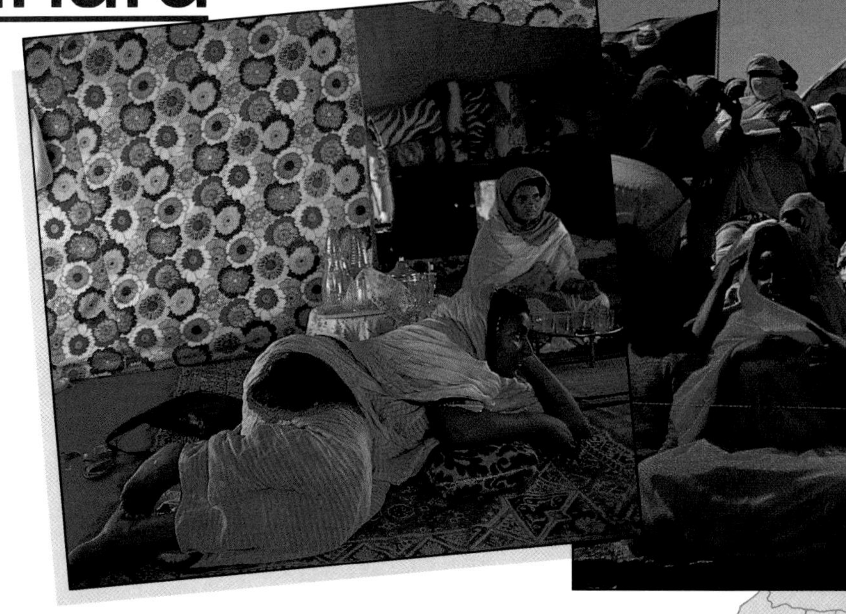

Berber women in the south of Western Sahara relax on beautiful carpets inside a tent that shelters them from the merciless heat of the Sahara.

The Saharawis, the inhabitants of Western Sahara, are of mixed Arab and Berber descent. Since 1976, when the Polisario Front began fighting Morocco and Mauritania over control of the region, many Saharawis have settled in refugee camps in Algeria.

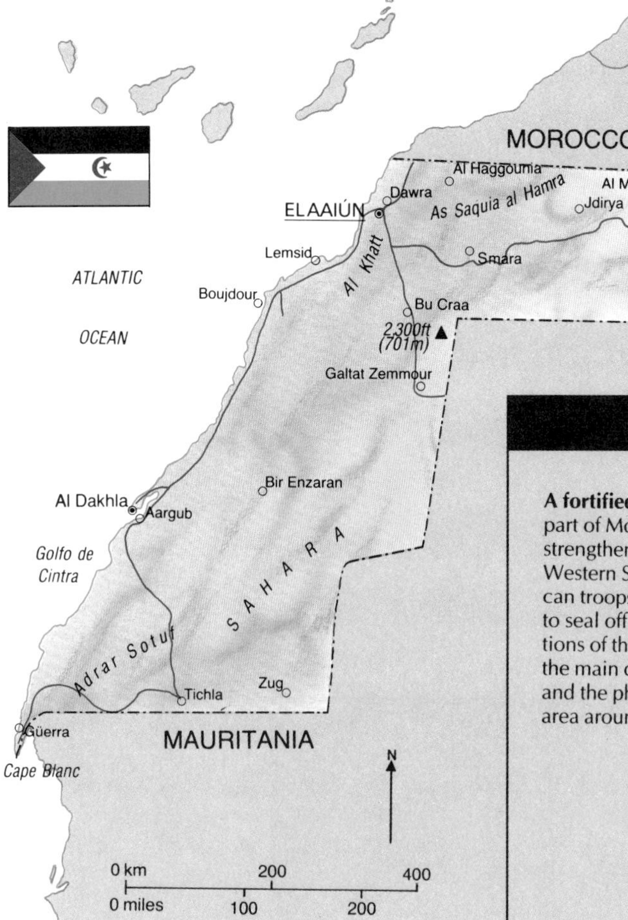

A fortified sand wall is part of Morocco's plan to strengthen its claim to Western Sahara. Moroccan troops built the wall to seal off important sections of the region, such as the main city of El Aaiún and the phosphate-rich area around Bu Craa.

Fighting broke out between the Polisario Front and Moroccan and Mauritanian troops. Algeria provided military aid for the Polisario Front. Later, Libya also aided the independence movement.

In 1979, Mauritania gave up its claim to the southern part of Western Sahara and withdrew its troops. Morocco then claimed the southern area as well.

Continuing conflict

During the 1980's, Moroccan troops built a 2,000-mile (3,200-kilometer) wall to seal off the most valuable areas of Western Sahara. A fortified defense line made of barbed wire and sandbanks and equipped with electronic sensors and minefields, the wall stretches from the Moroccan border southwest to the Atlantic coast.

In 1984, Morocco and Libya signed a treaty of unity, and Libya agreed to stop aiding the Polisario Front. But the agreement fell apart in 1986. Fighting continued until 1991, when a United Nations-sponsored cease-fire took effect.

Children celebrate the founding of the Polisario Front, *left,* a nationalist group that opposes Morocco's claim to Western Sahara.

The state in conflict

Under Moroccan control in 1984
Earthworks
Phosphate conveyor belt
MOROCCO
ALGERIA
EL AAIÚN
Al Mahbes
Jdirya
Smara
Bu Craa
MAURITANIA
WESTERN SAHARA
Dakhla
Zug

Official name: Western Sahara.
Main city: El Aaiún.
Land region: Sahara.
Area: 102,700 sq. mi. (266,000 km²).
Climate: Hot and dry.

THE GOVERNMENT
Administered by Morocco, territory disputed by Morocco and Polisario Front.

THE PEOPLE
Estimated 1990 population: About 180,000.
Languages: Arabic, Berber.
Religion: Islam (100%).

THE ECONOMY
Currency: Moroccan dirham.
Goods exported: Fish, phosphates.
No data are available for goods imported, gross national product, annual growth rate, balance of trade, or trading partners.

1509	Spain claims area.
1524-1860	Morocco rules region.
1860-1976	Spain rules region.
1958	Province of Spanish Sahara established.
1963	Large phosphate deposits found at Bu Craa.
1975	Moroccans move into Spanish Sahara.
1976	Spain gives area to Morocco and Mauritania. Region renamed Western Sahara. Fighting by Polisario Front begins.
1979	Mauritania gives up its claim. Morocco claims entire region.
1980's	Morocco builds sand wall. Attempts to reach peaceful agreement fail.
1991	U.N. cease-fire takes effect.

Western Samoa

Western Samoa is an independent island country in the Pacific Ocean, about 1,700 miles (2,740 kilometers) northeast of New Zealand. It is one of the smallest countries in the world. Western Samoa consists of two main islands, Upolu and Savai'i, and several smaller islands. The islands were formed by erupting volcanoes. Tropical rain forests cover the high volcanic peaks at the center of the islands, while the shores are lined with tall, graceful coconut palms and fringed with coral reefs.

Way of life

A Samoan *matai*, the chief of an extended family, is elected by the family group. The chiefs, in turn, elect the members of the country's Legislative Assembly.

Most Samoans are Polynesian and live with their relatives in extended family groups called *aiga*. The aiga elects a head of the family, called a *matai*. Some of the younger Samoans resent the matai's power, but the system is still strong.

The people speak Samoan, a Polynesian dialect. Some Samoans also speak English. Most of the people can read and write Samoan, and about 50 per cent can read and write English. Almost all Samoans are Christians.

The people of Western Samoa live in open-sided houses that have a thatched roof supported by poles. Most Samoan men wear a *lava-lava*, a piece of cloth that is wrapped around the waist like a skirt and sometimes worn with a blouse or shirt. Most of the women wear a long lava-lava and an upper garment called a *puletasi*.

Western Samoa's economy is based on agriculture, and about 60 per cent of the people are farmers. The chief food crops are bananas, coconuts, breadfruit, and *taro* (a starchy tuber). The people also raise pigs and chickens and catch fish for food. The average annual income in Samoa is very low by world standards, but most Samoans have little need for money. They raise most of their own food, build their own houses, and make most of their own clothing.

History and government

People have lived in Samoa for at least 2,000 years, probably migrating there from what are now Fiji and Vanuatu. The Samoans began forming their own nation about 1,000 years ago. Many chiefs ruled the people until a woman, Salamasina, united them in the 1500's.

The first European to visit the islands, a Dutch explorer named Jacob Roggeveen, arrived in 1722, but few others followed until the first mission was established in Savai'i in 1830. During the mid-1800's, two royal families ruled different parts of Samoa and fought over who would be king. Germany, Great Britain, and the United States supported rival

FACT BOX

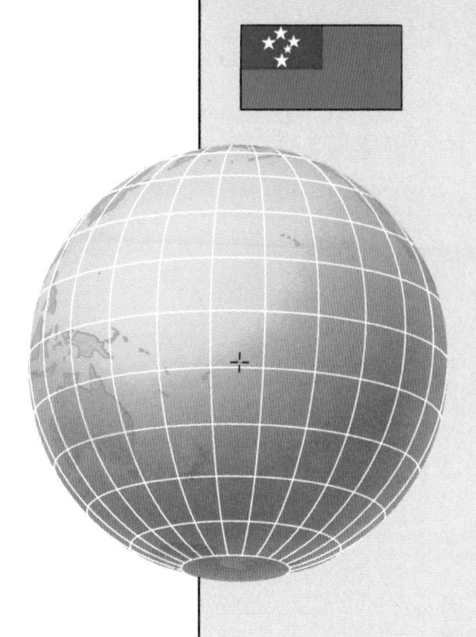

THE COUNTRY
Official name: Samoa i Sisifo (Western Samoa).
Capital: Apia.
Land regions: Two main islands and several smaller ones.
Area: 1,093 sq. mi. (2,831 km²).
Climate: Tropical and humid.
Highest elevation: Mt. Silisili, 6,095 ft. (1,858 m).
Lowest elevation: Sea level.

THE GOVERNMENT
Form of government: Constitutional monarchy.
Head of state: Head of State (current head holds office for life; future heads will be elected to 5-year terms).
Head of government: Prime minister.
Administrative areas: 11 districts.
Legislature: Legislative Assembly with 47 members elected to 3-year terms.
Court system: Supreme Court, Court of Appeal, magistrates' court, and land and title court.

THE PEOPLE
Estimated 1996 population: 160,000.
Official languages: Samoan and English.
Religions: Protestant (68%), Roman Catholic (21%).

THE ECONOMY
Currency: Tala.
Gross national product (GNP) in 1992: $153 million U.S.
Real annual growth rate (1985–92): −0.1%.
GNP per capita (1992): $940 U.S.
Balance of trade (1990): −$66 million U.S.
Goods exported: Bananas, cacao, and copra.
Goods imported: Manufactured goods, petroleum, and processed foods.
Trading partners: Australia, Germany, Great Britain, Japan, New Zealand, and the United States.

Western Samoa, one of the smallest countries in the world, lies about 1,700 miles (2,740 kilometers) northeast of New Zealand. The nation consists of two main islands—Upolu and Savai'i—and several smaller islands.

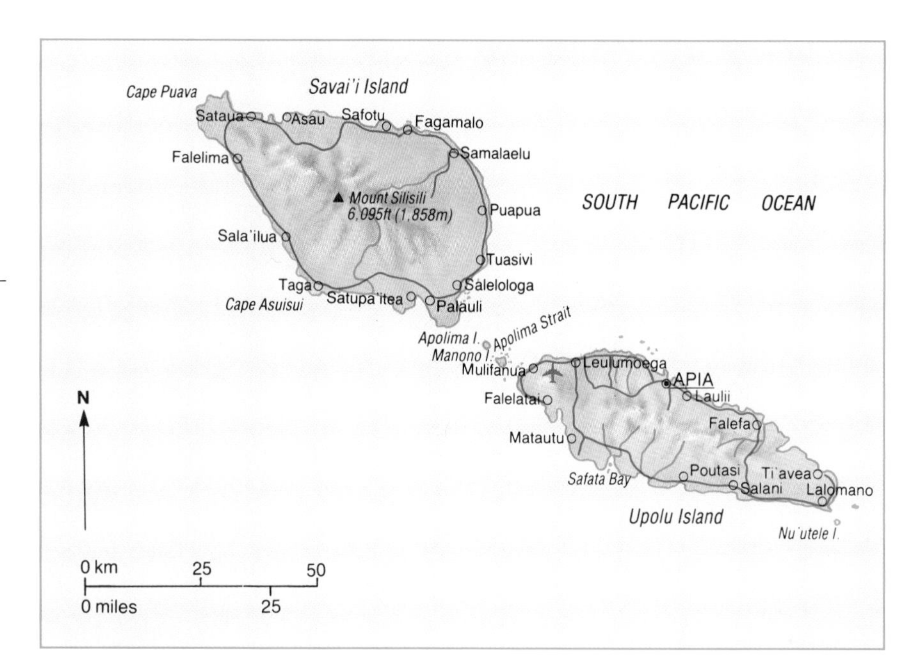

groups. In 1899, the three countries agreed that Germany and the United States would divide the islands and, in 1900, Germany took control of Western Samoa.

During World War I (1914–1918), New Zealand occupied the islands. The New Zealand government became increasingly unpopular, and eventually Samoans refused to obey laws or cooperate with the government. After World War II (1939–1945), the United Nations made Western Samoa a trust territory and asked New Zealand to prepare the islands for independence. Western Samoa became independent in 1962.

The country has a 47-member Legislative Assembly that elects the prime minister and passes laws. The prime minister runs the government with a Cabinet selected from among the Assembly members. Laws passed by the Assembly do not go into effect until the head of state approves them.

Rich vegetation, *top,* covers the fertile land near a coastal inlet. Farther inland, tropical rain forests blanket high volcanic peaks.

A beach in Western Samoa provides a scenic location for a kindergarten class. Education is free but not compulsory in Western Samoa. Most villages have government-run elementary schools.

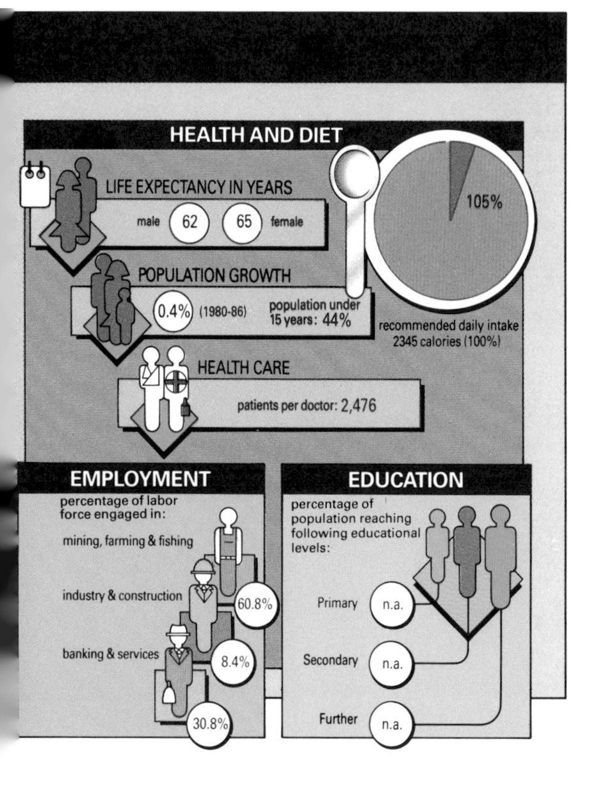

Yemen

Along the southern tip of the Arabian Peninsula lies the elbow-shaped country of Yemen. Its shores touch the Red Sea to the west and the Gulf of Aden to the south. The deserts of Saudi Arabia and Oman lie to the north and east.

Although most of Yemen is hot and dry, the country's high northwestern interior is the most beautiful and cultivated part of the Arabian Peninsula.

Lowlands, highlands, and desert

Yemen has three major land regions. A coastal plain called the Tihamah lies along the shore of the Red Sea. In the south along the Gulf of Aden, the plain is mostly sand, with some fertile spots.

Both the Tihamah and the southern coastal plain are hot, with temperatures ranging from 68° to 130° F. (20° to 54° C) in the Tihamah, and from 61° to 106° F. (16° to 41° C) in Aden on the gulf. The Tihamah is humid, yet little rain falls on either lowland.

East of the Tihamah, cliffs rise up sharply from the plain. As much as 30 inches (76 centimeters) of rain fall on the cliffs each year, cutting into the rock and creating steep valleys. The cliffs form the western border of the highland region of Yemen.

The high interior is a land of broad plateaus lying 6,000 feet (1,800 meters) above sea level and surrounded by steep, rugged mountains rising more than 12,000 feet (3,000 meters) in the northwest. The altitude makes this region—called High Yemen—cooler and wetter than the coast.

As the highland region curves into southern Yemen, it becomes a dry, hilly plateau. Deep valleys called *wadis* cut into the plateau, providing some rich farmland.

East and north of the highlands, the land slopes to the stony desert called the *Rub al Khali* (Empty Quarter). The desert stretches past Yemen's undefined northern border into Saudi Arabia.

In Yemen's fertile highland region lies Sana, the capital. Sana is an ancient city—no one knows exactly when it was founded. A long wall encloses Sana and its distinctive

buildings and mosques. Eight gates in the wall allow traffic to enter and leave the city. Many buildings in Sana are decorated with white plaster trim that looks like lacy icing against the reddish-brown mud-brick walls.

Mud-brick dwellings are a common sight in Yemen. Many people in the cities live in mud-brick houses, while the town of Shibam has tall mud-brick buildings that seem to grow out of the land itself. Today, Western styles have begun to influence the country. Some of Yemen's city people live in modern apartments or comfortable houses along wide streets.

An ancient land, a young nation

The area we now call Yemen has a long history. Semitic people are thought to have invaded what is now northwestern Yemen about 2000 B.C. They introduced farming and building skills to the herders who were already living in the region. The area later grew rich as an ancient center of trade in frankincense and myrrh and other luxury goods.

But Yemen itself is a fairly new country. From the 1700's until 1990, the territory that is now Yemen was made up of two countries—Yemen (Sana) and Yemen (Aden). The two Yemens had different histories: northwestern Yemen, or Yemen (Sana), was ruled by Muslim imams and was part of the Ottoman Empire. Southern and eastern Yemen, or Yemen (Aden), was a British protectorate. The two Yemens had somewhat different religious populations: Yemen (Sana) was largely divided between Shiite Muslims of the Zaydi sect and Sunni Muslims of the Shafii sect. Yemen (Aden) had mostly Shafii Sunnites. The two Yemens also had different economies and politics—Yemen (Sana) relied on agriculture and had an anti-Communist government, while Yemen (Aden) depended on its port at Aden and had a socialist government.

But the two Yemens also had much in common, and in 1990 they united to form the Republic of Yemen. Continuing tensions between North and South led to an eruption of civil war in May 1994. The North claimed victory on July 7, and President Ali Abdallah Salih declared the country reunited.

Yemen Today

Yemen is a Middle Eastern country that wraps around the southern tip of the Arabian Peninsula. Its full name in Arabic, which is the country's official language, is Al-Jumhuriyah al Yamaniyah, or the Republic of Yemen. Sana is Yemen's capital and largest city. Aden is the country's economic center.

The Republic of Yemen marks its date of birth as May 22, 1990. On that day, two separate nations—Yemen (Sana), which was also called North Yemen or Northern Yemen, and Yemen (Aden), which was also called South Yemen or Southern Yemen—announced their union.

A developing economy

Yemen remains one of the least developed countries in the world, and the nation depends on extensive foreign aid. Many of Yemen's young men leave the country to work and send some of their earnings home to their families.

Most Yemenis make a living by farming or herding. However, Aden is an important port with a prosperous service economy. Ships of many nations use the port for refueling, repairs, and transferring cargoes. Aden's oil refinery processes oil shipped from other countries, mostly those on the Persian Gulf.

Petroleum was discovered in northwestern Yemen in the mid-1980's, and the oil industry may help the country's development.

FACT BOX

THE COUNTRY
Official name: Al-Jumhuriyah al Yamaniyah (Republic of Yemen).
Capital: Sana.
Land regions: Coastal plain, including Tihamah on west coast; cliffs to the east of the Tihamah; high plateaus and mountains inland; desert farthest inland.
Area: 203,850 sq. mi. (527,968 km²).
Climate: Hot and humid along coast; cooler and wetter in highlands; hot and dry in desert.
Highest elevation: Hadur Shuayb, 12,336 ft. (3,760 m).
Lowest elevation: Sea level along the coast.

THE GOVERNMENT
Form of government: Republic.
Head of state: President.
Head of government: Five-member presidential council.
Administrative areas: 17 governorates.
Legislature: Council of Representatives.
Court system: Supreme Court and commercial courts (*sharia* [Islamic law] and traditional law).
Armed forces: 64,000 troops.

THE PEOPLE
Estimated 1996 population: 14,361,000.
Official language: Arabic.
Religion: Islam (100%).

THE ECONOMY
Currency: Rial.
Gross national product (GNP) in 1992: $6.7 billion U.S.
Real annual growth rate (1980–88):
Sana: 5.5%.
Aden: −3.2%
GNP per capita (1991): $520 U.S.
Balance of trade (1990): −$1.2 billion U.S.
Goods exported: Coffee, cotton, crude oil, fish, and hides.

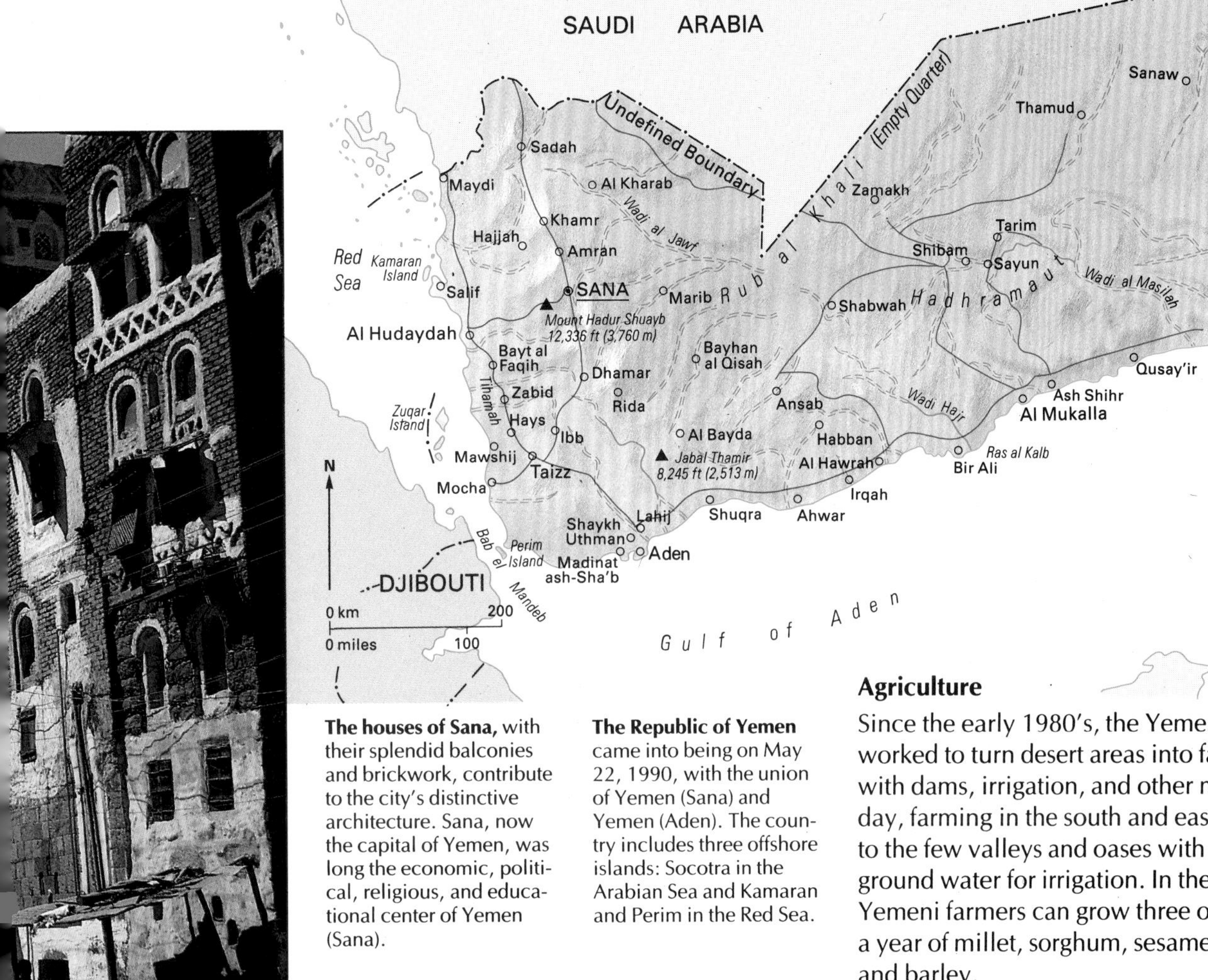

The houses of Sana, with their splendid balconies and brickwork, contribute to the city's distinctive architecture. Sana, now the capital of Yemen, was long the economic, political, religious, and educational center of Yemen (Sana).

The Republic of Yemen came into being on May 22, 1990, with the union of Yemen (Sana) and Yemen (Aden). The country includes three offshore islands: Socotra in the Arabian Sea and Kamaran and Perim in the Red Sea.

Petroleum mining already supports a growing construction industry. Building projects include new hotels, office buildings, and roads.

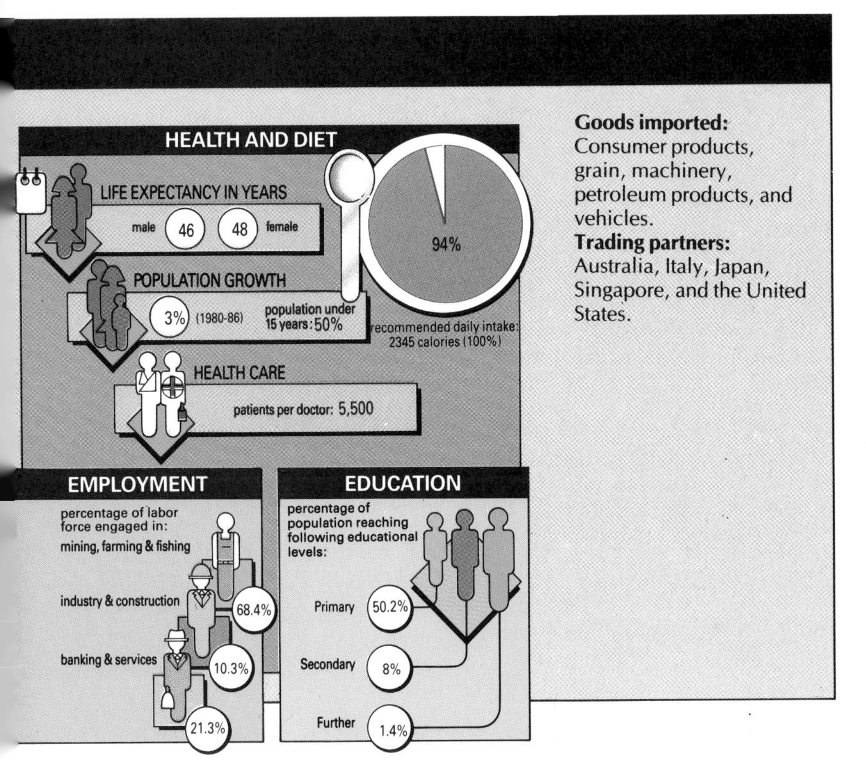

Goods imported: Consumer products, grain, machinery, petroleum products, and vehicles.
Trading partners: Australia, Italy, Japan, Singapore, and the United States.

Agriculture

Since the early 1980's, the Yemenis have worked to turn desert areas into farmland with dams, irrigation, and other methods. Today, farming in the south and east is limited to the few valleys and oases with underground water for irrigation. In these areas, Yemeni farmers can grow three or four crops a year of millet, sorghum, sesame, wheat, and barley.

The plateaus and hills of the northwestern interior highlands are the most productive agricultural region of Yemen. Farmers there raise food grains, such as wheat, barley, and a type of sorghum called *durra*. Yemenis grow a wide variety of fruits, including apricots, bananas, grapes, papayas, and pomegranates. Beans, lentils, onions, tomatoes, and other vegetables are grown in gardens at the edges of the highland villages and towns.

The leading cash crop, however, is *khat* (sometimes spelled *kat* or *qat*)—a woody highland shrub whose leaves contain a stimulant. When chewed, khat leaves produce a mildly intoxicating feeling of well-being. Groups of men and groups of women often meet separately in the afternoon to chew khat.

Coffee is another important cash crop for Yemenis, and Mocha coffee is especially popular. Coffee plants grow on terraces that are cut into the hills and watered by ancient aqueducts.

On the coast and on Socotra Island, some people live by fishing. Near the shore, Yemeni men spear fish from dugout canoes called *sambugs;* in deeper water, they net fish from single-sailed *dhows*.

History

In ancient times, Yemen was known as *Arabia Felix* (Fortunate Arabia)—a land of frankincense and myrrh, which yielded highly valued incense and perfumes. Yemen also lay along important trade routes between Europe, Asia, and Africa. Arab merchants there handled gems, spices, silks, and other exotic goods.

Cities, castles, temples, and dams were built during this period. Farms were irrigated. In the 900's B.C., the Queen of Sheba ruled one of several kingdoms that flourished in the area.

But the region's prosperity ended in the A.D. 100's. Local tribal chiefs warred among themselves, and Abyssinia (now Ethiopia) conquered the land for a short time in the A.D. 300's. For hundreds of years afterward, Yemeni tribes and religious groups fought with one another, as well as with would be invaders.

The most important cultural and political event in the history of the region occurred in the 600's, when Islam was introduced to the people. By the end of the 800's, most Yemenis were Muslims.

The adoption of Islam did not solve all the tribal conflicts, however, partly because tribes in the region belonged to different Muslim sects. To a large degree, the tribes remained split socially, politically, and religiously. The history of the region split too.

Beginning in 897, a Muslim *imam* began to serve as the religious and political leader of northwestern Yemen. In 1517, this area fell under the control of the Ottoman Empire, which was centered in Turkey. However, the local imams kept considerable power. In 1924, the Treaty of Lausanne freed northwest Yemen from the Turks.

In 1962, a group of military officers supported by Egypt overthrew the imam and set up a republic. The imam's forces—called *royalists*—were supported by Saudi Arabia and fought from bases in the mountains to regain control. The fighting ended in 1970, when the republicans set up a government that included both republicans and royalists.

Meanwhile, southern and eastern Yemen had fallen under Western influence. In 1839, Great Britain had seized the city of Aden in southern Yemen after people of the town looted a wrecked British ship. Aden then became an important refueling stop for British ships on their way to India via the Suez Canal.

To protect Aden from the rest of southern Yemen, which claimed the town, Britain extended its control to the tribal states in the surrounding region and signed treaties with the tribal chiefs, promising protection and aid in return for loyality. The area came to be known as the Aden Protectorate.

In 1959, six tribal states in the protectorate formed a federation, and Britain promised to grant the federation independence in the future. By 1965, Aden and all but four of the tribal states had joined the federation.

But the British had trouble setting up a representative government to rule the federation after independence. Both the radical Arab nationalists in Aden and the tribal chiefs in the protectorate wanted control. The radicals launched terrorist attacks against both the British and the chiefs. Two radical groups—the National Liberation Front (NLF) and the Front for the Liberation of Occupied South Yemen (FLOSY)—also fought each other for control.

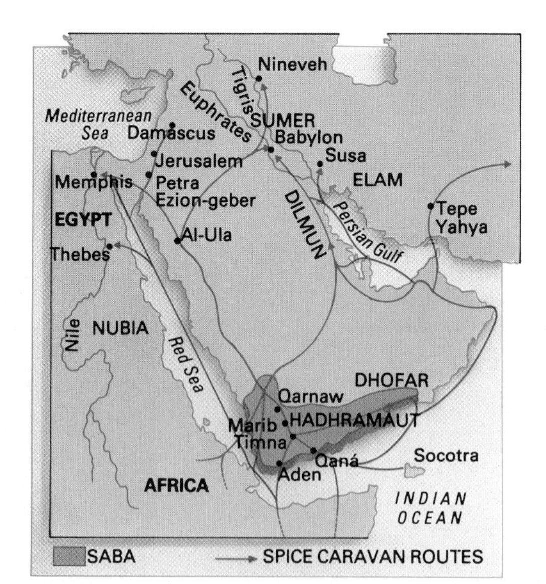

Ancient Yemen, or Saba, was part of a region ruled by the Biblical Queen of Sheba. This area, which included the Dhofar region of present-day Oman, was famous in the ancient world as the source of frankincense and myrrh and a center of spice trading.

Ruins of the Marib Dam, *right,* are evidence of the ancient civilization that flourished in Yemen. Built about 500 B.C., the dam provided enough water to irrigate an area that could have supported as many as 300,000 people.

In 1967, British troops finally withdrew, and the NLF, the most powerful group, formed a government for the new country, called Yemen (Aden). Later, the NLF and other groups reorganized as the Yemeni Socialist Party (YSP). National leaders then formed ties with Communist countries, which led to fighting with northwestern Yemen, then called Yemen (Sana). Anti-Communist army officers took over Yemen (Sana) in 1974. Relations between the Yemens began to improve in the 1980's, and in 1990, the two were at last united. Disputes over power sharing and oil resources led to civil war in May 1994. The fighting ended with victory for the North in July, and the country remained one.

The rugged hills of northern Yemen once supported forests of trees that yielded the rare and fragrant resins called *frankincense* and *myrrh.* Ancient peoples prized these resins for use in medicines, cosmetics, and incense.

Yemeni women wash clothes in a rocky stream, *below,* using a method that may have remained unchanged for centuries. Yemen no longer enjoys the position of wealth and importance it held in ancient times.

People and Government

Most of the people of Yemen are Arab Muslims, but they belong to different tribes and different religious sects. Small groups of Indians, Pakistanis, and Africans also live in Yemen.

Way of life

Most of Yemen's people are farmers or herders. Some make their living by fishing in coastal water. In the desert, a few people still live as nomadic herders. They travel constantly in search of water and food for their sheep and goats. Because of Yemen's lack of economic development, many Yemenis depend on wages sent home by family members working in neighboring oil-rich lands. Some areas of Yemen have no schools, and only about 16 per cent of Yemeni adults can read and write.

The basic foods of Yemen's people are rice, bread, vegetables, lamb, and fish. A spicy stew called *salta* is the national dish.

As in other developing countries, city life in Yemen differs from rural life. Some city people reside in modern houses or apartment buildings, and many others live in one-story brick houses. Many wear Western-style clothing.

Some farm families live in towns, such as Sayun, that have mud-brick houses three or four stories high. Others live in small villages close to the land they farm. Near the Red Sea coast, many people live in straw huts. Traditional Arab clothing is common in rural areas. The men's garments include cotton breeches or a striped *futa* (kilt). Many men wear skullcaps; turbans; or tall, round hats called *tarbooshes*.

Many Yemenis are craft workers in small one-room shops. Yemeni craft workers have been noted for their textiles, leatherwork, and ironwork since ancient times, and many such goods are still made by hand. Yemenis dye and weave beautiful cloth and make rope, glassware, wooden chests, *jambiyas* (daggers), jewelry, brassware, harnesses, saddles, and pottery. Some sell their goods in village bazaars, while others go to Aden's market district, where each trade has its own street.

A forbidding landscape of rock and sand makes up the northern interior of Yemen. A few nomadic herders wander through the desert. Most of the men own nothing but their clothes and their curved daggers called *jambiyas*. The women are unveiled, and many are tattooed with tribal marks.

East meets West as Yemeni men sport Western-style jackets over long tribal robes, *above*. Many Yemenis, however, prefer traditional Arab clothing. The men wear *futas* (kilts) or breeches, and turbans or round hats called *tarbooshes*, while women wear veils and dark, shapeless robes.

Conflict and division

Tribal divisions have been important in Yemen since ancient times. The Arab tribes' desire for self-rule and their rivalries often led to conflicts.

In northwestern Yemen, the Muslims are divided by their beliefs. One group—Shiites of the Zaydi sect—live mainly in the high interior and in Sana. The imams who ruled this section of the country from 897 to 1962 were Zaydis. A group of Zaydis called the Sayyids

A jambiya salesman displays his wares. In the past, the kind of jambiya a man owned and the position in which it was worn indicated the tribe to which he belonged.

A dark veil, embroidered with silver, hides the face of a Yemeni woman. Women in Yemen (Aden) enjoyed greater access to jobs and education than did women in Yemen (Sana).

A teacher instructs a class of eager children in a Yemeni school. Education was stressed more in Yemen (Aden), which had been controlled by the British, than it was in Yemen (Sana).

were government officials, and many Zaydis were soldiers. The second group—Sunnites of the Shafii sect—includes a wealthy merchant class. In the past, the Zaydis and Sunnites clashed. In southern and eastern Yemen, most of the Muslims also are Shafii Sunnites.

A united government

Before the two Yemens merged, each had its own national legislature. In 1990, the two legislative assemblies elected a president, a vice-president, and three other leaders to make up a five-member ruling council for the united country.

The legislatures then dissolved themselves and re-formed as one legislature called the Council of Representatives. The council has 301 members—159 from the former legislature of Yemen (Sana), 111 from the former legislature of Yemen (Aden), and 31 appointed members.

Tensions over power-sharing and oil resources led to civil war in May 1994. The South declared its independence and attacked the Northern capital of Sana. Despite the South's superior military power, the North captured military bases and oil fields. The war ended when the South's main city, Aden, fell on July 7. As many as 12,000 people died.

Yugoslavia

Lying on the Balkan Peninsula in southeastern Europe, Yugoslavia is a nation made up of two republics—Serbia and Montenegro. Yugoslavia was formerly a federation of six republics—Bosnia-Herzegovina, Croatia, Macedonia, Montenegro, Serbia, and Slovenia. In 1991 and 1992, all the republics except Serbia and Montenegro declared themselves independent nations and broke away from the federation.

The first modern Yugoslav state, known as the *Kingdom of the Serbs, Croats, and Slovenes,* was formed in 1918. King Peter I of Serbia became king, but he was old and sick, so his son Alexander ruled in his place. The kingdom united six major groups of South Slavs—the Bosnian Muslims, Croats, Macedonians, Montenegrins, Serbs, and Slovenes.

King Alexander succeeded his father to the throne in 1921, and, in 1929, he renamed the country *Yugoslavia,* which means *Land of the South Slavs.* In 1945, the nation fell under the control of the Communists and became the Federal People's Republic of Yugoslavia.

With six major nationality groups, three major religions, three official languages, and two alphabets, Yugoslavia was a country with a rich variety of cultures. While the people worked together to improve their living standards and meet their economic goals, they retained a strong ethnic identity within their nationality groups.

However, differences in religion, language, and culture made unity difficult. In addition, deep-seated resentments against the Serbs, who held most of the power in the federal government, also contributed to the breakup of the country. Tension between ethnic groups led to violence during the early 1990's. After Croatia and Slovenia declared independence in June 1992, fighting took place between their militias and Serbian forces. Fighting between Serbs and other ethnic groups also broke out in Bosnia-Herzegovina after that republic declared independence in March 1992.

As a result of these battles, Serbian forces occupied about a third of Croatia's territory and about two-thirds of Bosnia-Herzegovina. A cease-fire ended most of the fighting in Croatia in January 1992 but fighting continued in Serb-occupied Croatian lands. Serbia and Montenegro announced in April that they had formed a new, smaller Yugoslavia.

In May 1992, the United Nations imposed an oil and trade embargo against Yugoslavia in an attempt to end the fighting in Bosnia-Herzegovina. Also in May, the United States and member nations of the European Community recalled their respective ambassadors from Yugoslavia. In 1994, after the Bosnian Serbs refused the latest international peace plan which called for the partitioning of Bosnia, Yugoslavia severed its economic and political ties with them.

Yugoslavia Today

Yugoslavia became a Communist republic in 1945, after Josip Broz Tito and his anti-Nazi resistance forces took over the government, but the nation followed an independent path. In 1948, Yugoslavia was expelled from the Cominform, a group of Communist nations, because Tito refused to allow the Soviet Union to control Yugoslavia.

After the split with Soviet leaders, Yugoslavia began to develop its own type of Communist society based on a system of *self-management* that involves the people in the decisions of the businesses in which they work. Self-management blended the strengths of Communism and capitalism, while allowing the workers to control the economy.

In 1990, the Communist Party voted to end its monopoly on political power. Soon many non-Communist political parties were formed. When the first multiparty elections were held in all six republics, non-Communist parties gained control of the four republics that later left the federation— Bosnia-Herzegovina, Croatia, Macedonia, and Slovenia. Communists, renamed Socialists, continued to hold power in Serbia and Montenegro.

Both Serbia and Montenegro have their own governments, each headed by a popularly elected president and parliament. The provinces of Kosovo and Vojvodina, which are part of Serbia, enjoyed many powers of self-government until 1990, when Serbia stripped them of their special status.

Political problems

In 1987, Slobodan Milošević became chief of the League of Communists in Serbia, and he became president of Serbia in 1989 and was reelected in 1992. He censored the media in order to promote support from the Serbian people for his activities.

Milošević's vigorous support of Serbian nationalism and higher living standards for Serbia gained him widespread support among Serbs during his rise to power. For example, many Serbs supported the suppression of self-government in Kosovo and Vojvodina that Milošević helped engineer. Meanwhile, other ethnic groups feared they might lose some of their independence and economic strength to the Serbs, and this deepened ethnic divisions in Yugoslavia. After Yugoslavia broke up, Milošević's support for Serbs outside Serbia and Montenegro increasingly put his country at odds with the rest of the world. United States and European Community leaders accused Serbia of aggression for its military support of Bosnian

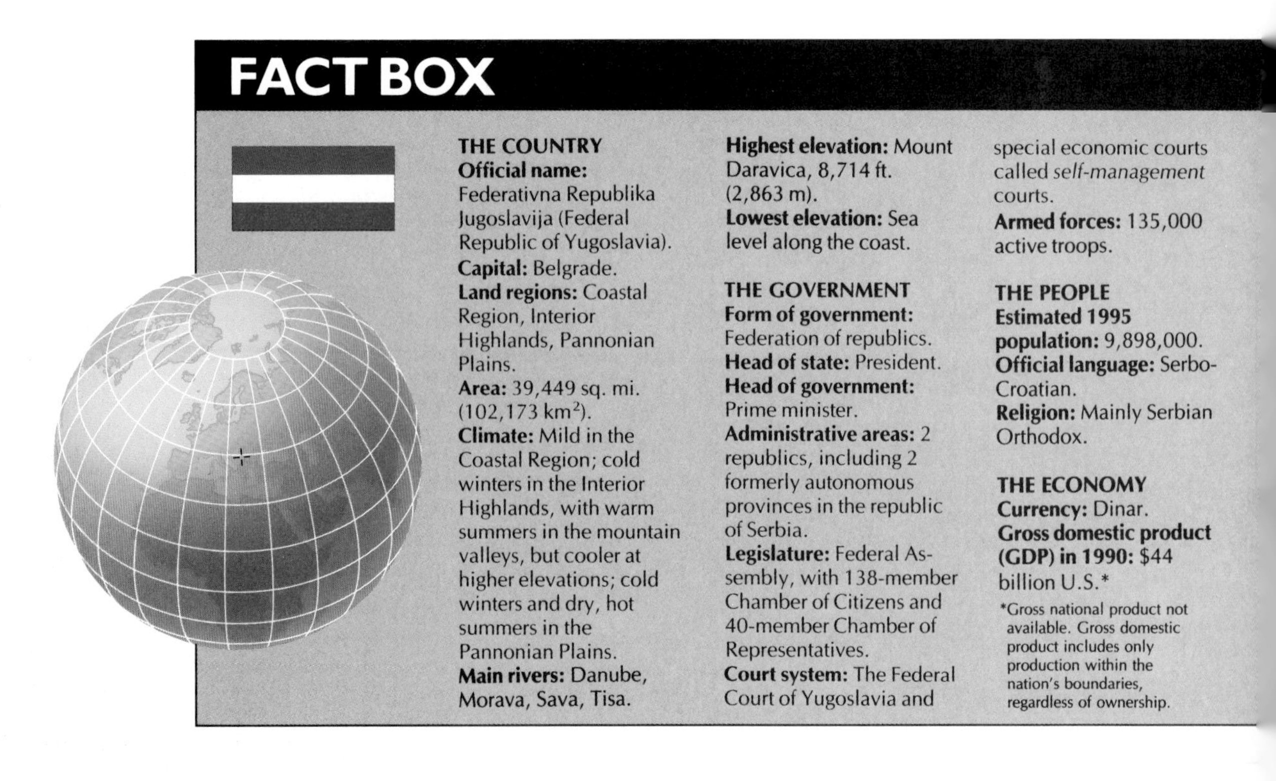

FACT BOX

THE COUNTRY
Official name: Federativna Republika Jugoslavija (Federal Republic of Yugoslavia).
Capital: Belgrade.
Land regions: Coastal Region, Interior Highlands, Pannonian Plains.
Area: 39,449 sq. mi. (102,173 km²).
Climate: Mild in the Coastal Region; cold winters in the Interior Highlands, with warm summers in the mountain valleys, but cooler at higher elevations; cold winters and dry, hot summers in the Pannonian Plains.
Main rivers: Danube, Morava, Sava, Tisa.
Highest elevation: Mount Daravica, 8,714 ft. (2,863 m).
Lowest elevation: Sea level along the coast.

THE GOVERNMENT
Form of government: Federation of republics.
Head of state: President.
Head of government: Prime minister.
Administrative areas: 2 republics, including 2 formerly autonomous provinces in the republic of Serbia.
Legislature: Federal Assembly, with 138-member Chamber of Citizens and 40-member Chamber of Representatives.
Court system: The Federal Court of Yugoslavia and special economic courts called *self-management* courts.
Armed forces: 135,000 active troops.

THE PEOPLE
Estimated 1995 population: 9,898,000.
Official language: Serbo-Croatian.
Religion: Mainly Serbian Orthodox.

THE ECONOMY
Currency: Dinar.
Gross domestic product (GDP) in 1990: $44 billion U.S.*

*Gross national product not available. Gross domestic product includes only production within the nation's boundaries, regardless of ownership.

Serbs in Bosnia-Herzegovina's civil war. The fighting was touched off by a Bosnian Serb rebellion when the republic withdrew from the Yugoslav federation in March 1992.

International efforts to take punitive action against Serbia for its support of the Bosnian Serbs were instituted. In May, the United Nations (UN) imposed an oil and trade embargo against Yugoslavia in an attempt to stop the fighting. In September, the UN General Assembly increased pressure on Serbia by voting to deny it and Montenegro the right to automatically continue Yugoslavia's membership. The Assembly said the two republics had to apply to the Security Council for membership as a new nation.

In April 1993, the United Nations imposed tougher sanctions against Yugoslavia after the Bosnian Serbs twice rejected the Vance-Owen peace plan. The plan, drawn up by mediators Lord Owen and former U.S. Secretary of State Cyrus Vance, would have left Serbs in control of 43 per cent of Bosnia. At the time of the proposal, the Serbs held 70 per cent of Bosnia.

In addition to reinforcing the May 1992 embargo, the new sanctions froze Yugoslav government and private assets around the world. They also blocked shipments going through Yugoslavia by way of the Danube River and shipments by land and water of most goods in and out of Yugoslavia, except medicines, food, and relief supplies.

In June 1994, a United Nations commission investigating war crimes in Bosnia formally accused Bosnian Serbs of genocide. In August 1994, Milosěvić announced that Yugoslavia was severing its economic and political ties with the Bosnian Serbs and closing their common border. Milosěvić indicated that he was cutting off the Serbs because they rejected the latest international peace proposal, which called for the partitioning of Bosnia between the Serbs and a Muslim-Croat federation. In return, the UN Security Council eased economic sanctions against Yugoslavia for 100 days, beginning Oct. 3.

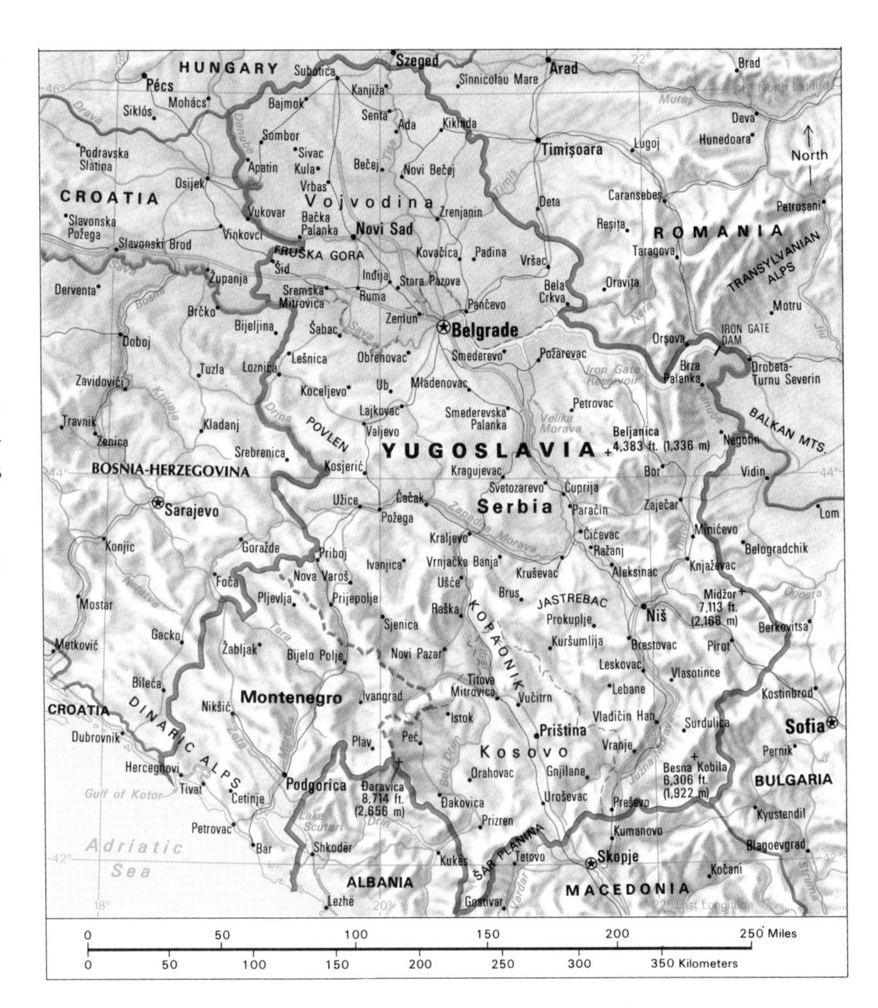

Yugoslavia, a federation of the republics of Serbia and Montenegro, occupies the northwestern part of the Balkan Peninsula. The country was formerly made up of six republics. However, four of them—Bosnia-Herzegovina, Croatia, Macedonia, and Slovenia—declared their independence in 1991 and 1992 and broke away from the federation.

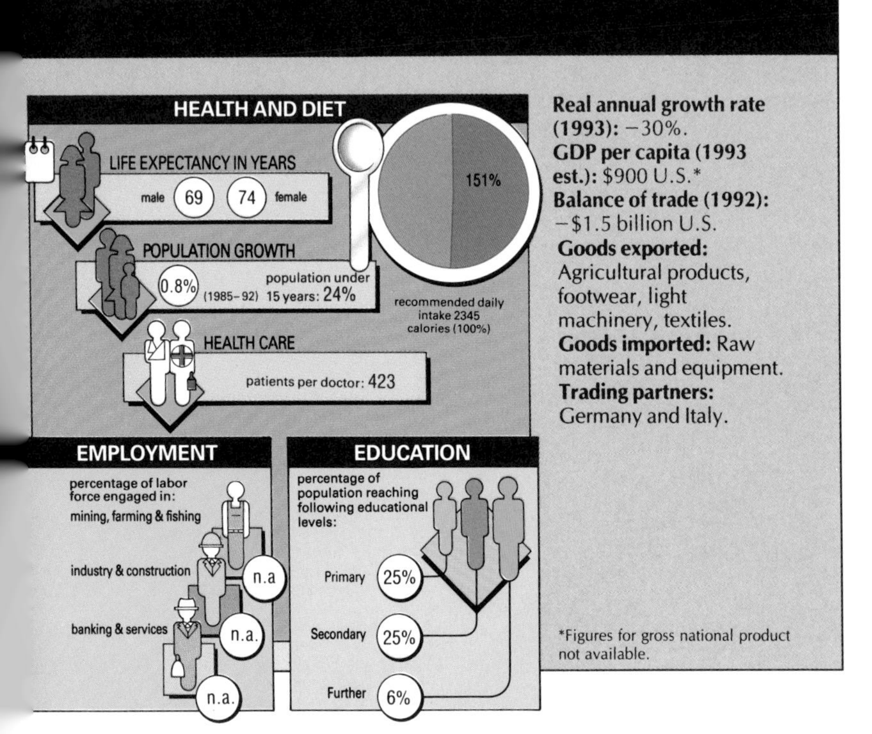

History

Although people have lived in what is now Yugoslavia for at least 100,000 years, the first known settlers were the Illyrians and the Thracians, who inhabited the region about 3,000 years ago. The Illyrians were known throughout the Greek and Roman world as raiders and pirates.

During the 500's B.C., the Greeks established colonies along the Adriatic coast, and about 300 years later, the Romans began their invasion of the Balkan Peninsula. The area became part of a Roman imperial province about 11 B.C. In A.D. 395, when the Roman Empire was divided into two parts, Serbia and Montenegro became part of the East Roman (Byzantine) Empire.

During the 500's and 600's, various groups of Slavs, including the ancestors of the Serbs, settled in the Balkan Peninsula. Each tribe had its own leader until the late 1100's, when Stephen Nemanja, a warrior and chief, formed the first united Serbian state, which also included Montenegro. After King Stephen Dušan died in 1355, the Serbian empire began to collapse, and Montenegro became an independent state. In 1389, the Ottoman Turks defeated Serbia in the Battle of Kosovo Polje. Serbia came under complete Ottoman control in the mid-1400's. Local nobles in Montenegro ruled on behalf of Ottoman overlords.

Serbia gained its independence from the Ottoman Empire in 1878, and called for the independence of other Slavic lands. When Archduke Francis Ferdinand of Austria-Hungary was assassinated in 1914 in Sarajevo by a Bosnian Serb, Austria-Hungary claimed Serbia had supported the killing and declared war on Serbia. The incident marked the beginning of World War I. After Austria-Hungary was defeated in 1918 by the Allied powers, the Slavs became free to form their own state.

The first united Yugoslav state consisted of territories that joined together in 1918 as the Kingdom of the Serbs, Croats, and Slovenes, *below*. In 1992, the second, smaller Yugoslavia included only the republics of Serbia and Montenegro.

c. 1000 B.C. Illyrians and Thracians live in what is now Yugoslavia.

600's B.C. Greeks establish colonies along the Adriatic coast.

c. 300's B.C. Romans invade the Balkan Peninsula.

229–228 B.C. and **219 B.C.** Romans war against the Illyrians.

168 B.C. Romans conquer the Illyrians.

13–9 B.C. Romans conquer Pannonia.

395 Serbia and Montenegro become part of the East Roman (Byzantine) Empire.

1100's The first united Serbian state is established.

1400's Ottoman Turks rule Serbia; nobles rule Montenegro on behalf of the Ottomans.

1516 Serbian Orthodox bishops rule part of Montenegro; by the late 1700's, they rule all of Montenegro.

1804 George Petrović, a Serbian peasant nicknamed Black George, leads an uprising against the Turks.

1815 Miloš Obrenović leads a second revolt against the Turks.

1851 Montenegro ruler takes the title of prince.

1878 Serbia gains independence from the Ottoman Empire.

1914 Archduke Francis Ferdinand of Austria-Hungary is assassinated by Bosnian Serb Gavrilo Princip.

1918 The Kingdom of the Serbs, Croats, and Slovenes is formed.

1929 King Alexander I establishes a dictatorship and changes the name of the country to Yugoslavia.

1941 Germany and other Axis powers invade Yugoslavia; Tito organizes a resistance movement.

1945 Yugoslavia becomes a Communist republic.

1974 Nine-member *Presidency* is formed to provide leadership after Tito's retirement or death.

1990 Four of Yugoslavia's six republics elect non-Communist governments.

1991 Croatia and Slovenia declare independence; civil war breaks out in Croatia. Macedonia declares independence.

1992 Bosnia-Herzegovina declares independence. Cease-fire takes effect in Croatia. Fighting breaks out in Bosnia-Herzegovina. Serbia and Montenegro announce they formed a new, smaller Yugoslavia.

Alexander I (1888-1934) ruled the first Yugoslav federation as regent from 1918 to 1921, and as king from 1921 until 1934.

Josip Broz Tito (1892-1980), *far left,* declared Yugoslavia a Communist republic in 1945.

Yugoslav author Ivo Andrić (1892–1975) won the Nobel Prize for literature in 1961.

The monastery of Manasija, built in the early 1400's along the banks of the Resava River in Serbia, houses some of the most splendid examples of Serbian Orthodox painting to be found in Yugoslavia.

Partisan troops march into Belgrade in 1944, liberating the city from Nazi occupation. The Partisans, led by Josip Broz Tito and the Communist Party, controlled all of Yugoslavia by the end of World War II.

On Dec. 1, 1918, Peter I of Serbia became king of the Kingdom of the Serbs, Croats, and Slovenes. The new nation, a constitutional monarchy, included Bosnia-Herzegovina, Croatia, Dalmatia, Montenegro, Serbia, and Slovenia. Problems soon developed, however, because the Slovenes and the Croats believed that the Serbs had too much power.

In 1929, King Alexander, Peter I's son, abolished the Constitution and began to rule as dictator. Alexander tried to unify the nation. He changed the country's name to Yugoslavia and created new political divisions that ignored the historical boundaries of the nationality groups. He also tried to enforce the use of only one language.

But instead of unifying the country, Alexander's actions made matters worse between the groups. He was assassinated by Croatian terrorists in 1934. Because Alexander's son was only 11 years old, his cousin Paul became regent.

The outbreak of World War II (1939–1945) found Yugoslavia ill-prepared to defend itself. Under pressure, the government agreed to join the Axis powers of Germany and Italy on March 25, 1941. The army rebelled against the action by overthrowing Paul and putting Alexander's son Peter on the throne. The Germans invaded Yugoslavia on April 6, and Yugoslavia surrendered 11 days later.

To counter the German occupation, the Yugoslavs formed two guerrilla resistance movements. The Chetniks were army officers and others who supported the king. The Partisans, led by Josip Broz Tito, were Communists. The two movements fought each other in addition to the Axis forces. At first the Allies helped the Chetniks, but in 1943 they started supplying the Partisans because Tito's forces were more effective against the Germans.

In November 1943, the Communists set up a temporary government in Jajce, and in 1944, with the help of the Allies, they freed Belgrade from German control. By the time World War II ended, Tito and the Communists firmly controlled all of Yugoslavia. Communist control of Yugoslavia continued until 1990, when the Communist Party voted to end its monopoly of power in the country.

Economy

After the Communists came to power in 1945, they set two main economic objectives. The first goal was to transform an economy based on agriculture into one based on industry. The second objective was to establish what they understood to be the ethic of Communism in the workplace.

When the Communists took over, Yugoslavia was one of the least developed agricultural countries in Europe. About 75 per cent of the 2-1/2 million peasant holdings were under 12.3 acres (5 hectares) in area. In addition, many hundreds of thousands of peasants had no land to work. Those who did own farmland used primitive equipment to work it.

The Communists were successful in transforming Yugoslavia into a modern, industrial nation. The rapid industrial growth, which required large imports of raw materials, fuel, and capital equipment, was largely made possible through credits and grants from the United States and Western Europe. This huge influx of financial aid allowed Yugoslavia to build up a massive trade deficit while transforming the economy.

However, most of the industrial development took place in the republics of Croatia and Slovenia, two of the republics that broke away from the Yugoslav federation in 1991. Today, many Yugoslavs still earn their living as farmers.

In 1945, to meet the second objective, Communist leaders nationalized most of Yugoslavia's businesses and industries. During the 1950's, they set up a system of self-management in these enterprises, in which economic planning was placed in the hands of workers' councils using government guidelines. In 1992, however, the new Yugoslav government announced plans to move toward a free enterprise system, in which business owners and managers would decide what to produce and how much to charge for their goods and services.

Agriculture, forestry, and mining

Much of Yugoslavia's agricultural production comes from the Pannonian Plains of Serbia, where farmers grow corn, sugar beets, and wheat. In the Interior Highlands, the major crops are barley, oats, and potatoes. Mon-

A sheepherder tends to his flock in the uplands of Kosovo, where livestock production is an important occupation. Farmers throughout the Interior Highlands of Yugoslavia raise cattle, hogs, and sheep.

Yugoslav workers assemble tractors in a Belgrade factory. The city is a major industrial center, and its factories and plants produce automobiles, electrical equipment, flour, paper, shoes, sugar, and woolen textiles in addition to farm machinery.

tenegro's farm produce consists mainly of corn, grapes and other fruits, olives, potatoes, tobacco, and wheat.

Forestry is also an important industry in Yugoslavia. Wood is processed into finished products or made into paper.

Yugoslavia also has mineral resources. Serbia's mines yield coal, copper ore, lead, and zinc, while Montenegro has deposits of bauxite, coal, and lead. In addition, wells in the Pannonian Plains and the Adriatic Sea produce petroleum and natural gas.

Manufacturing

Major products from the industrial centers in Serbia are aluminum, automobiles, cement, iron and steel, paper, plastics, textiles, and trucks. Montenegro's goods include aluminum, cement, iron and steel, and paper.

Industry has not yet reached its full potential in Yugoslavia. Under the Communists, only heavy industry was developed on a planned basis, and most of Yugoslavia's raw materials were exported in crude form and processed abroad. Today, the nation's processing industries remain underdeveloped because of the lack of skilled labor and shortage of investment capital.

Montenegro is less industrialized than much of Serbia. Its mountainous terrain has long isolated the republic from the rest of Yugoslavia, and its economic development has lagged behind. Government efforts to build up Montenegro's economy have largely failed.

In 1992, the UN-imposed trade embargo on Yugoslavia seriously threatened the country's economy. By the fall of 1992, supplies of raw materials for Serbian factories were becoming depleted, and plant closings and unemployment were increasing. In Montenegro, the embargo left ports idle.

In 1994, as the embargo continued to cause severe economic problems in Yugoslavia, Western nations threatened to tighten sanctions. Although the sanctions were often broken, unemployment was rampant throughout the country, and most of the population remained idle. Hyperinflation was also a serious problem. Yugoslavia severed its economic and political ties with the Bosnian Serbs after they rejected the international peace proposal, which called for the partitioning of Bosnia.

A vineyard worker picks grapes that will be used for making wine. Yugoslavia has experienced a steady migration of people from rural areas to the cities, where they go in search of industrial jobs.

People

The first modern Yugoslav state was formed with the goal of uniting six major groups of South Slavs. The two remaining republics that make up the new, smaller Yugoslavia consist mostly of two nationality groups—the Serbs, who live mainly in Serbia, and the Montenegrins, most of whom live in Montenegro.

The earliest references to Serbs as a distinct nationality group have been found in the writings of the Byzantine Emperor Constantine VII. In his work *De administrando imperio,* written in the A.D. 900's, Constantine referred to the Serbs as subjects of the Holy Roman Empire who had been converted to Christianity in the 800's.

The inhabitants of what is now Montenegro were culturally indistinguishable from the Serbs until the Turkish invasions of Serbia in the 1300's. Unlike Serbia, which fell to the Ottomans in 1389, Montenegro—then known as the principality of Zeta under the Serbian Empire—stood alone as the only Balkan region to succeed in preventing the Turks from conquering their land.

Today, Serbs make up about 65 per cent of Serbia's population. Other groups living in Serbia include Albanians, Croats, Hungarians, Montenegrins, Romanians, and Slovaks. In Montenegro, Montenegrins make up about two-thirds of the population, which also includes Albanians, Muslim Slavs, and Serbs.

Albanians represent about 90 per cent of the population in the formerly autonomous region of Kosovo, in southern Serbia. The remaining 10 per cent is made up mainly of Serbs. The province of Vojvodina is situated in northern Serbia. Many Hungarians live in Vojvodina, as well as Serbs, Croats, Montenegrins, Romanians, and Slovaks.

Cultural diversity and conflict

Each of Yugoslavia's nationality groups has its own cultural history and customs. This mixture of peoples enriches the cultural landscape of the country, but differences between ethnic groups have often led to violence and bloodshed.

For example, ethnic Albanians in Kosovo

A group of Yugoslavs enjoy the casual atmosphere of an outdoor cafe in Belgrade. The main meal of the day is usually lunch. It often includes soup, followed by a meat or fish dish, salad *(salate),* and dessert. A favorite snack is *burek,* a pastry layered with cheese, meat, or jam.

Folk dancers perform in traditional costume at a village square in Montenegro, *left.* Old-fashioned clothing is more common in the rural areas and worn mostly on holidays. City dwellers wear Western-style clothing.

Montenegrin farm women, *right,* prepare vegetables for sale at a market in Kotor. Farmers also grow tobacco and grapes, olives, plums, and other fruits in the mild climate of the Coastal Region.

have protested Serbian rule of the province and demanded greater independence. But in 1990, Serbia dissolved Kosovo's parliament. In declaring their independence from the first Yugoslav federation in 1991, Croatia and Slovenia accused the Serbs, who had the most influence in the national government, of trying to control the other republics.

The official language of Yugoslavia is Serbo-Croatian. Serbians and Montenegrins traditionally use the Cyrillic alphabet—the system of writing used in Russian and other Slavic languages. Many ethnic groups have their own languages, but most people also speak Serbo-Croatian.

Most Serbs and Montenegrins belong to the Serbian Orthodox Church. The Serbian Church played an important role in maintaining the Serbian culture during the Turkish occupation of Serbia between 1389 and 1878; it provided a framework for keeping alive a sense of national identity in the face of foreign rule. The wallpaintings that decorate Serbian churches built during the Middle Ages are considered to be the most important examples of early Yugoslav art.

City and country life

About half of Yugoslavia's people live in cities, and many of these urban dwellers live in apartments or older houses. Rural families in Yugoslavia live in small houses made of brick, stone, or wood.

Nearly 15 per cent of the country's population lives in Belgrade, the nation's capital and largest city. Belgrade's way of life combines modern Western influence with Balkan traditions. The city has skyscraper apartment buildings and supermarkets—and many of the problems of modern life, such as pollution and traffic congestion. Yet many coffee houses and restaurants still serve traditional Yugoslav dishes, such as grilled, highly seasoned meats, plum brandy, and thick, sweet Turkish coffee.

Environment

Yugoslavia has three major land regions: the Coastal Region, the Interior Highlands, and the Pannonian Plains. Each of these areas offers its own special beauty—from the sandy beaches of the Adriatic coast to the snow-capped Dinaric Alps and the peaceful, rolling countryside of the plains.

The Coastal Region

Yugoslavia's Coastal Region consists of a narrow, rocky strip of land along the Adriatic Sea. Montenegro's Gulf of Kotor—where the intense green of the landscape at sea level contrasts sharply with the surrounding mountains—provides one of the most spectacular sights in Yugoslavia.

The Coastal Region is made up of many striking *karst* formations. Karst is formed when water cuts through limestone over a long period of time, carving caves, sinkholes, and underground rivers. The white limestone formations against the deep blue of the Adriatic Sea create a magnificent seascape all along the coast.

The Coastal Region enjoys a Mediterranean climate, with dry, sunny summers and cool, rainy winters. Temperatures rarely fall below freezing.

The Interior Highlands

The Interior Highlands, the most rugged area of Yugoslavia, are mostly hilly or mountainous. The Dinaric Alps, made up of broad ridges and plateaus, run parallel to the Coastal Region, while the Balkan Mountains rise on Yugoslavia's eastern border.

The mountain ranges of Montenegro are desolate areas with harsh and snowy winters. Towering peaks, covered with pine and beech forests, overlook the coast. Clear mountain streams rush through the limestone rock, cutting deep canyons across the terrain. The spectacular scenery once prompted the Yugoslav political commentator Milovan Djilas to write: ". . . all living things, and all the works of mankind, can be lost on the stony heights of Montenegro; sound crumbles to nothing on the sharp contours of its cliffs, and light itself is ground to dust."

Throughout Montenegro's history, these almost impassable mountains provided a barrier against invaders and helped the Montenegrins hold off complete domination by the Ottoman Empire for about 500 years.

Some farmers in Kosovo still use farm animals to plow their fields. This formerly autonomous province of Serbia remains one of the most underdeveloped regions of Yugoslavia.

Beautiful, sandy beaches line the seaside resort town of Budva, *below,* which lies along Montenegro's Adriatic coast. One of the oldest settlements on the Adriatic coast, Budva was inhabited by many people—including the Phoenicians, Illyrians, Greeks, Romans, Venetians, and Austrians—before it became part of Yugoslavia.

Mountains form a backdrop for Lake Scutari, the largest lake in the Balkan Peninsula. The lake lies partly in Montenegro and partly in neighboring Albania. Famous for its abundance of fish, Lake Scutari is also one of Europe's largest bird reserves.

Earthquakes are an everpresent danger in the Interior Highlands. In 1979, a severe quake struck Montenegro, killing many people and destroying towns and villages. Since then, many historic areas have been carefully restored.

The Pannonian Plains

In northern Yugoslavia, the Interior Highlands flatten out to form the Pannonian Plains—a southwest extension of Hungary's Great Plain. The Pannonian Plains are mostly flat, with some low hills.

The ancient Pannonian Sea, which once covered this area, disappeared as the surrounding mountains gradually filled it with rich alluvial deposits. As a result, the Pannonian Plains have the most fertile soil in the country, making the region Yugoslavia's chief agricultural area.

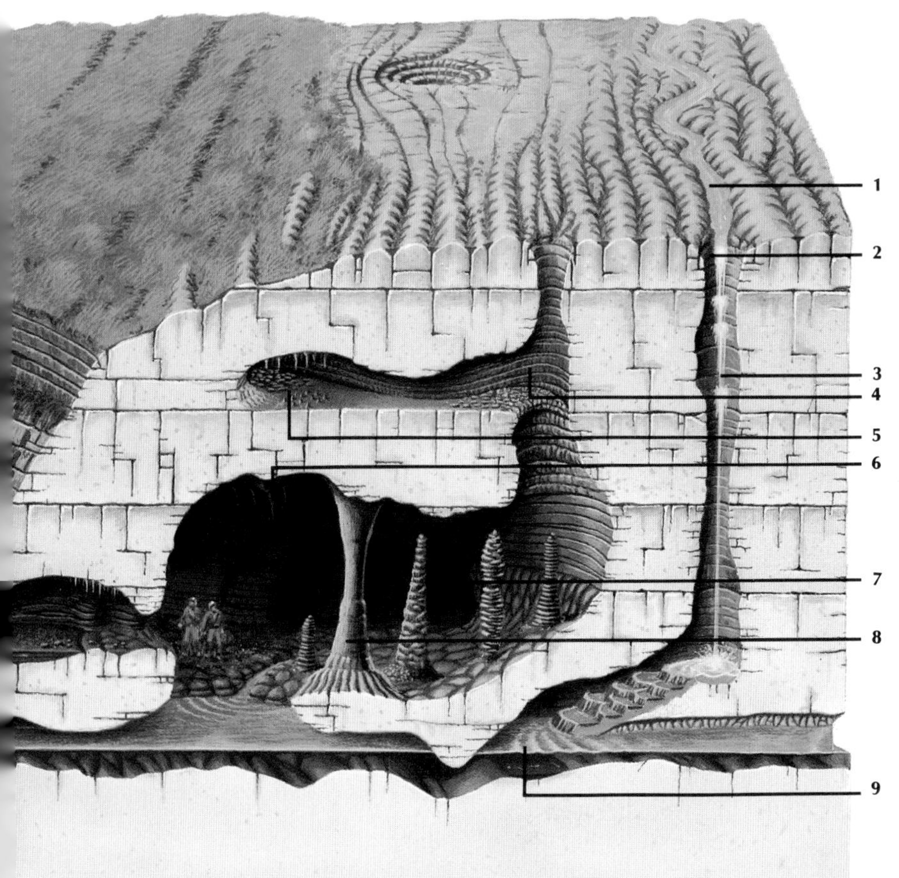

Karst features, *left,* are formed when rain falls onto certain types of rock, especially limestone (1). As the rain falls, it dissolves carbon dioxide from the air and becomes a weak acid. This acid dissolves the rock and creates a sinkhole (2). As the acid eats downward, it creates a chimney (3). Sometimes streams flow into the sinkholes and down the chimney. A dry chimney is known as a pothole (4). Eventually, caves (5) may be formed, often containing stalactites (6) and stalagmites (7), which may come together to form columns (8). Water gathers at the bottom of the cave and forms an underground stream (9). When the stream breaks the surface, it is known as a resurgence (10).

Montenegro

Montenegro is one of the two republics, along with Serbia, that make up the new, smaller Yugoslavia formed in 1992. It lies in the southern part of the country on the Adriatic Sea.

Montenegro, whose name in Serbo-Croatian, *Crna Gora,* means "black mountain," is a mountainous land with many towering summits that stretch down to the Adriatic coast. It covers about 5,333 square miles (13,812 square kilometers) and has about 583,000 people. Podgorica (formerly Titograd) is Montenegro's capital and largest city.

Dense beech and pine forests blanket the northern region, where the winters are harsh and snowy. The southernmost area along the Adriatic coast enjoys a mild, Mediterranean climate, and many tourists enjoy its warm, sunny weather and its beaches. However, tourism declined significantly in the early 1990's as a result of war in the neighboring republics of Croatia and Bosnia and Hercegovina—once part of the Yugoslav federation—and the UN-imposed trade embargo on Yugoslavia.

The rivers flowing through Montenegro to the Adriatic and Black seas are clear, fast-moving mountain streams that wind their way through deep canyons. The canyon of the Tara, for example, is one of the largest in the world in depth and length.

Montenegrins make up about 67 per cent of the republic's population, which also includes Albanians, Serbs, and members of other groups. Most Montenegrins speak Serbo-Croatian and belong to the Eastern Orthodox Church.

Because the Montenegrins speak the same language as the Serbs and trace their roots to a common ancestry, these two groups have long shared strong cultural ties. The close relationship between Serbs and Montenegrins became an economic advantage for Montenegro after World War II because the

The towering Morača Gorge, with its steep rock walls, is typical of Montenegro's rugged landscape. The region's mountainous terrain and thick forests once isolated the area from the rest of Yugoslavia.

Hoping to enjoy a morsel from the day's catch, a cat crouches next to a fisherman at the edge of a quay in Hercegnovi. A leading resort town on the Adriatic coast, Hercegnovi is known for its luxuriant vegetation.

central government—dominated by Serbs—invested more capital in Montenegro than in the other Yugoslav republics.

Montenegro was once part of the medieval Serbian kingdom. After 1355, when the isolated, mountainous kingdom began to collapse, Montenegro became an independent state ruled by nobles. In 1516, Eastern Orthodox bishops established a theocracy and governed the land until 1851, when Montenegro's ruler took the title of prince and the position of bishop became a separate office.

After World War I (1914-1918), Montenegro became part of what is now Yugoslavia, but it remained an economically backward region, mainly because of its poor transportation system. During World War II (1939-1945), the region was devastated by warfare.

Since the 1960's, Montenegro's transportation network has been vastly improved by new roads and a rail line linking the Montenegrin seaport of Bar with Belgrade, the capital of Yugoslavia. As a result, industry, tourism, education, culture, and health services developed rapidly.

In 1979, however, expansion stopped when a severe earthquake struck Montenegro. The eruption caused many deaths and widespread destruction. Rebuilding and restoration of the region, made possible in part through international aid, got underway.

Kotor Bay, *above,* offers one of the most spectacular sights on the Adriatic coast. The bay is a deeply indented and irregularly shaped inlet surrounded by steep and lofty mountains.

With its simple cottages set amid rolling hills, a small village, *left,* near the coastal town of Kotor reveals the pastoral charm of Montenegro. This southernmost area along the Adriatic coast enjoys a mild Mediterranean climate.

A child rests in her mother's arms, *top right,* in the city of Cetinje, the former capital of Montenegro. Cetinje lies on a barren plateau surrounded by mountains. It is snowbound at least five months of the year.

Serbia

Serbia is one of the two republics, along with Montenegro, that remain of Yugoslavia after four of its republics declared their independence in 1991 and 1992. Serbia also includes the formerly autonomous provinces of Kosovo in southern Serbia and Vojvodina, which lies in the northern part of the republic. A mostly hilly or mountainous country, Serbia is bordered by Hungary, Romania, Bulgaria, Macedonia, Albania, Montenegro, Bosnia-Herzegovina, and Croatia.

The ancestors of present-day Serbs settled in the center of the Balkan Peninsula during the A.D. 500's and 600's. In the late 1100's, one of the tribal chiefs, Stephen Nemanja, formed the first united Serbian state. During the 1300's, King Stephen Dušan led Serbia in victorious battles against the Byzantine Empire.

After Stephen Dušan's death in 1355, the Serbian kingdom began to break up, and in 1389, Serbia was conquered by the Ottomans. The Ottoman Empire ruled Serbia for nearly 500 years. In 1878, Russia defeated the Ottomans and Serbia regained its independence.

During the early 1900's, economic and political differences between Serbia and Austria-Hungary triggered the start of World War I (1914-1918). In June 1914, the heir to the throne of Austria-Hungary, Archduke Francis Ferdinand, was assassinated by Gavrilo Princip, a Serbian patriot from the province of Bosnia in Austria-Hungary. Austria-Hungary then declared war on Serbia.

After World War I ended, Serbia helped form the Kingdom of the Serbs, Croats, and Slovenes, which became Yugoslavia in 1929. Between World War I and World War II (1939-1945), the Serbs dominated Yugoslavia's central government. The overwhelming majority of important government posts went to Serbs, fueling tension between Serbia and the other republics.

The conflict between Serbia and the other republics was ultimately a contributing factor to the withdrawal of Bosnia-Herzegovina, Croatia, Macedonia, and Slovenia from the Yugoslav federation in 1991 and 1992.

Beginning in the late 1980's, tension grew within Serbia's own borders. In 1990, the Serbian government dissolved Kosovo's parliament in response to the province's demand to be recognized as a separate republic within the Yugoslav federation. That same year, an amendment to Serbia's constitution revoked the autonomy of both Kosovo and Vojvodina.

Rising on a rocky point high above the Danube, Golubac Castle, *top center,* is one of the largest and most beautiful buildings along the river. Built by the Serbs in the early 1300's, it was occupied by the Turks in 1391, then retaken by the Serbs in 1867.

A Serbian Orthodox monk living along the Crna River hangs his laundry out to dry. About 700 members of the Serbian Orthodox clergy were killed, and about a quarter of their churches were destroyed, during and after World War II.

In May 1992, however, ethnic Albanians in Kosovo—who make up about 90 per cent of the population—took further steps toward self-government. The Kosovo Albanians chose a president and parliament in elections that were declared illegal by the Yugoslav government.

Disagreements within Serbia's government have also added to the tension. Many Serbs have accused Slobodan Milošević, a Serb nationalist who became president of Serbia in 1987, of unfair practices during the elections. They have also protested the continued role of the League of Communists of Serbia, renamed the Socialist Party of Serbia, since the December 1990 multiparty elections in which they won a majority of seats in the republic's government.

Albanian resentment against Serbian authority can be traced back to 1946, when the constitution of Yugoslavia declared the Albanian-speaking areas of Kosovo and Metohija to be the Autonomous Region of Kosmet within the Serbian Republic. During that time, Albanians made up 70 per cent of the region's population, and many of them did not wish to be included in Yugoslavia, preferring to remain within the Greater Albania that had been created by Italy during World War II.

Belgrade's capitol provides an impressive sight on one of the city's boulevards. Few of Belgrade's historic monuments have been preserved, since invading armies have conquered and destroyed the city more than 30 times.

Zaire

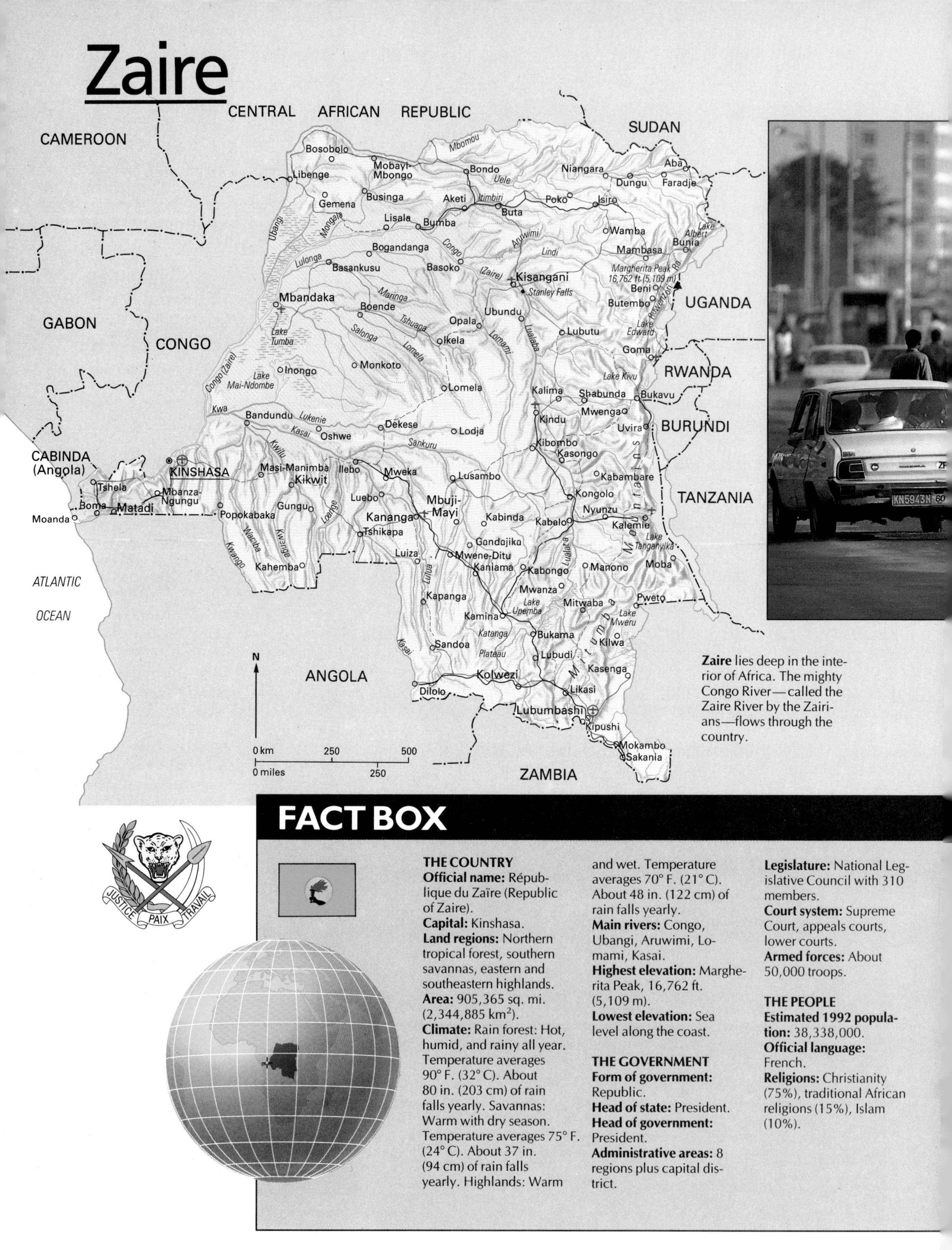

Zaire lies deep in the interior of Africa. The mighty Congo River—called the Zaire River by the Zairians—flows through the country.

FACT BOX

THE COUNTRY
Official name: République du Zaïre (Republic of Zaire).
Capital: Kinshasa.
Land regions: Northern tropical forest, southern savannas, eastern and southeastern highlands.
Area: 905,365 sq. mi. (2,344,885 km^2).
Climate: Rain forest: Hot, humid, and rainy all year. Temperature averages 90° F. (32° C). About 80 in. (203 cm) of rain falls yearly. Savannas: Warm with dry season. Temperature averages 75° F. (24° C). About 37 in. (94 cm) of rain falls yearly. Highlands: Warm and wet. Temperature averages 70° F. (21° C). About 48 in. (122 cm) of rain falls yearly.
Main rivers: Congo, Ubangi, Aruwimi, Lomami, Kasai.
Highest elevation: Margherita Peak, 16,762 ft. (5,109 m).
Lowest elevation: Sea level along the coast.

THE GOVERNMENT
Form of government: Republic.
Head of state: President.
Head of government: President.
Administrative areas: 8 regions plus capital district.
Legislature: National Legislative Council with 310 members.
Court system: Supreme Court, appeals courts, lower courts.
Armed forces: About 50,000 troops.

THE PEOPLE
Estimated 1992 population: 38,338,000.
Official language: French.
Religions: Christianity (75%), traditional African religions (15%), Islam (10%).

Kinshasa, *above,* is a busy, thriving city, but modern road transportation is rare in Zaire. Fewer than 1 per cent of Zairians own an automobile, and most roads are unpaved.

The huge country of Zaire lies in the heart of Africa. Only a narrow strip of land that stretches west to the Atlantic Ocean keeps the country from being landlocked.

One of the world's largest and thickest tropical rain forests covers most of northern Zaire. Its extraordinary variety of trees and plants grow so close together that sunlight seldom reaches parts of the forest floor. Grassy savannas cover much of southern Zaire.

History

Pygmies, the first known inhabitants of what is now Zaire, have lived in the rain forests of the region since prehistoric times. At least 2,000 years ago, other Africans began moving into the area, and by the A.D. 700's, several distinct civilizations were developing in southern Zaire. Kingdoms that formed in the south included the Kongo, the Kuba, the Luba, and the Lunda.

In 1482, Portuguese sailors began making contact with the Kongo people along the coast. Portugal soon established relations with the Kongo king.

Beginning in the early 1500's, thousands of Africans in the area were enslaved and sold to the Portuguese and other Europeans. The slave trade ended in the early 1800's. In 1878, King Leopold II of Belgium hired a British explorer, Henry M. Stanley, to set up Belgian outposts along the Congo River. Leopold eventually gained control of the entire region and made it his personal colony, called the Congo Free State.

The people of the Congo Free State suffered horribly under Leopold's rule. Other countries protested, and in 1908, the Belgian government responded by taking control from the king and renaming the colony the Belgian Congo.

Belgium profited greatly from the resources of its colony but refused to give the people any voice in their government. In 1959, rioting broke out against Belgian rule, and on June 30, 1960, the colony was granted independence. The name of the new nation was Congo.

Civil war followed independence, as rival groups fought for power and various regions tried to *secede* (break away) from the new country. Then in 1965, the Congolese army took control of the government, and General Joseph Désiré Mobutu became president.

Mobutu tried to unify the country and encourage African pride. His government began to change the European names of the nation's cities and physical features to African names. In 1971, the name of the country itself was changed to Zaire.

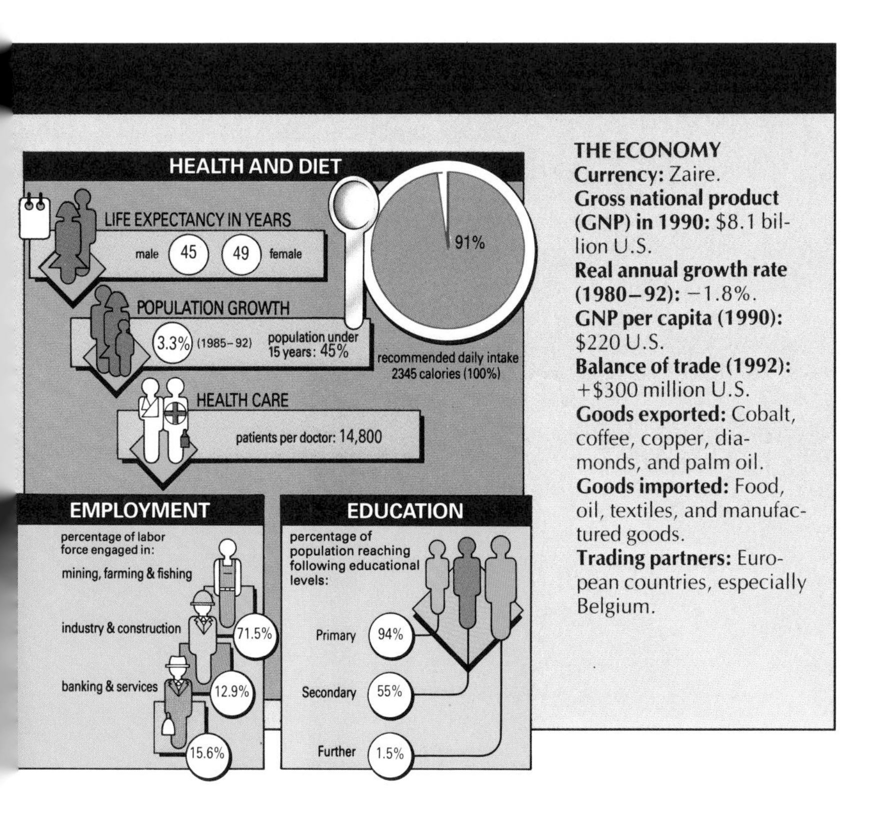

THE ECONOMY
Currency: Zaire.
Gross national product (GNP) in 1990: $8.1 billion U.S.
Real annual growth rate (1980–92): −1.8%.
GNP per capita (1990): $220 U.S.
Balance of trade (1992): +$300 million U.S.
Goods exported: Cobalt, coffee, copper, diamonds, and palm oil.
Goods imported: Food, oil, textiles, and manufactured goods.
Trading partners: European countries, especially Belgium.

Government

Today, the Constitution of Zaire gives the nation's president almost complete control of the government. In 1990, however, Mobutu announced that he would lift a 20-year ban on opposition parties, part of a process intended to lead eventually to multiparty elections.

Etienne Tshisekedi, an opponent of Mobutu, was elected prime minister at a national conference of government and opposition delegates in October 1991. Mobutu later tried to remove Tshisekedi, and rival governments emerged. In 1994, Mobutu named Kengo wa Dondo as a new prime minister and merged the two governments into one. Tshisekedi claimed he was still the legal prime minister. Zaire's first democratic elections in 29 years were expected to be held in 1995.

People and Economy

When Zaire became independent in 1960, Europeans greatly influenced the country's cultural life and economy. Deep divisions existed among Zaire's ethnic groups, and the country faced severe economic problems. Since independence, Zaire's leaders have worked to reduce European influence, unite the people, and improve the economy.

More than 99 per cent of Zairians are black Africans, but they belong to many different ethnic groups. Tension between these groups has caused conflict in Zaire from time to time.

Zaire's people also include the Pygmies, whose ancestors lived in the region thousands of years ago, and Europeans, especially Belgians. In addition, about a million refugees who have fled from neighboring war-torn countries, such as Angola, Burundi, Rwanda, and Uganda, live in Zaire.

French is the nation's official language. It is used by government officials and taught in many schools, but most of the country's ethnic groups have their own language that the people use in their everyday lives. About 200 languages are spoken in Zaire, but most belong to the Bantu language group and thus are closely related. In addition, most Zairians speak one of the country's four regional languages—Kikongo, Lingala, Swahili, and Tshiluba.

About 6 of every 10 Zairians live in rural areas, mainly in small villages that range from a few dozen to a few hundred people. Their houses are made from mud bricks or dried mud and sticks. Most of the homes have thatched roofs, but the houses of more well-to-do rural families have metal roofs. In some areas, people pound out rhythms on drums to send messages from village to village.

The great majority of rural families farm small plots of land and grow almost all their own food, including bananas, cassava, corn, peanuts, and rice. The basic

Zairian dancers sport fantastic costumes that express the ferocity of jungle beasts. Many local African religions include the *animistic* belief that all things in nature have a spirit.

A young miner, *left,* at Kalima, in east-central Zaire, removes tin from ore by repeated washings. Tin is just one of the country's many valuable mineral resources.

A Zairian villager, *below,* bathes in one of the many small rivers that flow into the Congo. Many rural people suffer from malnutrition because their diet often lacks protein.

Zairian dish is a thick porridge made from grain and cassava, served with a spicy sauce.

Crops raised for sale include cacao, coffee, cotton, and tea. Few farmers can afford modern equipment, so most use old-fashioned hand tools and methods. As a result, production is low, and most farm families are poor.

Since independence, large numbers of Zairians—especially young people—have moved to urban areas seeking work. Today about 40 per cent of Zairians live in cities, and this rapid urban growth has caused such problems as unemployment and crowded living conditions. Government officials and business people live in attractive bungalows, but large numbers of urban factory and office workers are crowded into small, flimsy houses made of cinder blocks or mud bricks.

Zaire is a poor country with a developing economy. Urban factory workers produce relatively small amounts of manufactured goods, mainly beer, cement, processed foods, soft drinks, steel, textiles, and tires. Many manufactured goods are imported.

However, Zaire's many natural resources give it the potential to become a wealthy nation. Besides the trees that grow in its rain forests, which yield valuable products such as rubber, Zaire is rich in minerals. Copper is the country's most important mineral resource. Zaire ranks among the leading copper-producing nations and leads the world in producing industrial diamonds, its second most important mineral. Oil deposits lie off the coast, and the nation also has deposits of cadmium, cobalt, gold, manganese, silver, tin, and zinc. Zaire's railroads, which operate mostly in the southeastern section of the country, connect its mines with river ports on the Congo or its branches.

A thick blanket of mist covers the dense tropical rain forest of Zaire. Because of the lack of open space, few people live in the forest, but its trees yield palm oil, rubber, and timber.

The Congo River

The fifth longest river in the world, the Congo River flows 2,900 miles (4,667 kilometers) through the heart of Africa. Carrying more water than any other river except the Amazon, it drains an area of about 1.4 million square miles (3.6 million square kilometers). The Congo is the main waterway of Zaire.

The first European to see the river was Portuguese navigator Diogo Cão, who reached its mouth in 1483. Portuguese settlers established an outpost on the Congo's southern bank near the Atlantic Ocean in the 1490's. But Europeans knew little about the rest of the great river until after the British explorer Henry M. Stanley completed an expedition from its source to its mouth in 1877.

The Congo begins south of Kabalo, Zaire, where the Lualaba and Luvua rivers meet. The river is often called the Lualaba from this point until it tumbles over Stanley Falls, when it is known as the Congo. The people of Zaire, however, have now named it the Zaire River.

Near Stanley Falls, the river turns westward and flows through the rain forest of northern Zaire, where several major rivers empty into the Congo, including the Aruwimi, Lomami, and Ubangi. Near the town of Mbandaka, the Congo turns southwestward to form a natural boundary between the countries of Zaire and Congo for about 500 miles (800 kilometers).

Near Kinshasa, Zaire, the Congo widens so much that it forms a lake called Stanley Pool. The river then drops about 800 feet (240 meters) in altitude, forming a series of spectacular waterfalls between Kinshasa and Matadi, Zaire. These falls prevent riverboats from sailing all the way to the Atlantic Ocean.

The Congo empties into the Atlantic about 90 miles (140 kilometers) west of Matadi. Unlike the Mississippi and the Nile, the Congo does not form a delta at its mouth. Instead, the river's muddy waters flow into a deep trench that extends far into the ocean.

Commercial ships sail the Congo between the Atlantic and Matadi and between Kinshasa and Kisangani, and the river also serves as a major transportation route for local people. Fishing ranks as the most important economic activity in all areas of the Congo River Basin, but little agricultural activity is possible in the dense forest.

People have settled in areas where the riverbanks are relatively firm and permanent. But elsewhere, swampy conditions and the possibility of floods make living conditions much more difficult. In the densely forested, hard-to-reach northern areas of the Congo River Basin, pygmies carry on their traditional ways, hunting and gathering food as they travel in small groups from one area to another.

The rain forests that lie along the mighty Congo are also home to a remarkable variety of wild animals. Crocodiles and hippopotamuses live in or near the river, while baboons, chimpanzees, gorillas, and monkeys thrive in the forests. The okapi, a forest-dwelling animal related to the giraffe, lives nowhere else in the world but the Congo River Basin of Zaire. The okapi was unknown to Europeans until the year 1900, more than 400 years after the first European saw the river itself.

The Congo River, *right,* drains a vast area of equatorial Africa. Despite its many waterfalls and rapids, the Congo is Zaire's main waterway and an important transportation route. Oceangoing ships use the river between the Atlantic and Matadi, and other commercial ships navigate its waters between Kinshasa and Kisangani. Goods are transported between Kinshasa and Matadi by railroad.

Canoe travel, *center,* is widespread on the Congo because of the lack of bridges and roads in the forests that border the river. Rapids and waterfalls prevent navigation in some sections of the Congo, however.

Barge passengers and their belongings travel on the upper course of the Congo River, above Kisangani in Zaire. Here, the great river is usually known as the Lualaba. The waters of the Congo and its branches are navigable for about 7,200 miles (11,500 kilometers) in Zaire, making it one of the country's most important transportation systems.

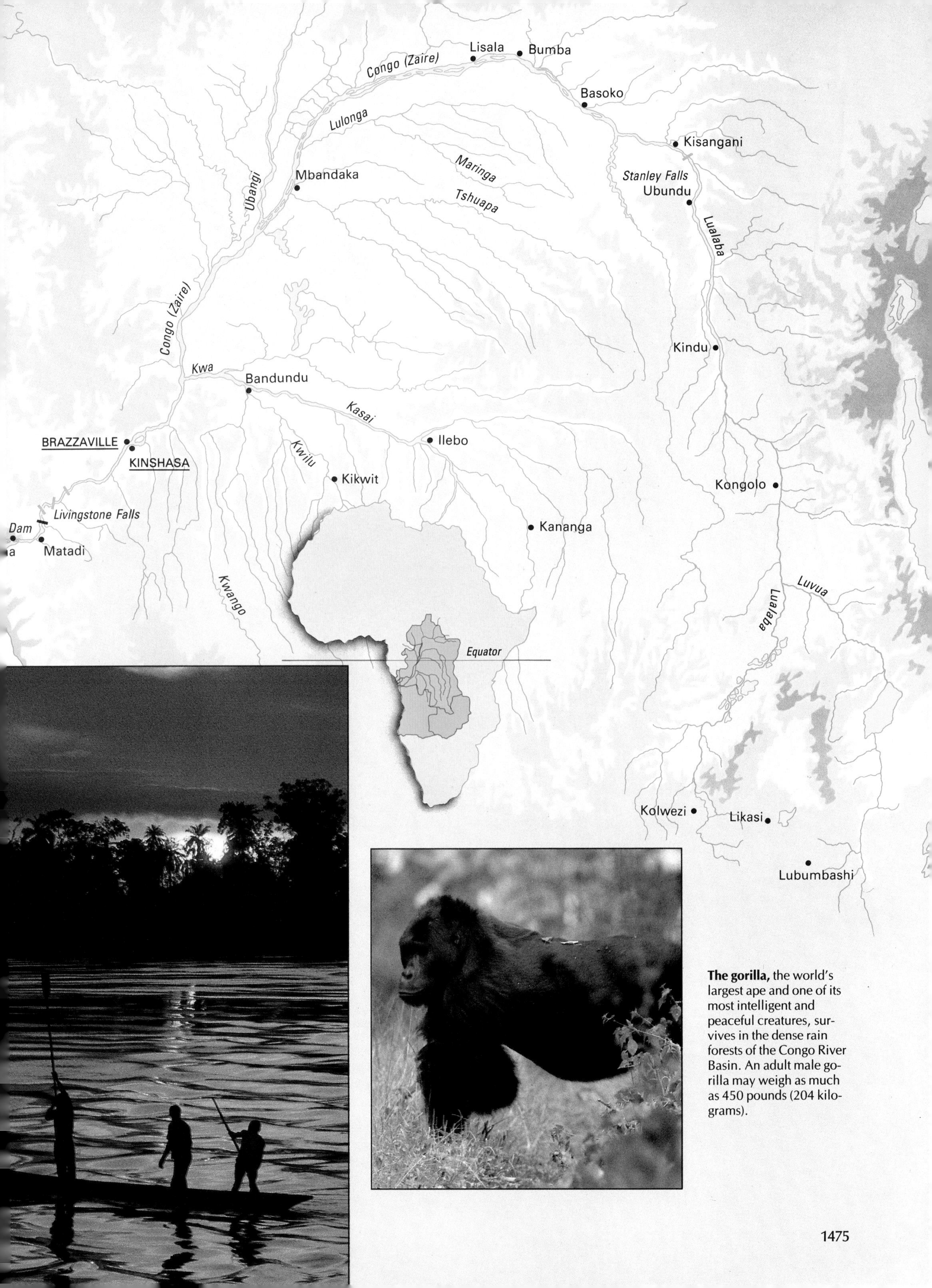

The gorilla, the world's largest ape and one of its most intelligent and peaceful creatures, survives in the dense rain forests of the Congo River Basin. An adult male gorilla may weigh as much as 450 pounds (204 kilograms).

Zambia

The Republic of Zambia in south-central Africa took its name from the great Zambezi River, which forms most of its southern border. Once a British protectorate called Northern Rhodesia, Zambia became an independent nation in 1964.

Government

All Zambian citizens over the age of 18 may vote. The people elect a president as well as the 150 members of the National Assembly, the country's legislature. The president appoints certain Assembly members to Cabinet posts.

Kenneth Kaunda, who led the movement that resulted in independence, served as president from 1964, when Zambia became independent, until 1991. Kaunda became known for his moderate policies.

In 1972, the United National Independence Party (UNIP) became the only legal political party in Zambia. However, in 1990 the National Assembly approved a constitutional amendment permitting the formation of opposition parties. In a multiparty election in October 1991, voters elected Frederick Chiluba of the Movement for Multiparty Democracy as Zambia's new president.

Recent events

Zambia experienced severe economic difficulties during the 1970's and 1980's, due partly to its strained relations with neighboring Rhodesia (now Zimbabwe). Rhodesia was also a former British protectorate, but it had declared its independence without British consent. The Rhodesian government was ruled by whites, even though blacks greatly outnumbered them. Relations between Zambia and Rhodesia deteriorated over the white Rhodesian government's refusal to give the African majority a greater voice.

In 1973, Rhodesia prohibited Zambia from shipping goods across its territory, thus eliminating one of landlocked Zambia's main outlets to the sea. Rhodesia soon lifted the ban, but Zambia refused to ship goods across Rhodesia until 1978. In 1980, when blacks gained control of Rhodesia's government and changed the name of the country to Zimbabwe, relations between the two countries improved.

Zambia was also hurt economically when the price of copper dropped on the world market. Zambia ranks as one of the largest producers of copper, and the mineral accounts for more than 80 per cent of the country's export earnings. In addition,

FACT BOX

THE COUNTRY
Official name: Republic of Zambia.
Capital: Lusaka.
Land regions: Mainly flat plateau; Muchinga Mountains in northeast; sandy flood plain of Zambezi River in southwest.
Area: 290,587 sq. mi. (752,618 km^2).
Climate: Tropical, made milder by altitude, with three seasons: hot from September to November; rainy from November to April; mild to warm from May to August. Yearly rainfall averages 50 in. (130 cm) in north, 20 to 30 in. (51 to 76 cm) in south.
Main rivers: Zambezi, Luangwa, Kafue.
Highest elevation: 7,047 ft. (2,148 m) near eastern border.
Lowest elevation: About 1,600 ft. (500 m), along the Luangwa and Zambezi rivers.

THE GOVERNMENT
Form of government: Republic.
Head of state: President.
Head of government: President.
Administrative areas: 9 provinces.
Legislature: National Assembly with 150 members elected by the people. Members serve five-year terms.
Court system: Supreme Court, High Court, magistrates' courts.
Armed forces: 16,200 troops.

THE PEOPLE
Estimated 1996 population: 9,623,000.
Official language: English.
Religions: Christianity (75%), traditional African religions (24%).

THE ECONOMY
Currency: Kwacha.
Gross national product (GNP) in 1992: $2.6 billion U.S.
Real annual growth rate (1985–92): –2.1%.

Victoria Falls, called *Mosi oa Tunya*—smoke that thunders—by local people, is one of Africa's most awesome sights. The falls lies between Zambia and Zimbabwe on the Zambezi River.

The mining and refining of copper is the basis of Zambia's economy, *below left*. Copper, shown here being processed in a Zambian refinery, accounts for more than 80 per cent of the country's export earnings.

Zambia is a landlocked country in south-central Africa. It takes its name from the Zambezi River, which flows through southwestern Zambia and forms part of its southern border.

HEALTH AND DIET

LIFE EXPECTANCY IN YEARS

male 45 46 female

POPULATION GROWTH

3.5% (1985–92) population under 15 years: 49%

86%

recommended daily intake 2345 calories (100%)

HEALTH CARE

patients per doctor: 7,000

EMPLOYMENT

percentage of labor force engaged in:

mining, farming & fishing 50.2%

industry & construction 25.4%

banking & services 24.4%

EDUCATION

percentage of population reaching following educational levels:

Primary 96%

Secondary 17%

Further 1.5%

GNP per capita (1992): $290 U.S.
Balance of trade (1992): −$200 million U.S.
Goods exported: Copper and cobalt.
Goods imported: Chemical products, food, fuels, machinery, and vehicles.
Trading partners: China, Germany, Great Britain, Japan, South Africa, and the United States.

the production of copper products is the country's most important manufacturing activity. Without copper, Zambia would be one of the poorest countries in Africa.

The economy depends heavily on the mining of other minerals as well. Under President Kaunda, the government controlled the economy. It tried to lessen Zambia's dependence on mining and increase the importance of other economic activities. However, these measures largely failed, and Zambia's economy weakened further. After he took office, President Chiluba promised to privatize industries and introduce market economics in an effort to strengthen the economy.

Land and People

The land of Zambia is mostly a plateau lying about 4,000 feet (1,200 meters) above sea level. Because of its altitude, the country has a milder climate than might be expected in tropical Africa. Trees and bushes cover most of its relatively flat expanse.

The plateau is broken by the Muchinga Mountains, which rise 7,000 feet (2,100 meters) in the northeast. In the southwest, a broad, sandy plain lies on either side of the Zambezi River. Every year during the rainy season, the river waters flood this plain.

The wet season lasts from November through April, and violent storms swell the rivers of the country by March. Northern Zambia gets about 50 inches (130 centimeters) of rainfall a year, while the south gets 20 to 30 inches (51 to 76 centimeters). Because of this decrease in rain from north to south, trees in the south are smaller and large open areas are found there.

Many of Zambia's people farm the land for a living, but Zambian farmers cannot grow enough food to feed its rapidly growing population. Only about 5 per cent of the country's land area is cultivated, but a much larger area is suitable for farming. Every year, Zambians clear many square miles of forests to create much-needed farmland.

In the *bush,* or rural areas, where most Zambians live, the people plant their crops in November and December, at the beginning of the rainy season. In these remote parts of the country, life goes on much as it has for hundreds of years. The people live in villages of circular, grass-roofed huts and go out to the surrounding land to raise their food crops. Corn is the country's most important farm product and the people's main food. A favorite dish is *nshima,* a thick corn porridge. Other crops include cassava, coffee, millet, peanuts, sorghum, sugar cane, and tobacco.

However, the development of mining in Zambia has drawn thousands of jobseekers to mining towns. Other Zambians live and

Roman Catholic worshipers, *left,* take part in a religious ceremony. The majority of Zambians are Christians, but traditional African beliefs and religious rituals are still widely practiced.

A spirit dancer, wearing a bright red mask framed by a black wig, *right,* is a member of one of Zambia's *animistic* groups. Animists believe all things in nature have souls.

Shouldering their tools, Zambian boys return to their village after a hard day's work on their families' farms. Zambia's soil is generally poor, and the people make only a bare living off the land.

The Zambian landscape is made up mostly of wide expanses of trees and bushes. This stretch of land lies along the course of the Luangwa River, where water levels fall considerably during the dry season.

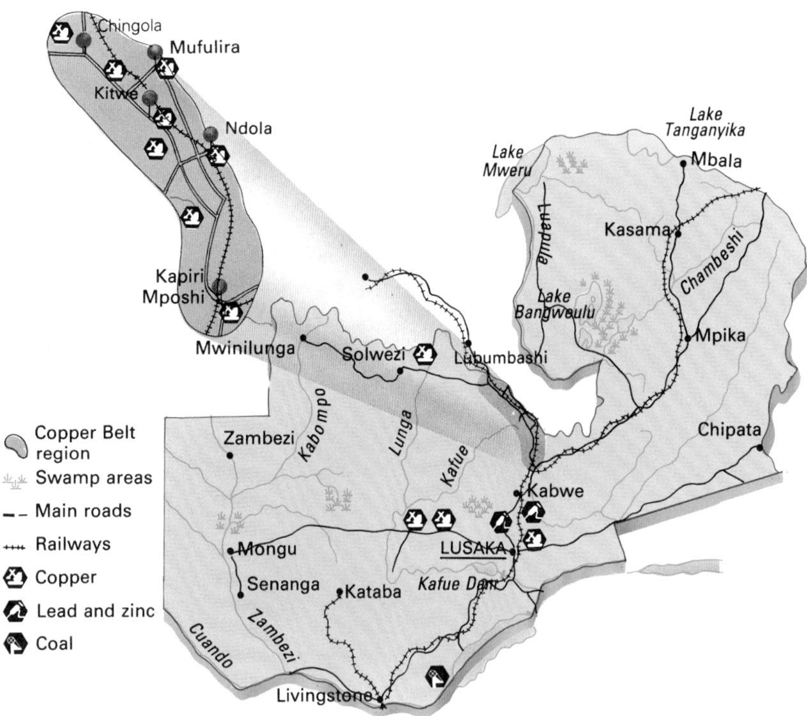

The copperbelt section of Zambia, which lies along the country's border with Zaire, has four large copper mines and several smaller ones. Valuable amounts of cobalt are obtained as by-products of copper mining. Copper mines exist in other parts of Zambia as well, and Zambia also has lead and zinc mines at Kabwe and coal deposits near Kariba Lake on its southern border. Because the nation has no outlet to the sea, rail lines have been built to connect its important mines with Atlantic seaports in Angola and Indian Ocean seaports in Mozambique and Tanzania.

work in the capital city of Lusaka, where the government employs many people. Lusakan factory workers help produce such goods as beverages, cement, food products, furniture, shoes, textiles, and tobacco. Nevertheless, less than half of all Zambians—44 per cent—live in urban areas.

Most Zambians are black Africans who belong to more than 70 different ethnic groups and speak one of eight major Bantu languages. Many Zambians also speak English, the country's official language.

The majority of Zambians are Christians, but traditional African beliefs strongly influence the village people. Traditional herbal medicine is still practiced in some rural areas, and old customs such as *polygyny* (one man marrying several wives) and *bride price* (a man paying parents in order to marry their daughter) are still followed. However, these traditions are slowly dying out in the towns.

The vast majority of Zambian children attend elementary school, but less than 20 per cent go on to secondary school. Those who graduate may enter the country's only university, the University of Zambia, or attend one of the nation's trade or technical schools.

Zimbabwe

The country of Zimbabwe, once known as Rhodesia, lies on a high rolling plateau in tropical southern Africa. Most of Zimbabwe is 3,000 to 5,000 feet (910 to 1,500 meters) above sea level. This high altitude helps create a pleasant climate.

Landscape

Zimbabwe's beautiful scenery includes the famous Victoria Falls on the Zambezi River, which runs along the country's northern border. About halfway between its mouth and its source, the Zambezi—about 1 mile (1.6 kilometers) wide at this point—drops suddenly into a narrow, deep chasm. The mist and spray created by this magnificent waterfall can be seen from several miles away. Because of this permanent cloud and the constant roar of the falling water, the people of the area named the falls *Mosi oa Tunya* (smoke that thunders). When Scottish explorer David Livingstone first sighted the falls in 1855, he named it after Queen Victoria of England.

A canyon about 40 miles (64 kilometers) long permits the water to flow out of the chasm. The height of Victoria Falls varies from 256 feet (78 meters) at the right bank to 343 feet (105 meters) in the middle.

Most rivers in Zimbabwe flow away from the center of the country—either northwest into the Zambezi or southeast—because the High Veld, a central grassy plateau, crosses Zimbabwe from northeast to southwest. The Middle Veld lies on either side of the High Veld. The Low Veld consists of sandy plains in the basins of the Zambezi, Limpopo, and Sabi rivers.

The people and their work

Most of the High Veld grasslands are owned by white farmers, even though whites make up only about 1 per cent of the population. Many blacks work on these commercial farms. Crops include coffee, cotton, peanuts, sugar, sunflower seeds, tea, tobacco, and wheat. Cattle are also raised on large ranches.

Most black Africans, who make up about 98 per cent of Zimbabwe's population, are farmers who raise only enough

Miners, like the one shown here, play an important role in Zimbabwe's economy. Gold, asbestos, and nickel are among the country's valuable mineral exports.

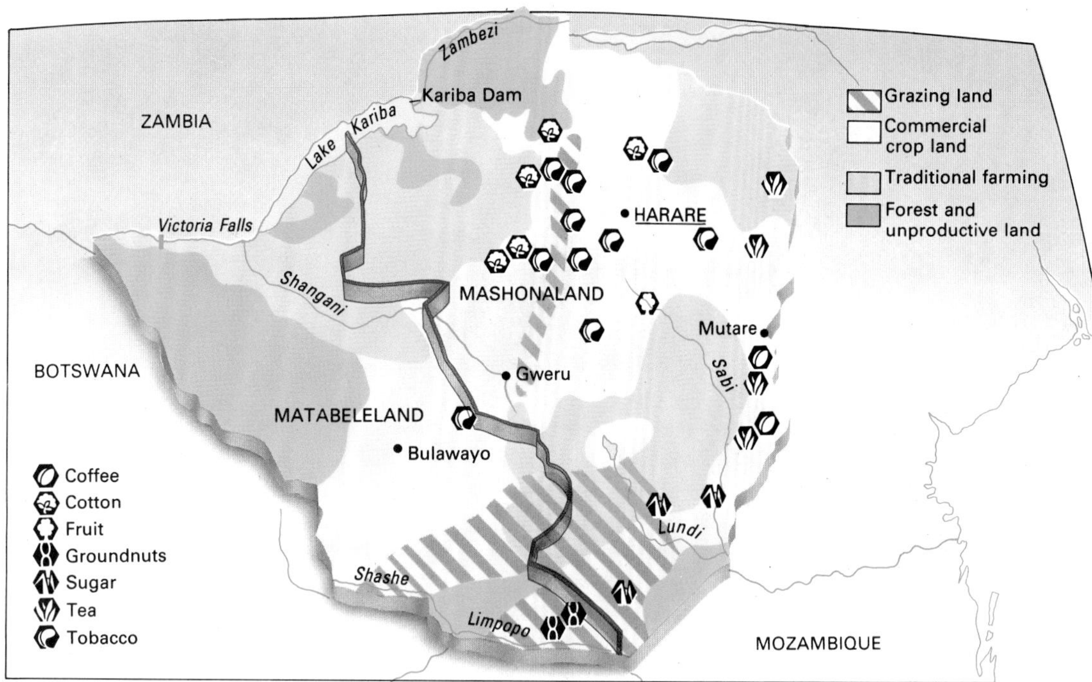

The Chimanimani Mountains rise along Zimbabwe's eastern border. Chimanimani National Park, one of the country's land and animal reserves, lies in this area.

Agriculture helps support Zimbabwe's economy, *above*. In addition to the ones shown here, important crops also include corn and sunflower seeds.

food for their families. Their main crop is corn, which they pound into flour to make a dish called *mealies* or *sadza*.

About 1 per cent of Zimbabwe's population is made up of Asians and *Coloreds* (people of mixed ancestry). Most of the whites, Asians, and Coloreds live in the nation's urban areas, such as the city of Harare, where many whites are business and professional people. Harare is a trading center for products raised on the fertile High Veld. Modern high-rise hotels and office buildings dominate downtown Harare, but crowded slums as well as upper-class suburbs lie on the outskirts of the city.

Most blacks in Zimbabwe live in rural areas, in thatched huts. The Shona people—often called the Mashona—make up the largest black African group and speak a language called Chishona. The Ndebele—often called the Matabele—are the second largest ethnic group, and their language is Sindebele.

English remains the official language of Zimbabwe and the language of business. However, since the black majority gained control of Zimbabwe's government in 1980, many whites have left the country.

Farmers inspect their corn on Zimbabwe's fertile plateau. Many of the country's commercial farms are owned by whites and worked by blacks. White farmers own most of the high grasslands.

A masked dancer, *left,* invokes spirits at a religious gathering near Harare. Most blacks in Zimbabwe follow Christianity blended with traditional African beliefs, which often include *animism*—the belief that everything in nature has a soul—and ancestor worship.

Abundant mineral wealth

Europeans originally came to Zimbabwe because of its mineral wealth. Cecil Rhodes, a British-born businessman, gained mineral rights from the Ndebele in 1888, and reports of gold brought more Europeans to the area in the 1890's.

Today, Zimbabwe is still an important producer of gold, as well as asbestos and nickel. A smelter at Kwekwe (formerly Que Que) removes iron from ore mined in the area, and coal comes from the Hwange (formerly Wankie) region. Zimbabwe also has deposits of chromite, copper, tin, and gems. Although Zimbabwe must import oil, the huge Kariba Gorge hydroelectric complex on the Zambezi River supplies electricity to most of the country.

Zimbabwe Today

Zimbabwe has a long history. Since the late 1800's, that history has been marked by troubled, and often violent, political events.

In the late 1800's, the region that is now Zimbabwe was called Rhodesia, after British businessman Cecil Rhodes, whose company controlled the area. Although the vast majority of Rhodesia's people were black Africans, whites controlled the government. Black African uprisings were crushed in 1896 and again in 1897. Then in 1922, the white settlers of Southern Rhodesia voted for self-government, and the area became a colony separate from Northern Rhodesia in 1923.

In the 1960's, black Africans in Southern Rhodesia began asking for a greater voice in the government. The white government eventually banned two black African parties.

In 1964, when Northern Rhodesia became the independent nation of Zambia, Southern Rhodesia became simply Rhodesia. The white government demanded independence for Rhodesia, but Britain refused to grant independence unless the white government would first guarantee more political power for blacks.

Therefore, when Prime Minister Ian Smith of Rhodesia declared independence on Nov. 11, 1965, Britain claimed the act

FACT BOX

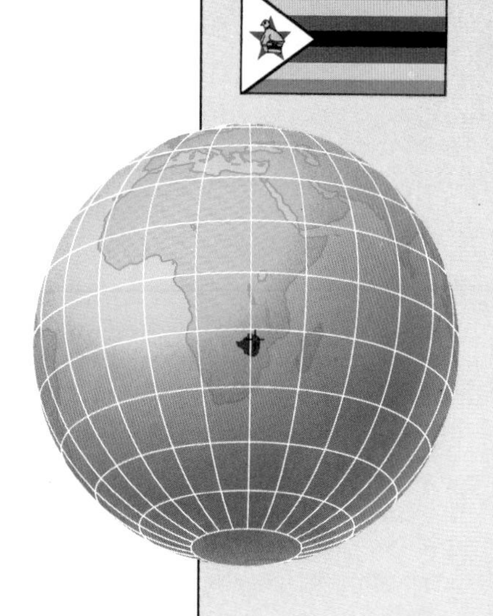

THE COUNTRY
Official name: Republic of Zimbabwe.
Capital: Harare.
Land regions: High Veld (central plateau), Middle Veld (either side of High Veld), Low Veld (sandy plains in river basins).
Area: 150,804 sq. mi. (390,580 km^2).
Climate: Hot, wet summers and cool, dry winters. Temperatures average from 54° to 85° F. (12° to 29° C). Yearly rainfall averages 15 in. (38 cm) in west, 50 in. (130 cm) in east.
Main rivers: Zambezi, Limpopo, Sabi, Shangani.
Highest elevation: Mount Inyangani, 8,514 ft. (2,595 m).
Lowest elevation: About 3,000 ft. (910 m).

THE GOVERNMENT
Form of government: Republic (single-party rule).
Head of state: Executive president.
Head of government: Executive president.
Administrative areas: 8 provinces.
Legislature: House of Assembly with 150 members, 120 of whom are elected by the people, 20 appointed by executive president, and 10 appointed by traditional chiefs. All members serve six-year terms.
Court system: Supreme Court, High Court, local courts.
Armed forces: 54,600 troops.

THE PEOPLE
Estimated 1996 population: 11,845,000.
Official language: English.
Religions: Mixture of Christianity and traditional African religions (25%) and Christianity (25%).

THE ECONOMY
Currency: Zimbabwe dollar.
Gross national product (GNP) in 1992: $6 billion U.S.
Real annual growth rate (1985–92): −0.6%.

Harare, the capital and largest city of Zimbabwe, was founded by white South African settlers in 1890. The city, *left*, was called by the English name of Salisbury until 1982, when it was given its current African name.

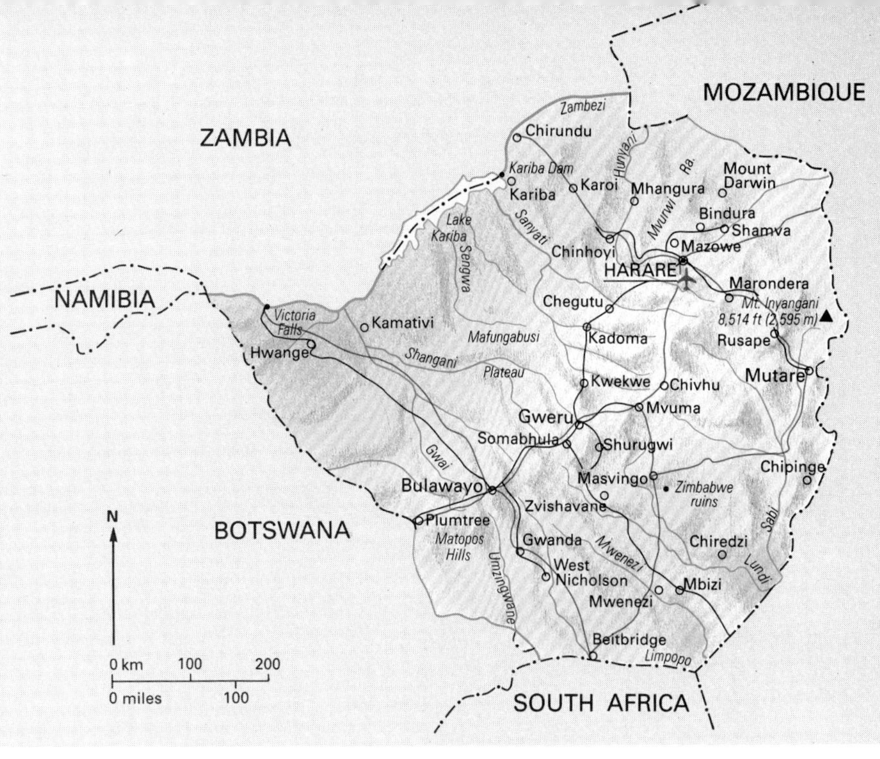

Zimbabwe, *right*, is a landlocked country on a high plateau in southern Africa. The vast majority of its people are black Africans, but whites controlled the government and the economy from about 1890 until 1979.

was illegal and banned trade with Rhodesia. In 1966, the United Nations imposed economic sanctions on Rhodesia, and many other countries then stopped or reduced their trading with Rhodesia.

In 1969, Rhodesian voters—mostly whites—approved a new constitution designed to prevent the black majority from ever gaining control. Rhodesia was declared an independent republic on March 2, 1970, but no country recognized it, and most continued to apply economic and political pressure to end white rule. Then black nationalists began fighting the government within Rhodesia.

These measures finally forced Smith to agree to hand some political power to blacks. The first black-majority government was elected in April 1979, with Abel T. Muzorewa as prime minister. But many blacks rejected this government because they felt it did not truly represent the majority and it still gave whites privileges. Guerrilla violence continued until an agreement was reached to create a new government.

In February 1980, the Zimbabwe African National Union-Patriotic Front (ZANU-PF) party won a majority of seats in the country's Parliament, and Robert Mugabe, the party's leader, became prime minister. On April 18, 1980, Britain recognized the independence of the new nation, now called Zimbabwe. Most other nations recognized the new country and lifted trade sanctions.

But the violence was not over. In 1981, fighting broke out between two black ethnic groups—the Ndebele and the Shona, and the conflict increased when Mugabe, a Shona, dismissed Joshua Nkomo, a Ndebele, from his Cabinet. Most of the fighting ended in 1983. In 1987, after the office of prime minister had been dropped, Mugabe was elected to the new office of executive president. In 1989, the parties of Mugabe and Nkomo merged, and Mugabe was reelected in 1990.

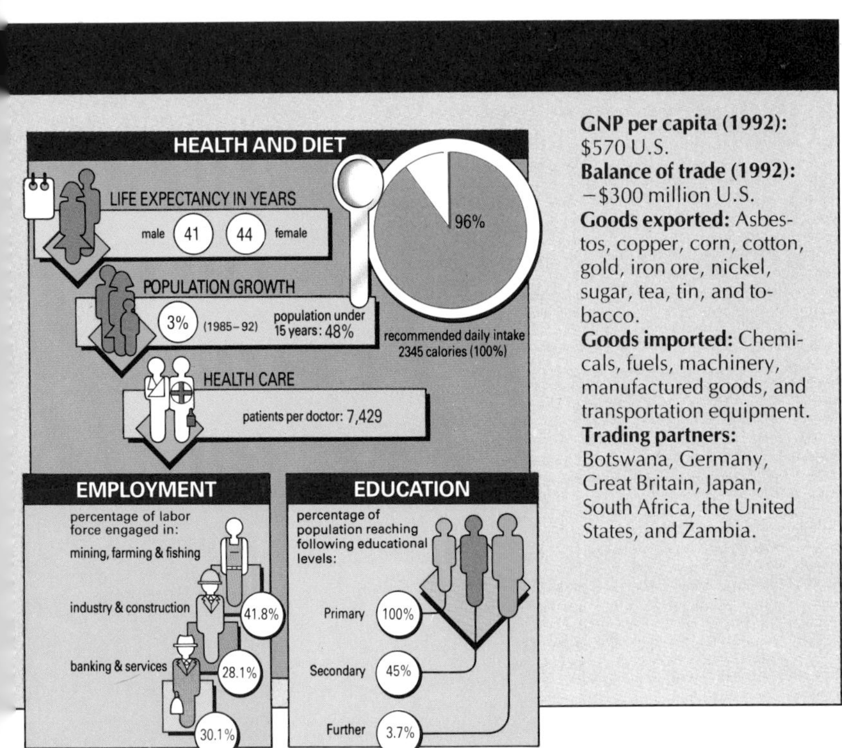

GNP per capita (1992): $570 U.S.
Balance of trade (1992): −$300 million U.S.
Goods exported: Asbestos, copper, corn, cotton, gold, iron ore, nickel, sugar, tea, tin, and tobacco.
Goods imported: Chemicals, fuels, machinery, manufactured goods, and transportation equipment.
Trading partners: Botswana, Germany, Great Britain, Japan, South Africa, the United States, and Zambia.

Great Zimbabwe

Since the late 1800's, Zimbabwe has suffered political troubles and violence, but the region has a long and great history that began thousands of years before the arrival of Europeans. In fact, the name *Zimbabwe* comes from an important part of that history.

Bushmen paintings and tools found in the region indicate that Stone Age people lived in what is now Zimbabwe. By the A.D. 800's, people were mining and trading minerals there. Then about A.D. 1000, the Shona people established their rule over the region.

The Shona built a city called Zimbabwe, or Great Zimbabwe, out of huge granite slabs that were skillfully fitted together, mostly without mortar. The word *zimbabwe* means *house of stone* in Chishona, the language of the Shona.

The ruins of Great Zimbabwe lie near the modern town of Masvingo (once called Fort Victoria). They include a conical tower 30 feet (9 meters) high and part of a wall that rises up to 32 feet (10 meters) high and measures 800 feet (240 meters) around.

The city of Great Zimbabwe, the center of the Shona's Zimbabwe kingdom, eventually became the capital of two African empires. The first was the Mwanamutapa Empire, established during the 1400's by a branch of the Shona people called the Karanga. Their empire included what is now the country of Zimbabwe and part of Mozambique. At eastern African ports on the Indian Ocean, the Karanga traded ivory, gold, and copper for porcelain from China and for cloth and beads from India and Indonesia.

The Rozwi, a southern Karanga group, rebelled against the Mwanamutapa Empire in the late 1400's and conquered it. They founded their own empire, called the Changamire Empire, which became even stronger than the Mwanamutapa.

The Rozwi took over the city of Zimbabwe and built its largest structures. For more than 300 years, the Changamire Empire was prosperous and peaceful. Then in the 1830's, the empire was conquered by the Nguni people from the south, and the city of Great Zimbabwe was abandoned.

European explorers, who came upon the ruins of Great Zimbabwe in the late 1800's, refused to accept the structures as the work of Africans. Some believed they must have been built by non-African settlers from the Middle East or India because the site contained so many goods from those areas.

However, no one had trouble believing that the ruins concealed vast quantities of gold. Treasure hunters plundered the ruins, stole the gold objects, and melted them down. In 1902, a law prevented the looters from ravaging the area any further, but so much had already been destroyed that there was little evidence left of the city's past.

The conical tower, *above,* still stands gracefully amid the ruins of Great Zimbabwe.

Double walls, *right,* skillfully constructed without the benefit of mortar, may have served as a ceremonial walkway during the height of the empire.

Archaeologists have since determined that Great Zimbabwe thrived on foreign trade, and that its buildings included the royal court, markets, warehouses, and religious shrines of the Shona people.

The British had named the whole region around the ruins Rhodesia, after the businessman Cecil Rhodes, whose company had gained control of the area. But when Rhodesia became a modern independent

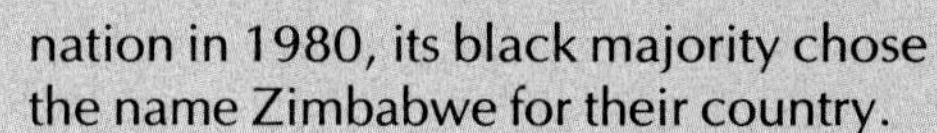

nation in 1980, its black majority chose the name Zimbabwe for their country.

Images of Great Zimbabwe are seen throughout the country today. A white triangle on the nation's flag contains a yellow Great Zimbabwe bird on a red star, while pictures of the conical tower appear on some of Zimbabwe's stamps and paper money.

The view from the Acropolis, or Hill Ruins, *left,* includes the valley of Great Zimbabwe and the town's majestic ruins in the High Veld region near Lake Kyle.

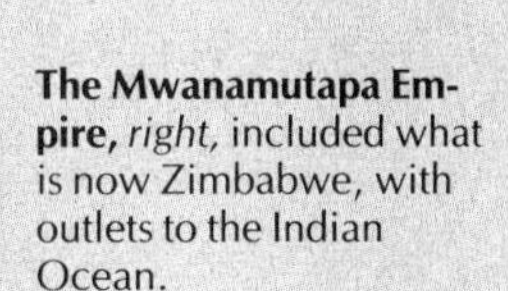

The Mwanamutapa Empire, *right,* included what is now Zimbabwe, with outlets to the Indian Ocean.

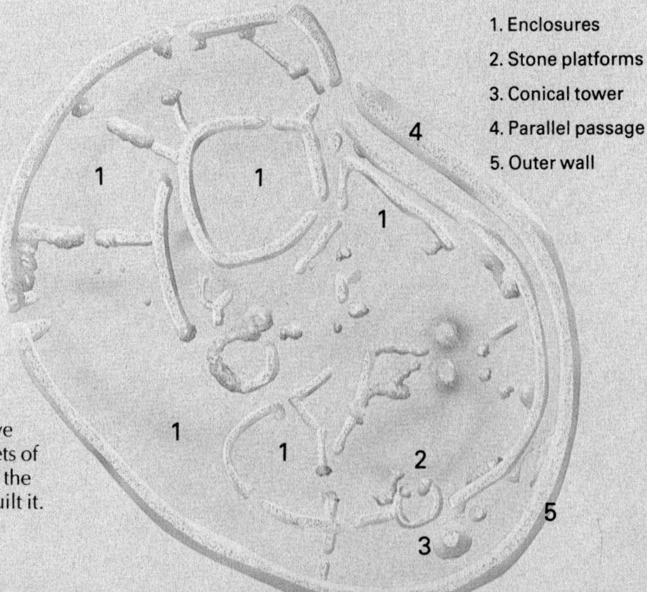

The Great Enclosure, *right,* of the Zimbabwe ruins guards the secrets of the ancient culture of the Shona people who built it.

Index

Note: Page numbers in *italic* type are references to illustrations. Page numbers in **boldface** type are references to maps.

Vol. 1, pages 1-336.
Vol. 2, pages 337-600.
Vol. 3, pages 601-848.
Vol. 4, pages 849-1152.
Vol. 5, pages 1153-1352.
Vol. 6, pages 1353-1580.

A

B

C

E

F

G

H

I

J

K

M

N

O

Q

R

U

V

W

X

Y

Acknowledgments

Maps
Kartographisches Institut Bertelsmann, Gütersloh
Swanston Graphics
Euromap Ltd.
Het Spectrum B.V., 1974

Layouts
Terry Sego
Malcolm Smythe

Diagrams
Eugene Fleury
Ted McCausland
Jean Jottrand

Illustrations
John Davies
Bill Donahoe
Michael Gillah
Tom McArthur
Michael Saunders
John Francis
R. Lewis
Leslie D. Smith
Ed Stuart
George Thompson

Photographic acknowledgments
Abbreviations
t top; b bottom; l left; r right; c center

APA/Apa Photo Agency
APWW/AP Wide World
BPK/Bildarchiv Prerissischer Kulturbesitz
BOV/Britain on View
B&U/B&U International Pictures
CP/Camera Press
CS/Colorsport
DP/Das Photo
FS/Frank Spooner
GAM/Gamma-Liaison
GFS/Gamma/Frank Spooner
HL/Hutchison Library
HPC/Hulton Picture Company
JEP/Jürgens Ost und Europa Photo
MC/Mansell Collection
MPL/Magnum
MTX/Matrix International
NOV/Novosti
PCP/Paul C. Pet
PH/Photo Researchers
PEP/Planet Earth Pictures
PP/Popperfoto
RF/Rex Features
RHL/Robert Hunt Library
RHPL/Robert Harding Picture Library
SA/Survival Anglia
SAP/South American Pictures
SC/Scala
SCL/Spectrum Colour Library
SG/Susan Griggs
SLMG/Soviet Life Magazine
SOV/Sovfoto-Eastfoto
SP/Sipa Press
SYG/Sygma
TAS/Tass
TIB/The Image Bank
TSM/The Stock Market
WC/Woodfin Camp, Inc.
Z/Zefa.

4-5 World Book map; **6-7** George Hunter/*APA;* **8** The Flag Research Center; **9** Eric Bouvet/*GFS;* **10** Disappearing World/*HL;* **10-11t** Thomas Ives/*SG,* **10-11b** *HL,* **11** *APA,* **12** Herman Schlenker/*Z,* **12-13** Heinz Stucke/*GFS,* **13t** Victor Englebert/*SG,* **13b** *MC;* **14** Andre Singer/*HL,* **14-15t** Dr M Beisert/*Z,* **14-15b** J Hatt/*HL;* **17** *SCL;* **18** Th. Foto/*Z,* **18-19t** *SCL,* **18-19b** *SCL,* **19** Th. Foto/*Z;* **20-1** Adam Woolfitt/*SG;* **23** Adam Woolfitt/*SG;* **24** *B&U,* **24-5t** Sarah Errington/*HL,* **24-5b** Victor Englebert/*SG,* **25t&b** *HL;* **26-7t** Julian Calder/*SG,* **26-7b** *HL,* **27** Cyril Isy-Schwartz/*TIB;* **28t** Michael MacIntyre/*HL,* **28b** *SCL,* **28-9t** Michael MacIntyre/*HL,* **28-9b** *SCL;* **30-1** Tor Eigeland/*SG;* **32-3** *HL;* **34-5** *HL;* **36-7** Rick Price/*SA;* **38-9** Rick Price/*SA,* **39l** US Department of the Interior, **39r** Rick Price/*SA;* **40-1** Rick Price/*SA,* **41t** Edwin Mickleburgh/*SA;* **42, 42-3** Prof Dr Franz, **43** Laboratory for Atmospheres, NASA Goddard Space Center/Science Photo Library; **44-5, 45** Richard Laird/*SG;* **46-7** Stephen Pern/*HI;* **49** Mecky Fögeling; **50-1t** Mecky Fögeling, **50-1b, 51** Mike Andrews/*SG;* **52** Robert Frerck/*SG,* **52-3t** Goebel/*Z,* **52-3b** Nancy Durrell McKenna/*HL,* **53** Colorsport; **54** Mecky Fögeling, **54-5** N Russell/Liaison/*GFS,* **55t&b** Stephen Pern/*HL;* **56** Reflejo/*SG,* **56-7** Hallinan/Stockphotos/*TIB,* **56-7b** Mecky Fögeling; **58** Reflejo/*SG,* **58-9t&b** Tony Morrison/*SAP,* **59** Rafael Wollman/*GFS;* **60t** Mansell Collection, **60bl** Magnum/*PP,* **60br** *PP,* **60-1t** International News Photo/*PP,* **60-1b** Rafael Wollman/*GFS;* **63** TAS from *SOV;* **64-5** Paul Steel/*APA;* **68t** Al Satterwhite/*TIB,* **68b** Alastair Scott/*SG,* **68-9t** Guido Alberto Rossi/*TIB,* **69t** Keith Job/*HL,* **69b** David Austen/*SG;* **70** Dallas & John Heaton/*APA,* **70-1t** Jen & Des Bartlett/*SA,* **70-1b** Robin Morrison, **71t** Dallas & John Heaton/*APA,* **71c** L Kuipers/*B&U,* **71b** Jen & Des Bartlett/*SA;* **72t** Pete Turner/*TIB,* **72b** Dallas & John Heaton/*APA,* **72-3t** Robin Smith/*Z,* **72-3b** Pete Turner/*TIB,* LK/*B&U;* **74-5t** Philip Little/*APA,* **74-5b** R Woldendorp/*SG,* **75t** *APA,* **75c** D Baglin/*Z,* **75b** Richard Woldendorp/*SG;* **76t** *B&U,* **76b** Otto Rogge/*TSM,* **76-7t** *APA,* **76-7b** Paul Steel/*APA,* **77t** Bill Bachman/*PH;* **77b** Paul Steel/*APA;* **78-9t, 78-9b** *APA,* **79t** Paul Steel/*APA,* **79c** *APA,* **79b** Paul Steel/*APA;* **80-1t** *B&U,* **80-1b** *Z,* **81t** J Kugler/*APA,* **81b** Ted Spiegel/*SG;* **82t, bl&br** Australian Overseas Information Service, **82-3** Art Seitz/*GFS,* **83** Australian Overseas Information Service; **84-5t** *Z,* **84-5b** Richard Woldendorp/*SG,* **85t** Peter Hendrie/*TIB,* **85b** Guido Alberto Rossi/*TIB;* **86** Alastair Scott/*SG,* **86-7t** *Z,* **86-7b** Philip Little/*APA,* **87** Christine Pemberton/*HL;* **88t** Carl Roessler/*PEP,* **88b** Manfred Gottschalk/*APA,* **88-9** APL/*Z,* **89t** Carl Roessler/*PEP,* **89b** M Kerstitch/*PEP;* **90-1** Scholz/*Z;* **93** Damm/*Z;* **94-5t** Heeresgeschichtlichtes Museum, Vienna, **94** *HPC,* **94-5b** *MC;* **96-7** M Thonig/*Z,* **97t&b** Adam Woolfitt/*SG;* **98-9** Adam Woolfitt/*SG;* **100-01** Adam Woolfitt/*SG;* **102-03t** W L Berssenbrugge/*Z,* **102-03b** Damm/*Z* Rex Features, **102, 103bl** Adam Woolfitt/*SG,* **103br** John Lewis Stage/*TIB;* **104-05** Damm/*Z,* **104, 105** Adam Woolfitt/*SG;* **107** Serguei Fedorov/*WC;* **108t** J Richardson/*SCL,* **108b** Sunak/*Z,* **108-09** *PCP;* **110** F R Damm/*Z;* **112-13** John Lewis Stage/*TIB;* **114-15** Trevor Page/*HL;* **117** Jehangir Gazdar/*SG;* **118** Nicholas Cohen/*SG,* **118-19t** Sarah Errington/*HL,* **118-19b** Jehangir Gazdar/*SG;* **120** Nicholas Cohen/*SG,* **120-21t** *HL,* **120-21b** Sarah Errington/*HL,* **121** Jehangir Gazdar/*SG;* **122** Bartholomew/Liaison/*GFS,* **122-23t** Naray Angants/*HL,* **123** Nicholas Cohen/*SG;* **124** Reflejo/*SG,* **125** Ted Spiegel/*SG;* **126** TAS from *SOV;* **128-29** E Streichan/*Z;* **130-31** Charles W Friend/*SG;* **132-133** *Z,* **133t** Agence Belga, **133bl** *PCP,* **133br** Weinberg Clark/*TIB;* **134** James Davies/*HL,* **134-35t** *PCP,* **134-35b** *SCL,* **135** *SCL,* **135b** Bullaty Lomeo/*TIB,* **136, 136-37** John Heseltine/*SG,* **137t** *HL,* **137b** Charles W Friend/*SG;* **138** *PCP,* **138-39** Melanie Friend/*SG,* **139** Louis De Poortere; **139-40** P Montgomery/*RF,* **141** P Montgomery/*RF;* **142, 141-42** Victor Englebert/*SG;* **145tl** Nik Wheeler/*SG,* **145tr** Larry Dale Gordon/*TIB;* **146-47** Sarah Errington/*HL;* **148-49** Brian Moser/*HL;* **150** Mecky Fögeling, **150-51** Brian Moser/*HL;* **153** Ron Sanford/Black Star; **154, 155** Rob Cousins/*SG;* **156-57** Rob Cousins/*SG;* **160tl** Mary Evans Picture Library, **160bl** *RHL,* **160br** Sipa/Colorsport, **160-61t** Wodder/*TIB,* **161t** Mary Evans Picture Library, **161b** Michael MacIntyre/*HL;* **162** H J Anders/C&J Images/*TIB,* **162-63** S Jorge/*TIB,* **163t** Barbosa/*TIB,* **163b** J L Taillade/Colorsport; **164** *B&U,* **164-65t** *HL,* **164-65b** Jesco von Puttkamer/*HL,* **165** Vautier-De Nanxe; **166** S Barbosa/*TIB,* **166-67t** Reflejo/*SG,* **166-67b** J L Taillade/Colorsport; **168t** *HL,* **168b** Peter Frey/*TIB,* **168-69** Giuliano Colliva/Colorsport; **170** Dr Nigel Smith/*HL,* **170-71t** Marcel Isy-Schwartz/*TIB,* **170-71b** Peter Frey/*TIB,* **171** Sarah Errington/*HL;* **172-73t** Embraer/Brazil, **172-73b** Jesco von Puttkamer/*HL,* **173t** Dr Nigel Smith/*HL,* **173c** Carlos Freire/*HL;* **174-75t** Tony Morrison/*SAP,* **174-75b** R Halin/*Z,* **175t** Victor Englebert/*SG,* **175c** Richard House/*HL,* **175b** Michael MacIntyre/*HL;* **176** S Tucci/*GFS,* **176-77t** Michael Coyne/*GFS,* **176-77b** S Tucci/Liaison/*GFS;* **178-79** Jürgens Ost und Europa Photo; **180, 180-81t** Jürgens Ost und Europa Photo, **180-81b** Adam Woolfitt/*SG,* **181** Jürgens Ost und Europa Photo; **182t&b** Jürgens Ost und Europa Photo, **183-84, 183t** Adam Woolfitt/*SG,* **183b** Jean Michel Nossant/*GFS;* **185** Chris Johnson/*HL;* **186-87** Joe Lynch/*APA;* **189** Michael MacIntyre/*HL;* **190** Tony Martorano/*APA,* **190-91t** *Z,* **191-91b** *HL,* **191** S Giles/*HL;* **192t** Kal Muller/*APA,* **192b** Alain Evrard/*APA,* **192-93t** *HL,*

192-93b H Schmied/*Z;* **194** *HL,* **194-95t&b** Michael MacIntyre/*HL,* **195t** *HL,* **195b** Liba Taylor/*HL;* **197tl&tr** *HL,* **197b** Dr Nigel Smith/*HL;* **198-99** Leon Schadeberg/*SG;* **200-01** Leon Schadeberg/*SG;* **202** Leon Schadeberg/*SG,* **202-03t** John Bulmer/*SG,* **202-03b** Leon Schadeberg/*SG,* **203** Terry Madison/*TIB;* **204, 204-05** John Bulmer/*SG,* **205** Dr H Ginsburg; **206t** Victor Englebert/*SG,* **206b** *HL,* **206-07** Bernard Regent/*HL,* **207t** Victor Englebert/*SG;* **208-09** Victor Englebert/*SG;* **210** Victor Englebert/*SG,* **210-11** Bernard Regent/*HL,* **211t** Heinz Stucke/*FS,* **211b** V & A Wilkinson/*HL;* **212-13** H Wendler/*TIB;* **216** *Z,* **217t** Dallas and John Heaton/*APA,* **217c** Gary Cralle/*TIB,* **217b** Earl Roberge/*TIB;* **220t** *MC,* **220bl** *MC,* **220br** Canadian High Commission, **221** Guido Alberto Rossi/*TIB;* **222t** R Vroom/Canadian High Commission, **222b** Canadian High Commission, **222bl** Canada House Film and Video Library, **222-23** *DP,* **222-23b** Robert Holmes/*SG,* **223l** D Wilkins/*APA,* **223r** Greenpeace/Baptist/*GFS;* **224-25t** Bernard Regent/*HL,* **224-25b** Hunter/*Z,* **225t** Melchior Di Giacomo/*TIB,* **225c** DC Productions/*TIB,* **225b** Grant V Faint/*TIB;* **226** Marc Romanelli/*TIB,* **226-27t** K Kummels/*Z,* **226-27b** Damm/*Z,* **227** Ted Speigel/*SG;* **230tl** The Flag Research Center, **230, 230-31** Heinz Stucke/*FS;* **233t&b** Victor Englebert/*SG;* **234-35** Wendy Watriss/*SG;* **236-37t&b** Wendy Watriss/*SG,* **237t** Chris Johnson/*HL,* **237b** *HL;* **238-39** Mike Andrews/*SG;* **241** Alexis Duclos/*FS;* **242, 242-43t** Mike Andrews/*SG,* **242-43b** Norwegian Archipelago Expedition/*SG,* **243** Rob Cousins/*SG;* **244l** Vautier-Decool, **244r** *B&U,* **244-45** Victor Englebert/*SG,* **245t** Brian Moser/*HL,* **245b** Rob Cousins/*SG;* **246** Brian Moser/*HL,* **246-47** Mireille Vautier, **246-47b** Goycolea/*HL;* **248-49** Don Klumpp/*TIB;* **252tl** Mansell Collection, **252br** Robert Hunt Library, **252-53** Hans Verkroost; **254tl** Mansell Collection, **254bl** Robert Hunt Library, **254br** Xinhua/*GFS,* **254-55** Eric Bouvet/*GFS,* **255** Sipahioglu/Sipa/*RF;* **256** Gulbenkian Collection, Durham, **256-57t** Freer Gallery of Art/*ET* Archive, **256-57b, 257** Hans Verkroost; **258-59t** Hans Verkroost, **258-59b** Earth Satellite Corp/Spectrum Colour Library, **259tl** Hans Verkroost, **259tr** Michael MacIntyre/*HL,* **259b** Guido Alberto Rossi/*TIB;* **260-61t** Thiele/*Z,* **260-61b** Sarah Errington/*HL,* **261** Dave Brinicombe/*HL;* **262** Mike Andrews/*SG,* **262-63t** Harald Sund/*TIB,* **262-63b** Christina Dodwell/*HL;* **264** *GFS;* **266-67t** *HL,* **266-67b** Michael MacIntyre/*HL,* **267t** *HL,* **267b** Janeart Ltd/*TIB;* **268t** Melanie Friend/*HL,* **268b** Leon Schadeberg/*SG,* **268-69** Sarah Errington/*HL,* **269** Don Klumpp/*TIB;* **270** Nik Wheeler/*APA,* **270-71t** Melanie Friend/*HL,* **270-71b** *HL,* **271t** Nik Wheeler/*APA,* **271b** Melanie Friend/*HL;* **272t** Felix Greene/*HL,* **272bl** Harald Sund/*TIB,* **272br** Hans Verkroost, **272-73** John Bryson/*TIB;* **274-75** Scholz/*Z,* **275** *HL;* **276-77t** *HL,* **276-77b** Adam Woolfitt/*SG,* **277** *HL;* **278t** Jules Zalon/*TIB,* **278b, 278-79t** *HL,* **278-79b** Paul Slaughter/*TIB;* **280** Nevada Wier/*TIB,* **280-81t** Leon Schadeberg/*SG,* **280-81b, 281** *APA;* **282** Marcus Brooke/*APA,* **282-83t** Jean Kugler/*APA,* **282-83b** Felix Greene/*HL,* **283t** *APA,* **283b** Felix Greene/*HL;* **284** N Navaro/*GFS,* **284-85** Pierrette Collomb/*HL,* **285t** *HL,* **285c&b** Melanie Friend/*HL;* **286-87** Adam Woolfitt/*SG;* **289** Patrick Rouillard/*TIB;* **290-91** Peter R Dickerson/*SG,* **291t** Brian Moser/*HL,* **291bl** Victor Englebert/*SG,* **291br** *HL;* **292t&b** Victor Englebert/*SG,* **292-93t** Brian Moser/*HL,* **293** Victor Englebert/*SG;* **294, 294-95** Tony Morrison/*SAP,* **295t** Adam Woolfitt/*SG,* **295b** Tony Morrison/*SAP;* **298-99, 299** Al Venter/*GFS;* **300-01** *Z;* **302, 302-03t, 303** Kal Muller/*SG;* **304bl&br** Gilles Merment/*GFS,* **304-05t** Peter Riley/South American Pictures, **305** Gilles Merment/*GFS;* **306-07** J H Carmichael Jr/*TIB;* **308** Gilles Merment/*GFS,* **308-09t** Peter Riley/South American Pictures, **308-09b** Gilles Merment/*GFS;* **311t, T** E Clark/*HL;* **311b** *SCL;* **312-13t** Damm/*Z,* **313t** Brian Moser/*HL,* **313b** John Griffith; **315** Felix Green/*HL;* **316** Felix Green/*HL,* **316-17t** Brian Moser/*HL,* **316-17b** Brian Moser/*HL,* **317** John Hatt/*HL;* **318** John Bulmer/*SG,* **318-19t** John Griffith, **318-19b, 319** Christine Pemberton/*HL;* **321** Brown/*FS;* **322** A Gasson/*RF,* **322-23t** *PCP,* **322-23b** *PCP,* **323t** Brown/*FS,* **323b** Thompson/*SCL;* **324-25** *HL;* **326-27** Jürgens Ost und Europa Photo; **328t,cl,bl** Mansell Collection, **328br** Jürgens Ost und Europa Photo, **328-29** Robert Hunt Library, **329t** Nathan Benn/*SG;* **329b** Michal Krumphanzl, CTK from Eastfoto; **330** Liba Taylor/*HL,* **330-31t** Jürgens Ost und Europa Photo, **330-31b** *Z,* **331** Liba Taylor/*HL;* **332t** Mary Evans Picture Library, **332b** Jürgens Ost und Europa Photo, **332-33t** British Film Institute, **332-33b** Jürgens Ost und Europa Photo, **333t** B&U International Pictures, **333c** Kobal Collection, **333b** Bouvet-Merillon/*GFS;* **334, 334-35t&b** Jürgens Ost und Europa Photo, **335l** Jaroslav Kubec/*TSM,* **335r** Peter Sellers/Impact; **339** W Saller/*Z;* **340-41** Paul C Pet; **342t** Paul C Pet, **342b** T Brettmann/*Z,* **342-43t** *Z,* **342-43b** Paul C Pet; **344-45** Victor Englebert/*SG;* **346** Bernard Regent/*HL,* **346-47** Adam Woolfitt/*SG;* **349** Martin Rogers/*SG;* **350-51t** Bernard Regent/*HL,* **350-51b** Martin Rogers/*SG,* **351t** Bernard Regent/*HL,* **351b** *DP;* **352-53t** J M Adamini/*GFS,* **352-53b** G Sirena/*Z,* **353t&b,** Michael Folco/*GFS;* **354-55** Victor Englebert/*SG;* **357tr** Mireille Vautier, **357c** Mike Andrews/*SG;* **358t** Mireille Vautier, **358b, 358-59t&b** Victor Englebert/*SG,* **359l** Mireille Vautier; **360t** Alan Root/*SA,* **360c** D & M Plage/*SA,* **360-61t** Jason Shenai/*SG;* **362-63** *Z;* **364-65** *HL;* **366l** *PCP,* **366r** NASA/Science Photo Library; **368t** Liba Taylor/*HL,* **368c** Sarah Errington/*HL,* **368b** Hutt/Mepha/*FS,* **369t** Dick Doughty/*Impact Visuals;* **369b** Robert Holmes; **370-71t** Charles W Friend/*SG,* **370-71b** Pasieka/*Z,* **371** C Osbourne/Mepha/*FS;* **372t** *PCP,* **372b** Dave G. Houser, **372-73t** *Z,* **373** A Hutt/Mepha/*FS;* **374t** *PCP,* **374bl** Mitchell Beazley, **374br** Egyptian Tourist Board, **374-75** *PCP,* **375bl** Melanie Friend/*HL,* **375br** *PCP;* **376-77t** Sacha Rocos/*GFS,* **376-77b** Hoagland/Liaison/*GFS,* **377** P F Bentley/Photoreporters; **379** Reflejo/*SG;* **380-81t** Jeremy Bigwood/*GFS,* **380-81b** Reflejo/*SG,* **381t** *HL,* **381b** M C Kiernan/*GFS;* **381b** Boccon/Sipa/*RF;* **383t** Heinz Stucke/*FS, Press/Picture Group;* **384** The Flag Research Center, **385b** Pascal Maitre/*MTX;* **386-87** Jürgens Ost und Europa Photo; **385t** Betty **388** N Colton/*SG,* **388-89** John Bulmer/*SG;* **390t** John Bulmer/*SG,* **390-91t** Kal Muller/*APA,* **390-91b** Photonews/*FS,* **391** Kal Muller/*APA;* **392t&b** Adam Woolfitt/*SG,* **392-93t** Zeidl/*Z,* **392-93b** Alastair Scott/*SG;* **394t** Goebel/*Z,* **394b** Ros Drinkwater/*RF,* **394-95t** Annie Price/*SA,* **394-95b** Cindy Burton & Annie Price/*SA,* **395** Ros Drinkwater/*RF;* **396** The Flag Research Center, **397t** *HL,* **397bl** Michael MacIntyre/*HL,* **397br** D Hiser; **399t** F Lochon/*GFS,* **399b** *RF;* **400** Maurice Harvey/*HL,* **400-01** *SCL,* **401t** Charles Zuber/*RF,* **401b** Maurice Harvey/*HL;* **402** Charles Zuber/*RF,* **402-03t** F Lochon/*GFS,* **402-03b** Dallas & John Heaton/*SCL,* **403t** Maurice Harvey/*HL,* **403c** *SCL,* **403b** Michael MacIntyre/*HL;* **404-05** Kotoh/*Z;* **407** G Sirena/*Z;* **408** Michael St Maur Sheil/*SG,* **408-09t** Kotoh/*Z,* **408-09b** Mosler/*Z,* **409t** Bernard Gerard/*HL,* **409b** Michael St Maur Sheil/*SG;* **410-11t** Andy Caulfield/*TIB,* **410-11b** Bernard Gerard/*HL,* **411t** Lr Villota/Stockmarket/*Z,* **411b** Das Photo; **412** Bernard Regent/*HL,* **412-13, 413t** *HL,* **413b** Bernard Regent/*HL;* **414-15** Ian Yeomans/*SG;* **418-19t** Kerth/*Z,* **418-19b** Knight/*APA,* **419b** Bordis/*Z;* **420-21t** Billon/Colorsport; **420-21b** Marvin Newman/*TIB,* **421t** Adam Woolfitt/*SG,* **421bl** Molyneux/*TIB,* **421br** Joyce/*APA;* **422tl** *MC,* **422bl** *MC,* **422br** *MC,* **423l** Jeremy Horner/*HL,* **423r** Victor Englebert/*SG;* **424** Adam Woolfitt/*SG,* **424-25t** Adam Woolfitt/*SG,* **425** Alexandra Allison/*SG;* **426tl&bl** *MC,* **426br** Robert Hunt Library, **426-27t** *MC,* **427c** Le Segnetau/*RF,* **427b** Robert Hunt Library; **428** *B&U,* **428-29t** Christine Pemberton/*B&U,* **428-29b** *Z,* **429t** Tim Motion/*HL;* **430** Bernard Regent/*HL,* **430-31t** Michel Braud/*APA,* **430-31b** *B&U,* **431** John Lewis Stage/*TIB;* **432t** Adam Woolfitt/*SG,* **432b** *HS/B&U,* **433** Alex Bartel/*APA;* **434t** Adam Woolfitt/*SG,* **434b** Oster/*Z,* **434-35t** Adam Woolfitt/*SG,* **434-35b** *SCL,* **435** *PCP;* **436-37t** John Lewis Stage/*TIB,* **436-37b** W-E Gudemann, **437b** John Lewis Stage/*TIB;* **438** Heinz Stucke/*FS,* **438-39** John Bulmer/*SG,* **439** Heinz Stucke/*FS;* **440** Guido Alberto Rossi/*TIB,* **440-41** Erwin Christian/*Z,* **441t** *Z,* **441b** Erwin Christian/*Z;* **442** Bernard

Regent/*HL,* **443** *HL;* **444t** Bernard Regent/*HL,* **444b** *HL,* **444-45t** C Francois/Figaro/*GFS,* **444-45b** *HL,* **445** Bernard Regent/*HL;* **447l** *HL,* **447r** Robin Laurance/*SG;* **449t** Steenmans/*Z;* **450-51** San Zarenber/*TIB;* **454br** *HPC,* **454t&bl** *MC,* **455t** Friedrichsruh/ Bismarck Museum/*BPK,* **455c** Bundesarchiv; **456tl** Vioujard/*GFS,* **456tr** Leon Schadeberg/ *SG,* **456bl** *HPC,* **456br** Patrick Piel/*GFS,* **456-57** *JEP,* **457** Popperfoto; **458t&b** Damm/*Z,* **459t** D Woog/*Z,* **459b** Helbing/*Z;* **460t** K Goebel/*Z,* **460b** F Brieg/*Z,* **460-61t** M Thonig/ *Z,* **460-61b** Horst Munzig/*SG;* **462-63t** Damm/*Z,* **462-63b** K Goebel/*Z,* **463** Hackenberg/*Z;* **464-65t** *DP,* **464-65b** Rossenbach/*Z,* **465t** Streichan/*Z,* **465b** Reinecke/Weichert/Bundesbildstelle; **466** Kolhas/*Z,* **466-67t** Damm/*Z,* **466-67b** Robert Hunt Library, **467** Paul Van Reil/*TIB;* **468** Lisl 75/*TIB,* **468-69t** *JEP,* **468-69b** Gert von Bassewitz/*SG,* **469** Damm/*Z;* **470** *JEP,* **470-71t** Waldkirch/*Z,* **470-71b** Rhise/*Z,* **471** Damm/*Z;* **472-73t** Damm/*Z,* **472-73b** K Lehnartz/*Z,* **473** *BPK;* **474-75t&b** *JEP,* **475t** Rossenbach/*Z,* **475b** *JEP;* **476, 476-77t&b, 477** *JEP;* **478-79** Hackenberg/*Z,* **479t&bl** *JEP,* **479br** Kotoh/*Z;* **480** Michael Pasdzior/*TIB,* **480-81** Horst Munzig/*SG,* **481t** T Schneiders/ *Z,* **481bl** N Bahnsen/*Z,* **481br** *JEP;* **482-83** Bavaria Verlag/*SCL,* **483t** M Thonig/*Z,* **483b** R Friedrich; **484** *SCL,* **484-85** *JEP,* **485** Mecky Fögeling; **486** Juergen Schmitt/*TIB,* **486-87** Streichan/*Z,* **487tl** Rosenfeld/*Z,* **487tr** H Lutticke/*Z,* **487c** Siemens Pressbild; **488-89** *JEP,* **489t** Damm/*Z,* **489cl** C Calais/*Z,* **489cr** Adam Woolfitt/*SG;* **490** Anna Tully/*HL,* **490-91t** Victor Englebert/*SG,* **490-91b** Anna Tully/ *HL,* **491** Michael St Maur Sheil/*SG;* **492-93** Victor Englebert/*SG;* **494-95t** K F Scholz/*Z,* **494-95b** John Bulmer/*SG,* **495t** *HL,* **495b** Tom Smith/Robert Harding Library; **496** Nathan Benn/*SG,* **496-97t&b, 497,** Robert Frerck/*SG;* **498-99** Brian Boyd/*BOV;* **500** O Henson/ *BOV;* **502** *BOV,* **502-503t&b** *BOV,* **503** Docklands Development Corporation; **504-05** Colin Molyneux, **505t** *CP,* **505bl&br** *BOV;* **506** Michael St Maur Sheil/*SG,* **506-07t** T Wood/Stockphotos/*TIB,* **506-07b** Adam Woolfitt/*SG,* **507t** Julian Nieman/*SG,* **507bl** Peter & Georgina Bowater/*TIB,* **507br** Bernard Gerard/*HL;* **508-09, 509t** Northern Ireland Tourist Board, **509c** Bradley/*GFS,* **509b** Shorts Brothers Plc; **510bl** Monique Jacot/*SG,* **510br** Barry Hicks/*BOV,* **511** Isle of Man Tourism; **512, 512-13t** *Z,* **512-13b** Barry Hicks/*BOV,* **513tl&tr** Adam Woolfitt/*SG,* **513b** *BOV;* **514-15t&b** Adam Woolfitt/*SG,* **513t&b** Liba Taylor/*HL;* **516-17** F Reglain/*GFS,* **517t** Romilly Lockyer/*TIB,* **517b** G de Keerle/*GFS;* **518** Rex Features, **518-19, 519t** Adam Woolfitt/*SG,* **519cl** David Stewart-Smith/*SG,* **519cr** Philip Little/*APA,* **519b** Nigel O'Gorman; **520t&br** *MC,* **520bl** *FPA,* **520-21t** Adam Woolfitt/*SG,* **520-21b** *BOV;* **522br** Oscar & Peter Johnson Ltd, London/ Bridgeman Art, **522bl** *APA,* **522tl** *MC,* **522tr** Alain Nogues, *SYG,* **522-23t** *MC,* **522-23b** *HPC;* **524-25** Michael Friedel/*RF,* **525** Stockmarket/*Z;* **526-27** Dallas & John Heaton/ *APA;* **528** Dallas & John Heaton/*APA;* **530** David Beatty/*SG,* **530-31** Rick Strang/*APA,* **531bl** *B&U,* **531br** Michael St Maur Sheil/*SG;* **532** Michael St Maur Sheil/*SG,* **532-33** G P Reichelt/*APA,* **533bl** David Beatty/*SG,* **533br** *PCP;* **534** Pierrette Collomb/*HL,* **534-35t** *PCP,* **534-35b** Key Color/*Z;* **536** David Beatty/*SG,* **536-37** *PCP,* **537t** Bernard Regent/*HL,* **537b** G P Reichelt/*APA;* **538tl** *MC,* **538bl** *MC,* **538br** Popperfoto, **538-39** K Kerth/*Z,* **539** Bernard Regent/*HL;* **540** *MC,* **540-41** Adam Woolfitt/*SG;* **542** John Egan/*HL,* **542-43t** Adam Woolfitt/*SG,* **542-43b** Robert Knight/ *APA,* **543** David Beatty/*SG;* **544** *PCP,* **544-45** *PCP,* **545** *Z;* **546-47t** Konrad Helbig/*Z,* **546-47b** H W Marmaras/*SG,* **547t** John Marmaras/ *SG,* **547b** John Marmaras/*SG;* **548, 548-49t** Ferchland/*Z,* **548-49b, 549** W Higgs/ Geoscience Features; **550** Jenny Allsopp/*SG,* **550-51** Cotton Coulson/*SG,* **551** Trevor Page/ *HL;* **552-53t** Adam Woolfitt/*SG,* **552-53b** Richard Laird/*SG,* **553c** Nicolas Sainte Luce/ *GFS;* **554-555t&c** J G Fuller/*HL,* **555t** *HL,* **555c** Michael MacIntyre/*HL;* **556t** *PCP,* **556b** *HL,* **556-57t** *PCP,* **557** *PCP;* **558-59** Reflejo/ *SG;* **560t** Robert Frerck/*SG,* **560b** *PCP,* **560-61t** J G Fuller/*HL,* **560-61b** *PCP;* **562-63** *Z;* **564t** Heinz Stucke/*FS,* **564c&b** J C Francolon/ *GFS,* **564-65t&b** M P Revelon/*GFS;* **566** Heinz Stucke/*FS,* **567** Boudin/*GFS;* **569** Heinz Stucke/*FS;* **570-71t** Nick Gordon/*SA,* **570-71b, 571** John Bulmer/*SG;* **572** John Hatt/*HL,* **573** Eric L Wheater/*TIB;* **574t** Jay Freis/*TIB,* **574b** Sarah Errington/*HL,* **574-75t** Dick Rowan/*SG,* **574-75b** Sarah Errington/*HL,* **575** Sarah Errington/*HL;* **576-77t** Simon Fisher/*RF,* **576-77b** R Haesler/Sipa/*RF,* **577** Issot/ Sergent/*GFS;* **578-79** Adams/*GFS,* **579t** John Madere/*TIB;* **580** Reflejo/*SG,* **580-81t** Reflejo/ *SG,* **581** Simon Fisher/*RF;* **582-83** R Ian Lloyd/*HL;* **584** Hans Verkroost, **584-85t** Keith MacGregor/*SG,* **584-85b** Jean Kugler/*APA,* **585t** Alain Evrard/*APA,* **585b** Rasmussen/Sipa/ *RF;* **586** Rasmussen/Sipa/*RF,* **586-587t** Manfred Gottschalk/*APA,* **586-87b** Hans Verkroost, **587** Keith MacGregor/*SG;* **588** TOM/*Z;* **590-91** Dr H Kramarz/*Z;* **592t&bl** Mansell Collection, **592br** Popperfoto, **592-93** Robert Hunt Library, **593** Adam Woolfitt/ *SG;* **594t** Horst Munzig/*SG,* **594b** *HL,* **594-95t&b** Jürgens Ost und Europa Photo, **595** *HL;* **596t&b** Jürgens Ost und Europa Photo, **596-97** John Bryson/*TIB;* **598-99** Art Zamur/ *GFS,* **599t** Adam Woolfitt/*SG,* **599c** Jürgens Ost und Europa Photo, **599b** Horst Munzig/ *SG;* **602-03** B&U International Pictures; **604** Prof Dr Franz-Dieter Miotke, **604-05t** J Behnke/*Z,* **604-05b** Sam Hall/*GFS,* **605l** Robert Francis/*HL,* **605r** Horst Munzig/*SG;* **606t** Robert Francis/*HL,* **606b** Paul C Pet, **606-07** Horst Munzig/*SG;* **608-09** Lyle Lawson/*APA;* **612t** *MC,* **612bl** *PP,* **612br** Adams/Liaison/*GFS,* **612-13** Robert Hunt Library; **614-15** *PCP;* **616-17** Stephanie Arnal/ *GFS,* **617** Jehangir Gazdar/*SG;* **618** *APA,* **618-19t** Adam Woolfitt/*SG,* **618-19b** *PCP;* **620-21t** Lyle Lawson/*APA,* **620-21b** K Debnicki/*APA,* **621t** Adam Woolfitt/*SG,* **621b** Jehangir Gazdar/*SG;* **622** Christine Pemberton/*HL,* **622-23t** Lisl Dennis/*TIB,* **622-23b** Andre Singer/*HL,* **623t** C Maurice Harvey/*HL,* **623b** M Saunders/*HL;* **624** Lyle Lawson/*APA,* **624-25t** Luca Invernizzi/*APA,* **624-25b** Carlos Freire/*HL,* **625t** J Zittenzieher/*Z,* **625b** Michael MacIntyre/*HL;* **626** David Beatty/*SG,* **626-27** Jehangir Gazdar/*SG,* **627** David Beatty/*SG;* **628** *PCP,* **628-29t** Simon Hughes/*APA,* **629t** Jenny Pate/*HL,* **629b** *PCP;* **630l** Craig Lovell/ *APA,* **630r** *HL,* **630-31** *PCP,* **631** Jehangir Gazdar/*SG;* **632-33** *PCP,* **633t** *PCP,* **633b** David Beatty/*SG;* **634-35t** Mary Grant/*SA,* **634-35b** Dr Nigel Smith/*HL,* **635l&r** Dieter & Mary Plage/*SA;* **636-37** Lyle Lawson/*APA;* **638** Pern/*HL,* **638-39t** Jehangir Gazdar/*SG,* **638-39b** Brett Froomer/*TIB,* **639** Jehangir Gazdar/*SG;* **640** *MC,* **640-41b** *APA,* **640-41t** *PCP;* **642** Leon Schadeberg/*SG,* **642-43t** Starfoto/*Z,* **643t** Charles Foale, **643b** Leon Schadeberg/*SG;* **644-45** Robert Francis/*HL;* **648** R Waldendorp/*SG,* **648-49t** Robert Francis/*HL,* **648-49b** *PCP;* **650c** R Ian Lloyd/ *HL,* **650b** Guido Alberto Rossi/*TIB,* **650-51t** R Ian Lloyd/*SG,* **651** Michael MacIntyre/*HL;* **652** Larry Dale Gordon/*TIB,* **652-53t&b** *PCP,* **653** Victor Englebert/*SG;* **654t** Don King/*TIB,* **654b** Victor Englebert/*SG,* **654-55t** Michael MacIntyre/*HL,* **654-55b** J G Fuller/*HL;* **656-57t** Nigel Westwood/*SA,* **656-57b** Heinz Stucke/ *FS,* **657c** Starfoto/*Z,* **657b** Dieter & Mary Plage/*SA;* **658-59** Coyne Productions/*TIB,* **662l** M Coyne/*TIB,* **662r** Robin Constable/*HL,* **662-63** Anthony Howarth/*SG;* **664-65** Globe Photos, **665t** Maroon/*Z,* **665c** Adam Woolfitt/ *SG,* **665b** Anthony Howarth/*SG;* **666t** Metropolitan Museum of Art, NY, **666bl** Hughes Vassal/*GFS,* **666br** Radesslami/*GFS,* **666-67** *HL;* **668** National Gallery of Art, Washington, **668-69** Cleveland Museum of Art, **669** Hutt/*FS;* **670-71** Fulvio Roiter/*TIB;* **673** Christine Osborne/*FS;* **674-75t&b** Christine Osborne/*FS,* **675** R Southwell/*HL;* **676-77t** J Brown/*FS,* **676-77b** Shehadeh/*FS,* **677** Christine Osborne/*FS;* **678-79** J Brown/ *FS,* **679t** Christine Osborne/*FS,* **679b** J Brown/ *FS;* **680-81** V Southwell/*HL,* **681** J Simson/*DP;* **682-83t** BM/*HL,* **682-83b** Robert Aberman/ *HL,* **683** Christine Osborne/*FS;* **684-85** Adam Woolfitt/*SG;* **686** Brian Lynch/Bord Fáilte; **688** *MC,* **688-89t** Michael St Maur Sheil/*SG,* **688-89b** Robert Hunt Library; **690** Adam

Woolfitt/*SG*, **690-91t** Adam Woolfitt/*SG*, **690-91b** Athlone Jerunladen/*APA*, **691** GP Reichelf/*APA*; **692-93** *Z*; **695** Bernard Regent/*HL*; **696t&bl** The Wiener Library, **696br** *GFS*, **696-97** A Sharon & Massada Publishing/Wiener Library; **698** Ina Block/*TIB*, **698-99t&b** Sara Binovic/*GFS*, **699** Ted Spiegel/Rapho Guillumette/*SG*; **700, 700-01t** *Z*, **700-01b** *HL*; **702** Nancy Durrell McKenna/*HL*, **702-03t** Marvin E Newman/*TIB*, **702-03b, 703** Nathan Benn/*SG*; **704-05** *PCP*; **708** Starfoto/*Z*, **708-09t** Studio Benser/*Z*, **708-09b** *PCP*; **710tl** *MC*, **710bl** *MC*, **710br** *MC*, **710-11t** Braennhage/*Z*, **710-11b** Adam Woolfitt/*SG*, **711b** K Scholz/*Z*; **712tl** *MC*, **712bl** *MC*, **712br** *MC*, **712-13t** *PCP*, **713** Robin Lawrence/*SG*; **714** *SCL*, **714-15t** Francesco Venturi/*KEA*/*SG*, **714-15b** Ted Spiegel/*SG*; **716** Gert von Bassewitz/*SG*, **716-17** John G Ross/*SG*, **717t** Adam Woolfitt/*SG*, **717b** Santi Visalli/*TIB*; **718-19t** Dennis/*TIB*, **718-19b** *HL*, **719bl** Adam Woolfitt/*SG*, **719br** John Bulmer/*SG*; **720c** Galleria degli Uffizi, Florence/Bridgeman Art Library, **720bl** Santa Maria della Victor, Rome/Bridgeman Art Library, **720-21t** Galleria dell'Accademia, Venice, **721** *Annunciation* (late 1470's), by Leonardo da Vinci; Uffizi Gallery, Florence, Italy (SCALA/Art Resource); **722** *RF*, **722-23t** K Kerth/*Z*, **722-23b** Heinz Stucke/*FS*, **723t** Heinz Stucke/*FS*, **723b** Sonja Bullaty/*TIB*; **724tl** John Heseltine/*SG*, **724tr** Matteini/Sipa-Press/*RF*, **724b** Hans Wolf/*TIB*, **724-25t** P Edward Parker/*HL*, **724-25b** Fiat; **726** John Heseltine/*SG*, **726-27t** *PCP*, **726-27b** Adam Woolfitt/*SG*, **727** Gary Gladstone/*TIB*; **728** John Heseltine/*SG*, **728-29t** John Heseltine/*SG*, **728-29b** Studio Benser/*Z*, **729** Juergen Schmitt/*TIB*; **731** M Isy-Schwart/*TIB*; **732** Nick Nicholson/*TIB*, **732-33t** Rentmeester/*TIB*, **732-33b** Nick Nicholson/*TIB*, **733** Rentmeester/*TIB*; **734** David W Hamilton/*TIB*, **734-35t** John Marmaras/*SG*, **734-35b** Hans Hofer/*APA*, **735** Nick Nicholson/*TIB*; **736-37** E Carp/*Z*; **738t** J H Carmichael Jr/*TIB*, **738b** Kaku Kurita/*GFS*, **738-39t** Tim Beddow/*HL*, **738-39b** Roger Job/*GFS*, **739t** Giacomoni/*GFS*, **739b** John Hatt/*HL*; **740-41** Orion Press/*Z*; **743** Morimoto/*GFS*; **744-45t** Orion Press/*Z*, **744-45b** G Coliva/*TIB*, **745b** Fred J Maroon/*SG*; **746t** Tony Martorano/*APA*, **746b, 746-47** Spectrum Colour Library; **748t** Paul C Pet, **748b** Donald Smetzer, TSW/Click Chicago, **748-49** Orion Press/Kuroda/*Z*, **749b** Paul Chesley; **750-51t** Grant V Faint/*TIB*, **750-51b** Ken Straiton/*RF*, **751t** Neil Beer, **751bl** Orion Press/*Z*, **751br** Kaku Karita/*GFS*; **752tl&bl** Mansell Collection, **752br** Kathy Tracy/*RF*, **752-53t** ET Archive, **752-53b** Paul C Pet, **753** Kurita-Wada/*GFS*; **754-55t** Michael Holford/Victoria & Albert Museum, London, **754-55b** Alain Evrard/*SG*, **755** Michael MacIntyre/*HL*; **756-57t** Spectrum Colour Library, **756-57b** Michael MacIntyre/*HL*, **757t** Spectrum Colour Library, **757b** *Z*; **758** J G Fuller/*HL*, **758-59t** *Z*, **758-59b** Adina Tovy/*APA*; **760** Hans Verkroost, **760-61t** Stockmarket/*Z*, **760-61c** Kazuyoshi Nomachi/*RF*, **760-61b** Paul C Pet, **761tl** B Edelhajt/*GFS*, **761tr** Robin Laurance/*SG*, **761b** David Ball/Spectrum Colour Library; **762-63t** D Schmidt/*Z*, **762-63b** Mitsuo Ambe/*GFS*, **763t** Ben Simmons/Sipa/*RF*, **763b** *RF*; **764-65t** A S I/Colorsport, **764-65b** Colorsport, **765t** John Bulmer/*SG*, **765c** Resource Foto/*SG*, **765b** Jim Anderson/*SG*; **766t&b** Paul C Pet, **766-67** *Z*, **767t** Resource Foto/*SG*, **767b** *Z*; **768-69t** Paul C Pet, **768-69b** Spectrum Colour Library, **769t** Jean Kugler/*APA*, **769b** Spectrum Colour Library; **770-71** Gerard Champlong/*TIB*; **773t** Michael Hardy/*SG*, **773b** Adam Woolfitt/*SG*; **774** Kay Chernush/*TIB*, **774-75t** Adam Woolfitt/*SG*, **774-75b** *Z*; **777** Yves Gellie/Odyssey from *MTX*; **778-79** Joseph B Brignolo/*TIB*; **780-81** Damm/*Z*; **782** *HL*, **782-83t** Timothy Beddow/*HL*, **782-83b** Victor Englebert/*SG*, **783** Hoffman-Burchard/*Z*; **785t** *MC*, **785b** Pete Atkinson/*PEP*; **787** De Vuadrey/*RF*; **788-89** Frilet/Sipa/*RF*; **790-91** Alain Evrard/*SG*; **793** Grant V Faint/*TIB*; **794** *HL*, **794-95t** J Reditt/*HL*, **794-95b** Alain Evrard/*SG*, **795t** Nathan Benn/*SG*, **795b** Alain Evrard/*SG*; **796t** Alain Evrard/*SG*, **796b** Nathan Benn/*SG*, **796-97t** Michael MacIntyre/*HL*, **796-97b** Alain Evrard/*SG*; **798** *APA*, **798-99** Alain Evrard/*SG*, **799** Barrie Rokeach/*TIB*; **801t** Croxford/*Z*, **801b** Tor Eigeland/*GFS*; **802-03t, 803** Tor Eigeland/*GFS*, **802-03b** Bernard Gerard/*HL*; **804-05** Mike Andrews/*SG*; **806-07** Jean-Leo Dugast/*APA*; **808-09** Jean-Leo Dugast/*APA*; **810-11t** Jean-Leo Dugast/*APA*, **810-11b** Giudicelli/*HL*, **811t** Jean-Leo Dugast/*APA*, **811b** Brian Moser/*HL*; **812** *HL*, **812-13t** Heinz Stucke/*FS*, **812-13b** Blair Seitz/*APA*, **813** Jean-Leo Dugast/*APA*; **814** Alvis Upitis/*TIB*, **814-15t** Jürgens Ost und Europa Photo, **814-15b** Steven Burr Williams/*TIB*, **815** Jürgens Ost und Europa Photo; **816-17** *B&U*; **818-19** Jill Brown/Mepha/*FS*; **820** John Bulmer/*SG*, **820-21t** J Brown/*FS*, **820-21b** John Bulmer/*SG*, **821** Christine Osborne/Mepha/*FS*; **823t&b** Nicholas Cohen/*SG*; **824** Paul C Pet, **824-25t** Ted Spiegel/*SG*, **824-25c** William Strode/*SG*; **826** James Davis World-wide Photographic Travel Library, **826b** Philip Wollmuth/*HL*, **826-27t** Dr Muller-Seeberg/*Z*, **826-27b** Adam Woolfitt/*SG*, **827** Dr Muller-Seeberg/*Z*; **828t** Philip Wollmuth/*HL*, **828b** Nathan Benn/*SG*, **828-29t** William Strode/*SG*, **828-29** Austin J Brown/*Z*; **830-31t** H Zahn/*Z*, **830-31b** John Bulmer/*SG*; **833** G Noel/Figaro/*GFS*; **834** John Bryson/*TIB*, **834-35t** B Regent/*HL*, **834-35b** *HL*, **835** Michael St Maur Sheil/*SG*; **836-37t** Charles W Friend/*SG*, **836-37b, 837t** Michael St Maur Sheil/*SG*, **837b** Mepha/*FS*; **839** *B&U*; **840-41** K Kerth/*Z*, **841t** Adam Woolfitt/*SG*, **841b** Chip Hires/*GFS*; **842-43t** Vladimir Birgus/*HL*, **842-43b** *Z*, **843t** British Museum (Natural History) Geological Museum, **843c** Vladimir Birgus/*HL*, **843b** Chip Hires/*GFS*; **845** A Davies/*Z*; **846-47t** Dallas and John Heaton/*APA*, **846-47b** Bazin Scorceletti/*GFS*, **847t** Patrick Doherty/Stockphotos/*TIB*, **847b** Bazin Scorceletti/*GFS*; **850** *HL*, **850-51t** Adina Tovy/*APA*, **850-51b** RCA Nichols/*APA*, **851bl** Sipa/*RF*, **851br** Julian Nieman/*SG*; **853** *SCL*; **854, 854-55t&b, 855b** Timothy Beddow/*HL*, **855t** Christina Dodwell/*HL*; **856-57,** Timothy Beddow/*HL*; **858-59** Timothy Beddow/*HL*, **859** A & E Bomford/Ardea; **861** Brian Moser/*HL*; **862-63** Wendy Chan/*TIB*; **864-65** P & G Bowater/*TIB*; **866** Frank Devlin/*SG*, **866-67t** Victor Englebert/*SG*, **866-67b** Alain Evrard/*SG*, **867t** Andrew Eames/*HL*, **867c** *HL*, **867b** R Ian Lloyd/*SG*; **868** David Alan Harvey/*SG*, **868-69t** R Ian Lloyd/*HL*, **869t** John Hatt/*HL*, **869b** Alain Evrard/*SG*; **870t** H James/*HL*, **870b** Alain Evrard/*SG*, **870-71** E L Wheater/*TIB*, **871** Victor Englebert/*SG*; **872t** Michael Salas/*TIB*, **872b** B Pougeoise/Sipa Press/*RF*, **872-73t** R Ian Lloyd/*HL*, **872-73b** David Alan Harvey/*SG*; **874-75** Adam Woolfitt/*SG*; **876-77** Wolfgang Freihen; **879** Mick Csaky/*HL*; **880** Timothy Beddow/*HL*, **880-81t** Horst Munzig/*SG*, **880-81b** *HL*, **881** Horst Munzig/*SG*; **882-83t** Mick Csaky/*HL*, **882-83b** Horst Munzig/*SG*, **883t** Haslam/*HL*, **883b** Bernard Regent/*HL*; **884** Adam Woolfitt/*SG*, **885l** *B&U*, **885r** Heinz Stucke/*FS*; **886** The Flag Research Center; **888-89** L Kuipers/*B&U*, **889t** Mike Andrews/*SG*, **889b** Das Photo; **890-91** Bernard Regent/*HL*; **892** John Wright/*HL*, **892-93t** *HL*, **892-93b, 893** Sarah Errington/*HL*; **895t** Derek Berwin/*TIB*, **895b** Damm/*Z*; **896-97** David Hiser/*TIB*; **900** Horst Munzig/*SG*, **900-01t** Paolo Gori/*TIB*, **900-01b** Kal Muller/*APA*, **901t** Kal Muller/*SG*, **901b** Dorates/*GFS*; **902-03** Robert Valladares/*TIB*; **904t** Liba Taylor/*HL*, **904b** Tor Eigeland/*SG*, **904-05t** Liba Taylor/*HL*, **904-05b** *DP*, **905** Liba Taylor/*HL*; **906** Liba Taylor/*HL*, **906-07t** *PCP*, **906-07b** Brett Froomer/*TIB*, **907** Kal Muller/*APA*; **908** Juergen Schmitt/*TIB*, **908-09t** Reflejo/*SG*, **908-09b** *PCP*, **909** Tony Morrison/South American Pictures; **910t** *MC*, **910bl** Mary Evans Picture Library, **910br** *PP*, **910-11t** Kal Muller/*APA*, **911t** *PCP*, **911b** Kal Muller/Woodfin Camp Associates/*APA*; **912** Liba Taylor/*HL*, **912-13t** Al Satterwhite/*TIB*, **912-13b** Kal Muller/*APA*, **913br** Peter R Dickerson/*SG*, **913c** Brett Froomer/*TIB*; **914-15** E Gormsen; **917** A Makarov/*NOV*; **918** De Nombel/Sipa Sport/Colorsport, **918-19** *B&U*, **919** *APA*; **920-21** Brian Moser/Granada TV/*HL*; **922** The Flag Research Center, **922-23** Francis Krachi/*GFS*; **924** Brian Moser/*HL*, **924-25t** Xinhua-News/*Z*, **924-25b** Brian Moser/*HL*, **925** *HL*; **926, 926-27t** Brian Moser/*HL*, **926-27b** *HL*, **927** Brian Moser/*HL*;

928-29 Nancy Durrell/*HL;* **931** *B&U;* **932t** *HL,* **932b** *B&U,* **932-33t** Tor Eigeland/*SG,* **932-33b** Tordai/*HL;* **934-35t** Don Klumpp/*TIB,* **935t, 935bl** Victor Englebert/*SG,* **935br** Dave Brinicombe/*HL;* **936** Adam Woolfitt/*SG,* **936-37t&b** Leon Schadeberg/*SG,* **937** *PCP;* **938-39t** Adam Woolfitt/*SG,* **938-39b** Julian Calder/*SG,* **939t** John Kelly/*TIB,* **939b** John Hatt/*HL;* **940-41** V Wentzel/*Z;* **942** Reardon/*RF,* **942-43t** A Aarhus/Sipa/*RF,* **942-43b** Reardon/*RF,* **943** Sarah Errington/*HL;* **944** Mecky Fögeling, **944-45** Rob Cousins/*SG;* **946-47** NASA/Science Photo Library, **947** Rod Borland/*SA;* **948** Michael Friedel/*RF,* **948-49** Frilet/Sipa/*RF,* **949** Frilet/*RF;* **950-51t** Charles Foale, **950-51b** *APA,* **951** Melanie Friend/*HL;* **953** Bartholomew/Liaison/*GFS;* **954** Joan Klatchko/*HL,* **954-55t** Charles Foale, **955t** Jeremy Horner/*HL,* **955b** Mick Csaky/*HL;* **956** *RF,* **956-57t** *RF,* **956-57b** *HL,* **957** *APA;* **958-59** N Presho/*Z,* **959** Joanna van Gruisen/*SA;* **960-61t** Jorgen Bitsch/*Z,* **960-61b** Sarah Errington/*HL,* **961** Neville Presho/*Z;* **963t** Sarah Errington/*HL,* **963c** Neville Presho/*Z,* **963b** Christine Osborne/*APA;* **964-65t** Sunak/*Z,* **964-65b, 965t** Dieter & Mary Plage/*SA,* **965b** *APA;* **966-67** Shuji Kotoh/*Z;* **968-69** PB/Rex Features; **970** Adam Woolfitt/*SG,* **970-71t** Adam Woolfitt/*SG,* **970-71b** Rijksmuseum, Amsterdam, **971t** Van Phillips/*APA,* **971b** *TIB;* **972b** D & J Heaton/*APA,* **972-73t** T Schneiders/*Z,* **972-73c** Puck-Kornetzki/*Z,* **972-73b** Puck-Kornetzki/*Z,* **973t** Adam Woolfitt/*SG;* **974-75t** Streichan/*Z,* **974-75b** Adam Woolfitt/*SG,* **975t** Van Phillips/*APA,* **975b** *PCP;* **976br** *PCP,* **976bl** Royal Netherlands Embassy/Scheermeijr; **978, 978-79** *PCP,* **979tl** Tor Eigeland/*SG,* **979tr** *DP,* **979b** Philips/*BV;* **980, 980-81t** Paul C Pet, **980-81b** Charles Weckler/*TIB,* **981** Paul C Pet; **982-83t** Michael MacIntyre/*HL,* **982-83b** Larry Dale Gordon/*TIB,* **983t** Pascule Sorgues/*GFS,* **983b** Witt/Sipa Press/*RF;* **984-85** Frances Furlong/*SA;* **987** Robin Morrison; **988** Adam Woolfitt/*SG,* **988-89t** *RF,* **988-89c** Adam Woolfitt/*SG,* **988-89b** Julia Hall/*HL,* **989** Annie Price/*SA;* **990t&b** Adam Woolfitt/*SG,* **990-91** Colorsport, **991t** Robin Morrison, **991b** R Ian Lloyd/*SG;* **992c** *RF,* **992b** Starfoto/*Z,* **992-93t** *RF,* **993t** Adam Woolfitt/*SG,* **993b** Colorsport; **994** Annie Price/*SA,* **994-95b** R Ian Lloyd/*SG;* **996-97** *HL;* **999** Enrico/*Z;* **1000** John Griffith, **1000-01** Gary Willis/South American Pictures, **1001tl** John Griffith, **1001tr** *HL;* **1003** Victor Englebert/*SG;* **1004, 1004-05** Dave Brinicombe/*HL,* **1005t** Victor Englebert/*SG,* **1005b** *HL;* **1006-07** *HL;* **1010t&b** *HL,* **1010-11t** Anna Tully/*HL,* **1010-11b** *Z;* **1012** *HL,* **1012-13t** *Z,* **1012-13b** Wendy V Watriss/*SG,* **1013** *HL;* **1014tl&tr** *HL,* **1015t** Werner Forman Archive, **1015b** *HL;* **1016-17** Paul C Pet; **1018-1019** Paul C Pet; **1020** John Kegan/*SG,* **1020-21, 1021** Paul C Pet; **1022, 1022-23t** Paul C Pet, **1022-23b** Tor Eigeland/*SG,* **1023t** Guido Alberto Rossi/*TIB,* **1023b** B&U International Pictures; **1024** Jack Lentfer/Survival Anglia, **1024-25t** B&U International Pictures, **1024-25b** Herta Gröndal/*Z;* **1026** Das Photo, **1026-27t&b** Paul C Pet, **1027** Tor Eigeland/*SG;* **1028-29** Jabal Hafit/*SG,* **1029** Robert Azzi/*SG;* **1034-35** Hanif Raza/*Z;* **1037** C Hires/*GFS;* **1038** David Fleming/*HL,* **1038-39** Christine Osborne/*APA;* **1040-41t** Leon Schadeberg/*SG,* **1040-41b** *HL,* **1041t** Lyle Lawson/*APA,* **1041b** Andre Singer/*HL;* **1042** Christine Osborne/*APA,* **1042-43t** Christine Osborne/*APA,* **1043l** Alain Evrard/*APA,* **1043r** Christine Osborne/*APA;* **1044-45t** Hanif Raza/*Z,* **1045** Jehangir Gazdar/*SG;* **1046tl** The Flag Research Center, **1047t** *HL,* **1047bl&r** T Bryant/Liaison/*GFS;* **1048-49** *RF;* **1050** Adam Woolfitt/*SG,* **1050-51t** Adam Woolfitt/*SG,* **1050-51b** J G Fuller/*HL,* **1051t** Adam Woolfitt/*SG,* **1051b** Robert Frerck/*SG;* **1053** Robert Frerck/*SG;* **1055l** Michael MacIntyre/*HL,* **1055r** Jose Reis/*GFS;* **1056** Jose Reis/*GFS,* **1056-57t&c** Michael MacIntyre/*HL,* **1056-57b** Charlie Nairn/Disappearing World/*HL,* **1057** Michael Coyne/*TIB;* **1059** Larry Dale Gordon/*TIB;* **1060-61t** Rob Cousins/*SG,* **1060-61b** Eric Sander/*GFS,* **1061l** Reflejo/*SG,* **1061r** Melanie Friend/*HL;* **1062-63** H Sunak/*Z,* **1063t** Noel/Figaro/*GFS,* **1063c** John Bulmer/*SG,* **1063b** P Aventurier/*GFS;* **1064-65** *B&U;* **1066-67** Victor Englebert/*SG;* **1068t** Victor Englebert/*SG,* **1068b** Mike Andrews/*SG,* **1068-69** Victor Englebert/*SG,* **1069t&b** Mireille Vautier; **1070** B Hyserbergh/*GFS,* **1070-71t** Robert Frerck/*SG,* **1070-71b** B Hyserbergh/*GFS;* **1072** Mireille Vautier, **1072-73t** H R Dörig/*HL,* **1072-73b** Robert Frerck/*SG,* **1073c** Cara Moore/*TIB,* **1073b** Mireille Vautier; **1076-77** E Streichan/*Z;* **1079** Joseph B Brignolo/*TIB;* **1080** Terry Madison/*TIB,* **1080-81t** Walter Ioos Jr/*TIB,* **1080-81b** Michael Friedel/*TIB;* **1082t&c** Ted Spiegel/*SG,* **1082-83t** Alain Evrard/*SG,* **1082-83b** Juergen Schmitt/*TIB,* **1083** Michael MacIntyre/*HL;* **1084** Frilet/Sipa Press/*RF,* **1084-85t** Alain Evrard/*SG,* **1084-85b** Terry Madison/*TIB,* **1085** Alain Evrard/*SG;* **1086t** Pamela J Zilly/*TIB,* **1086b** Charles Best/*SG,* **1086-87t** Maurice Harvey/*HL,* **1086-87b** Terry Madison/*TIB;* **1088** Maurice Harvey/*HL,* **1088-89t** Harald Sund/*TIB,* **1088-89b** Tom McHugh, Photo Researchers, Inc., **1089t** Walter Ioos Jr/*TIB,* **1089b** Ted Spiegel/*SG;* **1090t** *MC,* **1090bl** Mary Evans Picture Library, **1090br** Michael MacIntyre/*HL,* **1090-91t** Robert Hunt Library; **1092-93** *Z;* **1095** Jürgens Ost und Europa Photo; **1096tl&bl** Mansell Collection, **1096br** Chip Hires/*GFS,* **1096-97t&b, 1097** Jürgens Ost und Europa Photo; **1098-99t&b** Jürgens Ost und Europa Photo, **1099t&b** J Morek/Jürgens Ost und Europa Photo; **1100** Julian Nieman/*SG,* **1101t&c** Jürgens Ost und Europa Photo, **1101b** B&U International Pictures; **1102t&b** Jürgens Ost und Europa Photo, **1102-03t** CAF Warsaw/*Z,* **1102-03b** Jürgens Ost und Europa Photo, **1103** Marc Deville/*GFS;* **1104-05** Robert Frerck/*SG;* **1107** Charles Friend/*SG;* **1108** Robert Frerck/*SG,* **1108-09t** K Kerth/*Z,* **1108-09b** Jean Krugler/*APA,* **1109** Anthony Howarth/*SG;* **1110** Reflejo/*SG,* **1110-11** *B&U,* **1111t** Ian Yeomans/*SG* **1111bl** Bill Wassman/*APA,* **1111br** J Redditt/*HL;* **1112-13t** *HL/B&U,* **1112-13b** *PCP,* **1113t** Robert Frerck/*SG,* **1113b** Tor Eigeland/Blackstar/*SG;* **1114tl** *MC,* **1114bl** *MC,* **1114br** F Lochon/*GFS,* **1114-15** Michel Ginies/Sipa/*RF;* **1116t** Michael Friedel/*TIB,* **1116b** Cesar Lucas/*TIB,* **1116-17t** Robert Valladares/*TIB,* **1117** Fulvio Roiter/*TIB;* **1119l, 1119r** J Brown/Mepha/*FS;* **1120t** Skinnet-Vernon/Fig. Mag/*GFS,* **1120b** *HL,* **1120-21t** Bernard Regent/*HL,* **1120-21b** Heinz Stucke/*FS,* **1121** Bernard Regent/*HL;* **1123** Adam Woolfitt/*SG;* **1124, 1124-25t** Jürgens Ost und Europa Photo, **1124-25b, 1125t** Adam Woolfitt/*SG,* **1125b** Charles W Friend/*SG;* **1126t** Adam Woolfitt/*SG,* **1126b** Jürgens Ost und Europa Photo, **1126-27t** Charles Weckler/*TIB,* **1126-27b, 1127** Adam Woolfitt/*SG;* **1128-29** Mecky Fögeling; **1130-31** Steenmans/*Z;* **1132tl,bl,br, 1132-33t** Mansell Collection, **1132-33b** Dave Brinicombe/*HL;* **1134tl** Robert Hunt Library, **1134bl** Jürgens Ost und Europa Photo, **1134br** B Markel/Liaison/*GFS,* **1134-35** Shone/Gamma-Liaison, **1135t** Jürgens Ost und Europa Photo, **1135c&b** Robert Hunt Library; **1136t** Jürgens Ost und Europa Photo, **1136bl** B Meyer/*HL,* **1136br** *APWW,* **1136-37** Robert Francis/*HL,* **1137c** Heinz Stucke/*FS,* **1137b** Novosti/*GFS;* **1138** Havlicek/*Z,* **1139l&r** Jürgens Ost und Europa Photo; **1140** Leslie Woodhead/*HL,* **1140-41t** Jürgens Ost und Europa Photo, **1140-41b** Nik Wheeler/*SG,* **1141** Victoria Juleva/*HL;* **1142, 1142-43t&b** *Z,* **1143** Robert Francis/*HL;* **1144-45** *Z,* **1145t** Andreas Heumann/*SG,* **1145c** *HL,* **1145b** G Ricatto/*Z;* **1146, 1146-47t** Andreas Heumann/*SG,* **1146-47b, 1147t** Mecky Fögeling, **1147b** *Z;* **1148-49** Andreas Heumann/*SG,* **1149tl&tr** Mecky Fögeling, **1149b** *HL;* **1150-51** Bernard Gerard/*HL,* **1151** *HL;* **1154, 1154-55** Heinz Stucke/*FS,* **1155** John Hatt/*HL;* **1156** *Z,* **1157** Heinz Stucke/*FS;* **1158-59** L Kuipers/*B&U,* **1159** Ian Bradshaw/*SG;* **1160-61** *SCL,* **1161** *SCL;* **1162-63** Mary Evans, **1163** *HL;* **1164-65** Robert Azzi/*SG;* **1166** John Lewis Stage/*TIB;* **1168-69t** Anthony Howarth/*SG,* **1168-69b** Peter Ryan/*FS,* **1169t** Bernard Gerard/*HL,* **1169b** Tor Eigeland/*SG;* **1170** Lister/*HL,* **1170-71t** *PCP,* **1170-71b** R Azzi/*SG;***1173** Lisl Dennis/*TIB;* **1174** John Bulmer/*SG,* **1174-75t** J C Lozouet/*TIB,* **1174-75b** Bernard Regent/*HL,* **1175** Tavernier/Colorsport; **1176** M Friede/G&J Images/*TIB,* **1176-77** Damm/*Z;*

1178 David Clilverd/*HL*, **1178-79** Anna Tully/*HL*; **1181t** Tor Eigeland/*SG*, **1181b** Marc St Gil/*TIB*; **1182t** Banagan/*TIB*, **1182b** R Ian Lloyd/*HL*, **1182-83t** P & G Bowater/*TIB*, **1182-83b** R Ian Lloyd/*HL*, **1183** Michael Chua/*TIB*; **1185t** John Eastcott & Yva Momatiuk/*WC*; **1185b** Liba Taylor/*HL*; **1186, 1187** Adam Woolfitt/*SG*, **1188-89** Adam Woolfitt/*SG*; **1190-91** Leslie Woodhead/*HL*, **1191t&b** Michael MacIntyre/*HL*; **1193t** Timothy Beddow/*HL*, **1193b** *HL*; **1194-95** Harlicek/*Z*; **1196** The Flag Research Center; **1198tl,bl,br, 1198-99t&b** Mansell Collection, **1199** William Knost/*GFS*; **1200c** Magubane/Liaison/*GFS*, **1200-01t** Guy Hobbs/*GFS*, **1200-01b** De Keerle/UK Press/*GF*, **1201t** *Z*, **1201b** Eric Bouvet/*GFS*; **1202** Robert Aberman/*HL*, **1202-03t** Laurence Hughes/*TIB*, **1202-03b** Heinz Stucke/*HL*, **1203** J. Kuus, Sipa; **1204-05** Rosenbach/*Z*; **1208-09t** Rob Cousins/*SG*, **1208-09b** Jean Krugler/*APA*, **1209t** Robert Frerck/*SG*, **1209b** *APA*; **1210-11t** Ben Nakayama/*APA*, **1210-11b** Bill Wassman/*APA*, **1211** Adam Woolfitt/*SG*; **1212** *HL*, **1212-13t** *SCL*, **1213bl** Louis Castaneda/*TIB*, **1213br** Tor Eigeland/*SG*; **1214** Croxford/*Z*, **1214-15t** Robert Frerck/*SG*, **1214-15b** John Downman/*HL*, **1215** P Goycolea/*HL*; **1216** F R Damm/*Z*, **1216-17t** F R Damm/*Z*, **1216-17b** Robert Frerck/*SG*; **1218tl** *MC*, **1218bl** *MC*, **1218br** *MC*, **1218-19** Adam Woolfitt/*SG*; **1220tl** *MC*, **1220bl** *MC*, **1220br** Robert Hunt Library, **1220-21** Metropolitan Museum of Art, New York, **1221** C Vioujard/*GFS*; **1222** *PCP*, **1222-23t** K Kerth/*Z*, **1222-23b** Dr Mueller/*Z*, **1223** *PCP*; **1224** *MRE/B&U*, **1224-25t** *APA*, **1224-25b** *APA*, **1225** *MRE/B&U*; **1226-27t** Keresztes/*Z*, **1226-27b** Robert Frerck/*SG*, **1227** *B&U*; **1228-29** David Beatty/*SG*, **1231** Alain Evrard/*SG*; **1232-33t** Adam Woolfitt/*SG*, **1232-33b** Charles Friend/*SG*, **1233t** David Beatty/*SG*, **1233b** Adam Woolfitt/*SG*; **1234** Mat Naythons/Liaison/*GFS*, **1234-35** Wirtz/Liaison/*GFS*, **1235l** Mat Naythons/Liaison/*GFS*, **1235r** S Tucci/Liaison/*GFS*; **1236-37** Eric Wheater/*TIB*; **1238-39** Gezira/*HL*; **1240** *HL*, **1240-41t** Christine Osborne/Mepha/*FS*, **1240-41b** *HL*, **1241** Christine Osborne/Mepha/*FS*; **1242-43** Sarah Errington/*HL*, **1243l** John Ryle/*HL*, **1243c** Andre Singer/*HL*, **1243r** Sarah Errington/*HL*; **1244, 1244-45** Adam Woolfitt/*SG*; **1246-47** *Z*, **1247b** Paul Slaughter/*TIB*; **1248-49** Paul C Pet; **1251** Paul C Pet; **1252tl** Toni Sica/*GFS*, **1252tr** Popperfoto, **1252cl** United Nations, NY, **1252cr** Popperfoto, **1252b** E W W Fowler, **1253t&ct** Robert Hunt Library, **1253cb** J Claude Francolon/*GFS*, **1253b** Christian Vioujard/*GFS*; **1254t** Paul C Pet, **1254b** Mohn/*Z*, **1254-55, 1255t** Paul C Pet, **1255b** Mosler/*Z*; **1256** Paul C Pet, **1256-57t** D H Teuffen/*Z*, **1256-57b** Colin Molyneux/*TIB*; **1258, 1258-59t** Paul C Pet, **1258-59b** Haro Schumacher/*Z*, **1259** Paul C Pet; **1260-61** V Phillips/*Z*; **1262-63** Michael St Maur Sheil/*SG*; **1264-65t** Horst Munzig/*SG*, **1264-65b** Horst Munzig/*SG*; **1266-67** Monique Jacot/*SG*, **1267tl** Ruth L Aebi, Gstaad Aelper/*APA*, **1267tr** Michael Kuh/*TIB*, **1267b** Horst Munzig/*SG*; **1268** Ciba-Geigy, **1268-69t** Hans Verkroost, **1268-69b** Nestlé SA, **1269** Monique Jacot/*SG*; **1270** Andrew Hill/*HL*, **1270-71t** *GFS*, **1270-71b** Credit Suisse, **1271** CERN/Science Photo Library; **1272-73** Adam Woolfitt/*SG*; **1274** Chip Hires/*GFS*, **1275** Jamie Simson/*DP*; **1276** Fetzer/*Z*, **1276-77t** Kester J Eddy/*FS*, **1276-77b** Jamie Simson/*DP*, **1277** Dr Nigel Smith/*HL*; **1278** Ceasar Lucas/*TIB*, **1278-79t** Gunter Heil/*Z*, **1278-79b** Jamie Simson/*DP*, **1279** Dr Nigel Smith/*HL*; **1280-81t** G L Scarfiotti/*SG*, **1280-81b** K J Eddy/*FS*, **1281** G L Scarfiotti/*SG*; **1282** Guido Mangold/*TIB*, **1282-83t** Dick Rowan/*SG*, **1282-83b** Bernard Regent/*HL*, **1283** Dick Rowan/*SG*; **1284-85t** Charles Weckler/*TIB*, **1284-85b** L N Moyer/*FS*, **1285t** R Ian Lloyd/*HL*, **1285b** Alexis Duclos/*GFS*; **1286-87** Jeff Hunter/*TIB*; **1288** Robert Hunt Library, **1288-89** Bob Croxford/*Z*, **1289t&b** Alain Evrard/*SG*; **1290** The Flag Research Center, **1291** Pascal Le Segretain/*SYG*; **1292-93** Bruce Davidson/*SA*; **1294-95** Bullaty Lomeo/*TIB*; **1296** Bullaty Lomeo/*TIB*, **1296-97t** *HL*, **1297bl** Bullaty Lomeo/*TIB*, **1297br** Timothy Beddow/*HL*; **1298t** *HL*, **1298b** Alan Root/*SA*, **1298-99t** Paul C Pet, **1298-99b** *RF*, **1299** Matthews Purdy/*SA*; **1300-01** Alastair Scott/*SG*; **1302-03** Alain Evrard/*APA*; **1304** Chusak/*SG*, **1304-05t** Guido Alberto Rossi/*TIB*, **1304-05b** Sarah Errington/*HL*, **1305** Alain Evrard/*SG*; **1306t** Chiaroscuro Kessler/*APA*, **1306b** Paul C Pet, **1306-07t** Andrew Eames/*HL*, **1306-07b** *APA*, **1307** Guido Alberto Rossi/*TIB*; **1308-09t** *APA*, **1308-09b** Guido Alberto Rossi/*TIB*, **1309t** Adina Tory/*APA*, **1309c** R Ian Lloyd/*HL*, **1309b** Michael MacIntyre/*HL*; **1310t** Liba Taylor/*HL*, **1310b** Ivan Polunin/*SG*, **1310-11t** Dallas & John Heaton/*APA*, **1310-11b** Leon Schadeberg/*SG*, **1311** Paul C Pet; **1312** Paul C Pet, **1312-13t** John Lewis Stage/*TIB*, **1312-13b** Alain Evrard/*APA*, **1313** Dr H Ginsburg; **1314-15** Victor Englebert/*SG*; **1317** Michael MacIntyre/*HL*; **1318t** *HL*, **1318b** *SCL*, **1318-19t, 1319r** Michael MacIntyre/*HL*, **1319l** *SCL*; **1320-21** Adam Woolfitt/*SG*; **1322-23** Fulvio Roiter/*TIB*; **1324** Ch. Vioujard/*GFS*; **1326** *PCP*, **1326-27t** Bernard Regent/*HL*, **1326-27b** Bulmer/*SG*, **1327** Ben Partner/*Z*; **1328** *B&U*, **1328-29t** J Bulmer/*SG*, **1328-29b** Brown/*SS*, **1329** Mahaux/*TIB*; **1330** Hugh Sitton/*TSW*, Click/Chicago; **1333** Jamie Simson/*DP*; **1334** H J Burkard/*TIB*, **1334-35t** John Bulmer/*SG*, **1335** Maroon/*Z*; **1336-37t** W Steinmetz/*TIB*, **1336-37b** Stukke/*FS*, **1337** Charles Friend/*SG*; **1338-39t** Timothy Beddow/*HL*, **1338-39b** Richard T Nowitz/*APA*, **1339** Kester J Eddy/Mepha/*FS*; **1340** Brown/*FS*, **1340-41** Robert Aberman/*HL*, **1341** Robert Aberman/*HL*; **1342** *MC*, **1343** John Lewis Stage/*TIB*; **1344-45** Adam Woolfitt/*SG*; **1346-47t** K Benser/*Z*, **1346-47b** Dallas & John Heaton/*APA*, **1347** Brett Froomer/*TIB*; **1349** Christopher Rennie/*RHPL*; **1350** G Ricatto/*Z*; **1354** Kal Muller/*APA*; **1356-57t&b** Kal Muller/*APA*, **1357tl&tr** Michael St Maur Sheil/*SG*, **1357b** Dave Brinicombe/*HL*; **1359** Jürgens Ost und Europa Photo; **1361** B Croxford/*Z*; **1362-63** *HL*; **1364-65** J Ramey/Stockphotos/*TIB*; **1366-67** Adam Woolfitt/*SG*; **1370-71t** John Downman/*HL*, **1371tr** Peter Miller/*TIB*, **1371cr** Bill Wassman/*APA*, **1371b** Brad Markel/Liaison/*GFS*; **1372-73t** Harald Sund/*TIB*, **1373t** Karen A McCormack, **1373c** Nathan Benn/*SG*, **1373b** Michael Salas/*TIB*; **1374-75** Nathan Benn/*SG*, **1375tr** *DP*, **1375br** Guido Alberto Rossi/*TIB*, **1375bl** Frank Whitney/*TIB*; **1376t** Dick Rowan/*SG*, **1376-77t** Reflejo/*SG*, **1377t** A Boccaccio/*TIB*, **1377br** Dallas and John Heaton/*APA*; **1378-79** Bernard Regent/*HL*, **1378-79b** Paul Dix/*SG*, **1379t** F Grehan/*SG*, **1379b** Richard Rowan's Collection/*SG*; **1380t** Paul Dix/*SG*, **1380b** Anchorage Daily News/Liaison/*GFS*, **1380-81** Tibor Hirsch/*SG*; **1382-83** Adam Woolfitt/*SG*, **1383t** D Nicol/Geoscience Features, **1383b** Karl Kernberger/*APA*; **1384t, 1384bl, 1384br, 1384-85** *MC*, **1385b** Virginia Museum of Arts, Richmond; **1386tl** Library of Congress, **1386br** *RF*, **1386bl** Library of Congress, **1386-87** American Museum, Bath/The Bridgeman Art Library, **1387b** NASA; **1388-89** Novovitch, Gamma/Liaison, **1389c** David W Hamilton/*TIB*, **1389t** Leslie Woodhead/*HL*; **1390-91t** Richard Erdos/*APA*, **1391t** C Leroy/Sipa–Press/*RF*, **1391c** Adam Woolfitt/*SG*, **1391b** Insight/Liaison/*GFS*; **1392-93t** Susan Allen/*HL*, **1393t** John Marmaras/*SG*, **1393b** José Azel, Contact from Woodfin Camp, Inc.; **1394, 1394-95t** Brent Jones, **1394-95b** Bref R Lundberg/*APA*; **1396t** Robin Macey/Geoscience Features, **1397t** Adam Woolfitt/*SG*, **1397b** Art Street; **1398t** Nathan Benn/*SG*, **1398b** Adam Woolfitt/*SG*, **1399** Reflejo/*SG*; **1400-01t** Arthur D'Arazien/*TIB*, **1400-01b** Martin Rogers/*SG*, **1401t** P Guis–Figaro–Magaz/*GFS*, **1401c** Anne Heimann, The Stock Market; **1402** Adam Woolfitt/*SG*, **1402-03t** Sepp Seitz/*SG*, **1402-03b** Richard Laird/*SG*, **1403t** John Yates/*SG*, **1403b** Liaison/*GFS*; **1404t** *HL*, **1404-05t** Adam Woolfitt/*SG*, **1404-05b** Ted Spiegel/*SG*, **1405t** Tim Eagen/*SG*; **1406** Charles Gupton, TSW-Click/Chicago, **1406-07t** DiMaggio/Kelish, The Stock Market, **1406-07b** John Egan/*HL*, **1407** Peter Miller/*TIB*; **1408** *DP*, **1408-09t** Nils Jorgensen/*RF*, **1408-09b** Jeff Hunter/*TIB*, **1409t** John Downman/*HL*, **1409b** David J Maenza/*TIB*; **1411** *B&U*; **1412-13** Bernard Gerard/*GFS*; **1414-15**

Bernard Gerard/*GFS;* **1417** Kramarz/*Z;* **1418** Kal Muller/*SG,* **1419t** Larry Dale Gordon/*TIB,* **1419b** Philippe Metois/*GFS;* **1420l** Francolon/Hires/Magnam/*GFS,* **1420r** Adam Woolfitt/*SG,* **1421t** *B&U,* **1421b** Ted Spiegel/*SG;* **1422-23** Mireille Vautier; **1424-25** Mireille Vautier; **1426** Andi Spicer, **1426-27t** *HL,* **1426-27b** Mireille Vautier; **1428-29** Victor Englebert/*SG,* **1429t** John Bulmer/*SG,* **1429b** Mireille Vautier; **1430-31** Guido Alberto Rossi/*TIB;* **1432-33** Jean-Leo Dugast/*APA;* **1434** Francoise Demulber/*GFS,* **1434-35t** *HL,* **1434-35b** Gilles Caron/*GFS,* **1435t** Alain Evrard/*APA,* **1435b** Claude Johner/*GFS;* **1436-37t** Guido Alberto Rossi/*TIB,* **1436-37b** J C Labbe/*GFS,* **1437t** Leon Schadeberg/*SG,* **1437b** *HL;* **1438** Austin J Brown/*Z,* **1438-39t** *Z,* **1438-39b** Austin J Brown/*Z;* **1440-41t** Damm/*Z,* **1440-41b** Austin J Brown/*Z;* **1442-43** *HL;* **1444** Michael MacIntyre/*HL,* **1445t** *HL,* **1445b** Michael MacIntyre/*HL;* **1446-47** Magra/*B&U;* **1448-49** *PCP;* **1450-51t** Charles W. Friend/*SG,* **1450-51b** Peter Ryan/*FS,* **1451** *PCP;* **1452** *B&U,* **1452-53t** *PCP,* **1452-53b** *B&U,* **1453t** *B&U,* **1453b** Peter Ryan/*FS;* **1454-55** Schmied/*Z,* **1456** The Flag Research Center; **1458tl** Popperfoto, **1458bl** Robert Hunt Library, **1458br** Popperfoto; **1459t** Tessore/Bavaria, **1459b** *SOV;* **1460** Giaccone/Marka/Picture Group, **1460-61** Josef Pelleross/JB Pictures, **1461b** Linda Barrlett/*PH;* **1462** Picture Finders/Bavaria, **1462-63** *RHPL,* **1463b** Linda Barrlett/*PH;* **1464-65** Josef Pelleross/JB Pictures, **1464b** Hans Schmied/Bavaria, **1465t** Alon Reininger/*WC;* **1466bl** *SCL,* **1466br** Dave G Houser, **1467t** Jonathan Blair/*WC,* **1467tr&bl** Dave G Houser; **1468-69b** Steve McCurry/*MPL,* **1469t** Adam Woolfitt/*WC,* **1469b** Dončević/*RHPL;* **1470-71** Michael MacIntyre/*HL;* **1472** Andrew Hill/*HL,* **1472-73t** *HL,* **1473t** Andrew Hill/*HL,* **1473b** Bruce Davidson/*SA;* **1474** *HL,* **1474-75** David Beatty/*SG,* **1475** Lee Lyon/*SA;* **1476-77** *HL,* **1477** Marc & Evelyne Bernheim/*SG;* **1478t&b** Marc & Evelyne Bernheim/*SG,* **1478-79t** Campbell/*SA,* **1478-79b** Obremski/*TIB;* **1480-81** Ian Murphy/*SG;* **1482bl&br** Ian Murphy/*SG,* **1482-83t** Chris Johnson/*HL,* **1482-83b** Robert Aberman/*HL;* **1484** Heinz Stucke/*HL,* **1484-85t** *HL,* **1484-85b** Heinz Stucke/*FS*